THE PRACTICAL BOOK OF SMALL GARDENS

THE PRACTICAL BOOK OF SMALL GARDENS

gardening know-how for limited spaces

PETER MCHOY

SELECT EDITIONS

ABOVE: *An old wicker mannequin makes a witty and unexpected garden decoration.*

Select Editions imprint specially produced for Selectabook Limited

Produced by Anness Publishing Limited
Hermes House
88–89 Blackfriars Road
London SE1 8HA

A CIP catalogue record for this book is available from the British Library

Publisher: Joanna Lorenz
Senior Editor: Caroline Davison
Copy Editors: Polly Boyd, Lesley Riley
Designer: Bill Mason
Contributors: Susan Berry, Richard Bird, Steve Bradley, Valerie Bradley, Stephanie Donaldson, Tessa Evelegh, Andrew Mikolajski, Barbara Segall
Original Design: Patrick McLeavey and Partners

Previously published as *The Ultimate Small Garden*

Printed in Singapore

1 3 5 7 9 10 8 6 4 2

HALF TITLE PAGE: *Planting climbers, such as clematis, makes the most of a limited space.*

FRONTISPIECE: *The plants in these borders soften the hard edge of the paving.*

TITLE PAGE: Saponaria ocymoides *is a pretty mat-forming perennial for a dry bank.*

CONTENTS

Introduction 6

Elements of Design 8

Planning Your Garden 10

Difficult Sites 34

Features and Structures 52

The Garden Floor 54

Forming Boundaries 80

Finishing Touches 98

Container Choices 122

Rock and Water Gardens 142

Choosing Plants 156

Beds and Borders 158

Planning Borders 164

Maintaining Beds and Borders 196

Plants for a Purpose 204

The Kitchen Garden 238

Index 250

Acknowledgments 256

ABOVE: *A variegated hosta makes a striking contribution to this foliage-based planting.*

INTRODUCTION

SMALL GARDENS CAN STILL HAVE A BIG IMPACT, and this book shows you how to get the best from a limited area. Size is comparative of course, and if your gardening is confined to a tiny backyard or a balcony, even a small town garden can seem large. On the other hand, a medium-sized country garden may appear small to the owner of a large estate. But whether you garden on a rooftop, or you have a fairly typical small town garden or a larger plot that simply seems small to you, this book offers ideas and solutions.

Making the most of a small space depends partly on design and partly on planting. If you want a low-maintenance garden the emphasis should be on hard landscaping and the use of ground cover and low-maintenance plants. If you are a plant collector, a design with the emphasis on planting space will be important . . . but choosing the right plants in proportion to the available space is vital.

You will find lots of ideas for redesigning a small garden, from initial ideas to execution. But sometimes only minor modifications to your existing garden are necessary for a transformation, and the section on features and structures has plenty of thought-provoking ideas that you might like to consider.

Choosing appropriate plants can be the key to ensuring a small garden design works well. In the third section of the book you will find hundreds of recommended plants, arranged by use or purpose – from plants for colour theme beds and borders, and those providing colour in the cold months, to those grown for shade (a particular problem in small gardens) or fragrance. Many plants have more than a single role, of course, so to avoid repetition and to make space for more plants, multiple entries have been thoroughly cross-referenced.

Size is especially important in a small garden, so we have given an indication of likely heights and spreads. In the case of herbaceous plants these are typical dimensions after a couple of years, but for slower-growing trees and shrubs they are the probable size after 10–15 years. Bear in mind, however, that dimensions can be no more than a crude guide. Heights can vary greatly, according to soil, position, and local climate. Some trees and shrubs can be kept compact by regular pruning – for example, buddleias and eucalpytus are both too tall for a small garden if left unpruned, but will make compact shrubs with a good shape if cut back severely each spring.

Although you will find plenty of suggestions in the following pages, attractive gardens are not designed to a rigid formula, and there is always room for individual interpretation – and even eccentricity. Some gardens are designed to shock, some are traditional in concept, a few are strictly formal, and many are a compromise between formality and informality. There are as many garden styles as there are tastes, and the only criterion for success is whether the result pleases you personally.

Design does not become easier with decreasing size: rather, it becomes more difficult and demanding. A large garden tends to look good anyway, with the odd weedy bed going almost unnoticed among the overall impression of large lawns, stately trees and shrubs. In a small garden long vistas are out of the question and the use of trees and large shrubs is often severely limited. Every part of the garden comes under the spotlight, and errors of judgement are often emphasized.

All these handicaps can be overcome, however, and, as the illustrations in this book show, you can still make a big impact with a small garden.

OPPOSITE: *Pots and containers are a good means of incorporating herbs in a very confined space.*

Elements *of* Design

Attractive small gardens seldom just happen, they are designed. And despite the apparent contradiction, the smaller the garden, the more important good design becomes. A small garden can be taken in almost at a glance, and the difference between good and bad design, attention to detail or neglect, is immediately obvious. In a small garden there is always the temptation to try to cram in many more features than there is really space for. Keep the design simple, stick to a style, and follow the suggestions in this section for making a plan to scale. Then check the effect by marking out the shapes in the garden before you start work. This way you will be assured a success.

ABOVE: *Sometimes accommodating essentials, such as this tool shed, attractively can become a problem. Careful screening can help minimize their impact.*

OPPOSITE: *A small garden should not lack impact. Provided it is well planted and has some strong focal points, it becomes easy to ignore the limitations of size.*

Planning your Garden

Some successful gardens are worked out on the ground, in the mind's eye, perhaps visualized during a walk around the garden, or conceived in stages as construction takes place. This approach is for the gifted or very experienced, and it is far better to make your mistakes on paper first.

A major redesign can be time-consuming and expensive, especially if it involves hard landscaping (paving, walls, steps, etc). However, simply moving a few plants is rarely enough to transform an uninspiring garden into something special. It is worth having a goal, a plan to work to, even if you have to compromise along the way. Bear in mind that you may be able to stagger the work and cost over several seasons, but having a well thought out design ensures the garden evolves in a structured way.

Use the checklist opposite to clarify your 'needs', then decide in your own mind the *style* of garden you want. Make a note of mundane and practical considerations, like where to dry the clothes and put the refuse, plus objects that need to be screened, such as a compost area, or an unpleasant view.

Unattractive views, and necessary but unsightly objects within the garden, such as toolsheds, are a particular problem because they can dominate a small garden. Well-positioned shrubs and small trees can act as a screen. To improve the outlook instantly use a large plant in a tub.

ABOVE: *In this garden the bird table helps to draw the eye away from the practical corner of the garden.*

LEFT: *Make a small garden look larger than it really is by ensuring the sides are well planted and creating a striking focal point.*

OPPOSITE: *Shape and form can be as important as colour in creating a stylish garden.*

LABOUR-SAVING TIPS

- To minimize cost and labour, retain as many paths and areas of paving as possible, but only if they don't compromise the design.
- If you want to enlarge an area of paving, or improve its appearance, it may be possible to pave over the top and thus avoid the arduous task of removing the original.
- Modifying the shape of your lawn is easier than digging it up and relaying a new one. It is simple to trim it to a smaller shape if you want a lawn of the same area, and if you wish to change the angle or shape, it may be possible to leave most of it intact, and simply lift and relay some of the turf.

LEFT: *Strong lines and several changes of level give this small garden plenty of interest. In this kind of design, the hard landscaping is more important than the soft landscaping (the plants).*

CHOICES CHECKLIST

Before you draw up your design, make a list of requirements for your ideal garden. You will almost certainly have to abandon or defer some of them, but at least you will realize which features are most important to you.

Use this checklist at the rough plan stage, when decisions have to be made . . . and it is easy to change your mind!

Features

- Barbecue ☐
- Beds ☐
- Borders, for herbaceous ☐
- Borders, for shrubs ☐
- Borders, mixed ☐
- Birdbath ☐
- Changes of level ☐
- Fruit garden ☐
- Gravelled area ☐
- Greenhouse/conservatory ☐
- Herb garden ☐
- Lawn (mainly for decoration) ☐
- Lawn (mainly for recreation) ☐
- Ornaments ☐
- Patio/terrace ☐
- Pergola ☐
- Pond ☐
- Raised beds ☐
- Summerhouse ☐
- Sundial ☐
- Vegetable plot ☐
- Plus .... ☐

Functional features

- Compost area ☐
- Garage ☐
- Toolshed ☐
- Plus .... ☐

Necessities

- Children's play area ☐
  - Climbing frame ☐
  - Sandpit ☐
  - Swing ☐
- Clothes dryer ☐
- Dustbin area ☐
- Plus .... ☐

Choosing a Style

Before sitting down with pencil and paper to sketch out your garden, spend a little time thinking about the style that you want to achieve. In many gardens plants and features are used for no other reason than that they appeal; an excellent reason, perhaps, but not the way to create an overall design that will make your garden stand out from others in the street.

The styles shown in the following six pages are not exhaustive, and probably none will be exactly right for your own garden, but they will help you to clarify your thoughts. You should know roughly what you want from your garden before you start to design it.

FORMAL APPROACH

Formal gardens appeal to those who delight in crisp, neat edges, straight lines and a sense of order. Many traditional suburban gardens are formal in outline, with rectangular lawns flanked by straight flower borders, and perhaps rectangular or circular flower beds cut into them. Such rigid designs are often dictated by the drive for the car and straight paths laid by the house builder.

Although the gardens shown here are all very different, what they have in common is a structure as important as the plants contained within it. The designs are largely symmetrical, with no pretence at creating a natural-looking environment for the plants.

The very size and shape of most small gardens limits the opportunities for natural-looking landscapes, so a formal style is a popular choice.

Parterres and knot gardens

Parterres and knot gardens often appeal to those with a sense of garden history, though in a small garden the effect can only ever be a shadow of the grand designs used by sixteenth-century French and Italian gardeners.

Parterres are areas consisting of a series of shaped beds, or compartments, that fit together to form a pattern, often quite complex, on the ground. They were designed, often, to be viewed from the upper windows of grand houses.

Knot gardens, originally designed to be viewed from above, are similar but low-growing clipped hedges are used to form the geometric and often interwoven designs. The space between hedges can be filled with flowers or, more historically correct, coloured sands or gravel, or even crushed coal if black appeals.

ABOVE: *A knot garden. This kind of garden is not colourful, but the strong lines and formal shape, backed by a variety of greens, make it a restful place to relax.*

LEFT: *This small, enclosed courtyard garden balances a central focal point with a boundary that features this dramatic entrance.*

These are expensive gardens to create, slow to establish, and labour-intensive to maintain, but the results can be stunning. This kind of garden is unsuitable for a young family.

Formal herb gardens
Herb gardens are popular features and are much easier to create than knot gardens. Illustrations of both old and new herb gardens in books will often give you ideas for designs.

Rose gardens
A formal rose garden is easy to create, and it will look good even in its first season. To provide interest throughout the year, edge the beds with seasonal flowers and underplant the roses with spring bulbs or low-growing summer flowers.

Paved gardens
A small garden lends itself to being paved throughout. By growing most plants in raised beds or in containers, less bending is involved and many of the smaller plants are more easily appreciated. Climbers can be used to make the most of vertical space, and if you plant in open areas left in the paving, the garden can still look green.

Courtyard gardens
Space can be at a real premium in the heart of a town, but you can turn your backyard into an oasis-like courtyard garden, with floor tiles and white walls that reflect the light. Add some lush green foliage, an 'architectural' tree or large shrub, and the sound of running water. Although the plants may be few, the impact is strong.

Traditional designs
A small formal garden, with a rectangular lawn, straight herbaceous border, and rose and flower beds is still a popular choice with gardeners looking for the opportunity to grow a wide variety of plants such as summer bedding, herbaceous plants, and popular favourites such as roses. The design element is less important than the plants.

LEFT: *The use of white masonry paint can help to lighten a dark basement garden or one enclosed by high walls.*

BELOW: *This long, narrow plot has been broken up by strong lines: a useful design technique.*

INFORMAL EFFECTS

The informality of the cottage garden and the 'wilderness' atmosphere of a wild garden are difficult to achieve in a small space, especially in a town. However, with fences well clothed with plants so that modern buildings do not intrude, an informal garden can work even here.

Cottage gardens

The cottage garden style is created partly by design and the use of suitable paving materials (bricks for paths instead of modern paving slabs), and also by the choice of plants.

Relatively little hard landscaping is necessary for a cottage garden – brick paths and perhaps stepping-stones through the beds may be enough. It is the juxtaposition of 'old-fashioned' plants and vegetables that creates the casual but colourful look associated with this type of garden.

Mix annuals with perennials – especially those that will self-seed such as calendulas and *Limnanthes douglasii*, which will grow everywhere and create a colourful chaos. If flowers self-sow at the edge of the path, or between other plants, leave most of them to grow where they have chosen to put down roots.

Plant some vegetables among the flowers, and perhaps grow decorative runner beans up canes at the back of the border.

Wildlife gardens

A small wildlife garden seems almost a contradiction in terms, but even a tiny plot can offer a refuge for all kinds of creatures if you design and plant with wildlife in mind.

Wildlife enthusiasts sometimes let their gardens 'go wild'. However, this is not necessary. A garden like this one looks well kept and pretty, yet it provides long vegetation where animals and insects can hide and find

RIGHT: *The house itself will inevitably dominate a small garden, especially when you look back towards it. Covering the walls with climbers will help it to blend in unobtrusively.*

food. There is water to attract aquatic life, and flowers and shrubs to bring the butterflies and seeds for the birds.

An orchard can also be a magnet for wildlife of many kinds.

Woodland gardens

A woodland effect is clearly impractical for a very tiny garden, but if you have a long, narrow back garden, trees and shrubs can be used very effectively. Choose quick-growing deciduous trees with a light canopy (birch trees, *Betula* species, are a good choice where there's space, but they can grow tall). Avoid evergreens, otherwise you will lose the benefit of the spring flowers and ferns that are so much a feature of the traditional woodland garden.

RIGHT: *The woodland effect can be delightfully refreshing on a warm spring or summer day, but works best with trees that have a tall canopy that allows plenty of light to filter through. Although a pond is attractive in this situation, care will have to be taken to remove leaves in the autumn.*

BELOW: *A pretty pond is a super way to attract wildlife, and looks especially good if well integrated into the garden like this one.*

Use small-growing rhododendrons and azaleas to provide colour beneath the tree canopy, and fill in with ground cover plants, naturalized bulbs such as wood anemones and bluebells, and plant woodland plants such as ferns and primroses.

Use the woodland effect to block out an unattractive view or overlooking houses. As an added bonus it is low-maintenance too.

Rocks and streams

Rock or water features alone seldom work as a 'design'. They are usually most effective planned as part of a larger scheme. Combined, however, rocks and water can be used as the central theme of a design that attempts to create a natural style in an informal garden.

Meandering meadows

Instead of the rectangular lawn usually associated with small gardens, try broadening the borders with gentle sweeps, meandering to merge with an unobstructed boundary if there is an attractive view beyond. If the distant view is unappealing, take the border round so that the lawn curves to extend beyond the point of view. Use shrubs and lower-growing border plants to create the kind of border that you might find at the edge of a strip of woodland.

Bright beds and borders

If plants are more important than the elements of design, use plenty of sweeping beds and borders, and concentrate heavily on shrubs and herbaceous plants to give the garden shape. Allow plants to tumble over edges and let them grow informally among paving.

If you want to create a strong sense of design within such a plant-oriented small garden, use focal points such as ornaments, garden seats or birdbaths.

Distant Influences

Professional garden designers are frequently influenced by classic styles from other countries, especially Japan, but amateurs are often nervous of trying such designs themselves. Provided you start with the clear premise that what pleases you is the only real criterion of whether something works, creating a particular 'foreign' style can be great fun. Adapt the chosen style to suit climate, landscape and the availability of suitable plants and materials.

Japanese gardens

'Real' Japanese gardens are for the purist who is prepared to give the subject much study. Raked sand and grouped stones have special meaning for those briefed in the Japanese traditions, but can be enigmatic to untrained Western eyes.

Many elements from the Japanese style can be adapted for Western tastes, however, and many gardeners are happy to introduce the essential visual elements without concern for deeper meanings. This style is easily adapted to a small space, and the uncluttered appearance makes a confined area appear larger.

Stone and gravel gardens

Although stones and rocks are widely used in Japanese gardens, they can also be key components in creating a garden which is more reminiscent of a dry river bed in an arid region – the sort of garden that you might find in a rocky, semi-desert area.

This kind of garden needs minimal maintenance, and if you choose drought-tolerant plants it should look good even in a very dry summer.

Stone gardens appeal to those with a strong sense of design, and an adventurous spirit, rather than to plant-lovers. Although the plants play a vital role in the drama of the scene, opportunities for using a wide range of plants is limited.

Gravel gardens are also a practical choice where space is limited. You can add some large boulders or rocks as focal points, and plants can be used much more freely. It is easy to plant through the gravel, and a wide range of plants can be grown in groups or as isolated specimens.

LEFT: *You don't need a lot of plants to create a Japanese-style garden. Strong hard landscaping and the restrained use of plants is a hallmark of the Japanese garden style.*

OPPOSITE TOP: *The use of formal water, painted wall and patio overhead gives this garden a Mediterranean atmosphere.*

OPPOSITE: *The dry gravel slope and the use of plants like yuccas help to create the illusion of a garden in a warm, dry climate.*

Mediterranean gardens

The illusion of a Mediterranean garden is most easily achieved in a backyard or tiny walled garden. The effect is difficult to achieve if you view neighbouring homes and gardens over a low fence – guaranteed to kill any self-deception as to location!

Paint the walls white, or a pale colour, to reflect the light and create a bright, airy feeling. If possible include alcoves in which you can place plants, or build ledges on which you can stand pots.

Pave the area with bricks, terracotta-coloured pavers or tiles – but steer clear of paving slabs. Use plenty of decorative terracotta pots and tubs.

The illusion is completed by using plenty of appropriate plants, such as pelargoniums, oleanders, bougainvilleas, and daturas (brugmansias). Stand pots of large cacti and succulents outdoors too.

The success of this kind of garden owes less to its structural design than to the use of appropriate plants, ornaments, and garden furniture.

Exotic effects

You can give your garden an exotic appearance by concentrating on exotic-looking plants that are hardier than their appearance might suggest. Grow them in pots on the patio (which will enable you to move the tender kinds to a greenhouse or conservatory, or just a sheltered position, if you garden in a cold area), or in a gravel garden.

Tough, spiky plants to consider for this kind of garden are many of the hardy yuccas, and phormiums if they grow in your area without protection. Add some agaves such as *A. americana* if you live in a very mild area.

Palms are associated with warm climates, but some are tough enough to withstand moderately severe winters. *Trachycarpus fortunei* is particularly reliable. Just a few well-chosen plants can create images of far-away places.

Getting the Details Right

One of the most difficult tasks when planning a small garden is working out how best to use the available space. For most of us, it is the decorative features – the plants themselves – that take priority. But functional features are important, too, and it is best to allocate space for these first.

Once the fundamentals have been dealt with, it is much easier to decide where you want to have planting areas. Within this framework, you will be able to transform the space into a decorative outdoor room that you will want to use for much more of the year than just the few summer months.

Practical considerations

You will probably have decided that you want somewhere to sit. This need not necessarily be next to the house. For example, if evening is the time of day when you will most often be able to sit outside, and there's a spot at the far end of your garden that catches the evening sun, then it makes sense to site your seating area here.

If you have children, you will probably want somewhere for them to play. Common sense dictates that this is near the house, to make supervision easier. Try, if you can, to include a sandpit – children will be thrilled with one just 1m (3ft) square; if there is just a little more space, there will be room enough for a small play house.

Although there is a temptation to banish such mundane essentials as the tool shed and the compost bins to the bottom of the garden, with a long site this will not be very practical. Consider giving them a more central position, suitably screened from view all round.

Plan out in your mind the best place for each of these features in much the same way as you might plan your kitchen, where you also need to make the best possible use of the available space to make it efficient to work in and comfortable to be in.

RIGHT: *By dividing up the spaces, you can create visual depth. These two spectacular box orbs help to define a vista and lend perspective to the arbour at the end.*

Making changes

Once these priorities are fixed, it will be much easier to work out the layout of the garden. This is important, even if you don't have the resources for new paving and landscaping, at least for the foreseeable future. For example, there may be a flower bed just where you feel it would be best to create a seating area. With the garden layout left as it is, you would continually

ABOVE: *Even the smallest of spaces may be transformed with decorative touches such as pots of colourful primulas in a wooden holder.*

have to bring furniture in and out when you need it. That is no more comfortable than a living room would be if you had to bring in a chair every time you wanted to sit down. However, with a few little changes, like simply turfing over the flower bed, you can organize the garden so it is ready for relaxation any time you want.

Planning for privacy

Privacy and shelter are essential requirements for relaxation in the garden but, especially in built-up areas, they can be difficult to achieve. Try fixing trellis on top of walls and fences to create extra height. You can then grow decorative climbers to provide a wonderful natural wallpaper. You could plant fast-

ABOVE: *This wall hides part of the garden, offering privacy, while the archway frames a statue, bringing perspective to the whole space.*

BELOW: *Secret places can be created in even the smallest of spaces. This pathway winds through plantings in a tiny 3m (10ft) plot.*

growing conifers such as thuja, although you should always check their potential final height or you could end up deeply overshadowed, if not overlooked.

Seating areas in particular need privacy. Even if you live in the middle of the country, you will feel much more comfortable if you site these where, at least on one side, there is the protection of a wall of some sort. This could be the garden boundary wall, a hedge, or even a trellis screen to lend a more intimate feel.

Overhead screens

If you are closely overlooked, you may also want to create privacy from above. One of the most successful ways of doing this is to put up a pergola and let it become entwined with vines or other climbers. That way, you have a 'roof', which filters the natural light and allows a free flow of fresh air.

Creating the Right Atmosphere

Creating the right mood for your garden depends on stimulating the senses: sight, sound, touch, taste and smell, all of which are supplied free of charge by nature. And simply by being outside, you are closer to nature, so it should be even easier to bring atmosphere to the garden than to anywhere else in your home. For many people, the garden is just as important as any room in the house.

Sight and sound

You will find a wealth of suggestions for stimulating the senses throughout the following pages. These ideas can be set against the visual delights provided by the plants themselves. As well as the sound of birdsong and buzzing insects, you can add the music of wind chimes or the evocative trickling of water in even the smallest plot.

Smells galore

The outdoors also provides the most glorious fragrances, both sweet – from flowers such as roses, honeysuckle, and jasmine – and aromatic – from lavender and piquant herbs. Remember that scent develops in the warmth of the sun, so choose a sunny spot and that after a spring or summer shower, the air can smell heavenly.

Touch and taste

Touch, too, can be stimulated as it is impossible to walk through a garden without being touched by – or reaching out to touch – some of the plants. This is especially pleasing if they have interesting textures. Plan for a variety of these, using plants with fleshy, frondy and feathery leaves. Finally, eating out in the garden completes the sensory picture.

ABOVE: *A pretty Victorian-style wire plant stand, filled with flowering plants, brings flashes of bright white high up in the middle of a largely green planting area.*

LEFT: *The sound of trickling water enhances any outdoor area, and a water feature need not take up a large amount of space. Water flows over this wall-mounted, cast-iron shell.*

ABOVE: *A courtyard is set out as an outdoor room, with a cherry tree suggesting pretty 'wallpaper' and blossom forming a carpet.*

ABOVE: *Brick-shaped paviours set into a tiny lawn, then decorated with urns mimic the vistas set out on the floors of classical gardens.*

A hint of romance

The most romantic gardens hint at intimacy. They could literally be enclosed outdoor rooms, such as courtyards, balconies or roof gardens, which automatically offer intimacy. If your space is rather larger, you can add romantic interest by creating hidden places. This isn't difficult, even in the smallest garden. You can put a door in the fence or wall to hint at another space beyond; put up an archway to give the feeling of moving from one area to another; or add a trellis screen to section off an eating area or enclose a garden seat.

Creating an illusion

As well as creating intimacy, these dividing tactics also give the illusion of space. Adding an archway or screen means you are able to see beyond into another area, which lends perspective to the whole space, giving it structure and shape. However light the resulting screening is, it hints at secret places and romance.

LEFT: *A series of basic motifs painted over stripes of vibrant colours gives simple pots a rich Mexican look.*

FOCAL POINTS

Focal points are an essential part of good garden design, relevant whatever the size of garden. They help to take the eye to a favourable part and away from the less favourable. They can also act as signposts to lead the eye around the garden and placed at the end of the garden they can lead the eye into the distance, thus making the garden seem larger than it is in reality.

Adding interest to lawns
An expanse of even a well-kept lawn may look bare and a little boring, especially if all the interest is in the beds and borders around the edges. It can be useful to create a focal point within the lawn, but this often works best if offset to one side or towards one end of the lawn, rather than in the centre. Position it where you want to take the eye to an attractive view, or use it to fill an area that lacks interest. Try to avoid placing the focal point against a background that is already busy or colourful; otherwise one will fight against the other for attention.

Birdbaths and sundials
A sundial is a popular choice for a focal point on the lawn, but should be placed in a sunny position if it is to look in the least credible. A birdbath is another favourite option, and is especially delightful if it is close to the house where the visiting birds can be seen and enjoyed.

Statues and plants
In a small garden, a spectacular focal point such as a statue can be used to dominate a corner of the garden so that the limitations of scale and size become irrelevant for the moment. Bear in mind that plants can be used as well as inanimate objects. While a well-placed ornament or figure will serve as a simple focal point, when used in conjunction with plants, the effect can be particularly striking.

LEFT: *An exquisite, weathered wood and metal door makes a decorative garden entrance while the statue draws the eye towards the doorway.*

RIGHT: *A formal geometric pond with its oriental overtones makes a charming focal point in a terraced town garden.*

FAR RIGHT: *An enchanting little pond, complete with fountain and cherub, mimics designs on a much grander scale.*

Gateways and arches

Gateways and arches make excellent focal points in a garden, and can add a feeling of mystery and promise from whichever side you view them. Both gateways and arches work best if the areas on either side of them are laid out in contrasting styles or are visually very different to each other. In a long, narrow garden, for example, you could produce a series of arches or gates, taking the eye further on into a journey of exploration.

ABOVE: *A tripod can be used to draw the eye to the end of the garden. Once fully grown this* Clematis *'Jackmanii' will cover it completely.*

RIGHT: *Beneath this metal walkway, Greek pithoi in a bed of euphorbia and hellebores are used to great effect as a focal point.*

Screens and Disguises

Unless you are extremely fortunate, there will be a certain view or some objects within the garden that you really want to hide. Focal points can be used to take the eye away from some of them, but others will require some form of screening or disguise. A little bit of trickery can even be used to make the garden look a different shape – to shorten the appearance of a long thin site, for example, or to give apparent depth to a garden that is wide but shallow.

Living screens

Many common hedging plants can be allowed to grow taller than normal to form a shrubby screen. Space the plants further apart than for a hedge, so that they retain a shrubby shape, and clip or prune only when it is necessary to keep within bounds. Avoid a formal clipped shape unless you are screening within a very formal garden. Most hedging plants will grow to twice their normal hedge height if you give them more space and do not restrict them by frequent clipping and pruning.

Matching screen and setting

Choose plants appropriate to the setting. In a Japanese-style garden, many of the tall bamboos will make an excellent screen for, say, a garage wall or oil storage tank. Use shrubby plants in a garden where there are lots of shrubs, and especially if the shrub border can be taken up to the screening point. On a patio, a climber-covered trellis may look good.

Urban solutions

In town gardens, and particularly in the case of balcony and roof gardens, the problem is to minimize the impact of surrounding homes, offices and factories. These usually require impracticably huge walls to mask the view, which would also make the garden excessively dark. In a very small garden, trees may not be a practical solution for this type of screening either, although in a larger one they will probably provide the answer.

ABOVE: *Dense planting at the end of the garden suggests that the property goes further, even if the path leads nowhere in particular.*

A sensible compromise is to extend the wall or fence with a trellis, or similar framework, along which you can grow climbers. This will not block out the view completely, but it will soften the harsh impact of buildings and help to concentrate the eye within the garden by minimizing the distractions beyond. The boundary itself will be given extra height and interest.

Boundaries and beyond

A combination of plants and hard landscaping is often the most satisfactory way to screen a view beyond a boundary. Trees are a particularly pleasing solution. Even if they lose their leaves in winter, the network of branches is often sufficient to break up the harsh outline of buildings and beyond, and in summer – when you spend more

time in the garden and require more privacy – the canopy of foliage will usually block out most of the view. Trees are a particularly good solution if the aspect is such that most of the shadow falls away from your garden rather than over it.

Optical illusions

Although there are limits to how much you can change the site of your garden physically, it is possible to employ some optical tricks with which to alter its appearance.

A long, straight view will be foreshortened by a tall object or bright colours at the far end of it. If, on the other hand, the distant end has a scaled-down ornament and misty, pale colours, the ornament will appear to be further away.

Using colour and mirrors

A straight lawn can be narrowed towards the further end to make it seem longer, and the effect can be enhanced by using a bright splash of colour near the beginning. If your garden is wide but not very deep, you can give an impression of enhanced depth by positioning a mirror almost opposite the entrance and surrounding it with plants. As you step outside, you seem to see an entrance to another, hidden part of the garden.

If the area is surrounded by walls, they can be painted white (for extra light), green (to blend in), or with a floral mural where the planting is sparse. Shaped trellises can be added to give the impression of a distant perspective rather than a flat wall, and a false doorway with a *trompe l'oeil* vista disappearing away behind it can be wonderfully effective at enlarging a confined space.

OPPOSITE: *Here, painted square trellis has been used as a screen, dividing off one part of the garden from another.*

ABOVE: *A cleverly positioned mirror will reflect the plants back into the garden, suggesting that it is larger than it actually is.*

ABOVE: *An ordinary, wooden-slat garden door leads from an alleyway to a tiny but enchanting city garden.*

RIGHT: *A floral arbour makes a rich decorative frame for a piece of statuary, creating a very theatrical effect and hiding an unsightly view.*

UTILITIES AND STORAGE

The need to find room for less attractive bits and pieces of the garden – such as the dustbins (garbage cans) and the compost heap – is a fact of life, but utilities like these need not be on show. With a little imagination, they can be completely disguised or made to blend in with their surroundings. Storage space will also be needed for the amount of practical paraphernalia that gardening brings, from tools and pots and planters to potting compost (soil mix), seeds and string.

In an ideal world, dustbins (garbage cans) and recycling containers would be beautiful in themselves, but, unfortunately, in reality they are seldom an attractive sight. They are necessary, however, and they do need to be accessible. You can ignore your dustbins (garbage cans) or spend a little time and effort blending them in, by painting them to co-ordinate with the overall scheme (if this is feasible), using a screen of plants to hide them, or camouflaging them with a plant-covered trellis.

RIGHT: *A wire shelving unit, intertwined with clematis, makes a delightful garden detail that also serves a practical purpose.*

BELOW: *Shelving can be used for purely decorative purposes outside as well as in, no matter how small the garden.*

Compost bins

Compost is an invaluable aid for any gardener, no matter how small or large the plot. Material for composting can simply be piled in a heap in a corner and left to rot, but a manufactured container certainly looks more appealing. Various kinds of compost containers are available from garden centres. Those made of plastic tend to resemble rubbish bins (garbage cans), so why not treat them in the same way, either decorating them or screening them with plants. An alternative is to make your own container from suitably treated timber, painted to match the house or the rest of the garden furniture. The design can be very simple, with timber slats fixed to corner posts, or more imaginative – such as a compost bin in the shape of a traditional beehive!

Garden sheds

Garden sheds are the classic means of storing tools and equipment. Most gardens can accommodate one, although smaller gardens may be restricted to a mini-shed or tool store (cabinet), which can be as small as 30cm (12in) deep and so can be tucked into a corner. The shed need not be an eyesore: if painted and decorated it can become an attractive part of the garden architecture. Alternatively, you can camouflage the shed with plants climbing up a trellis. Fix the trellis to timber battens using catches rather than screws, so you will be able to remove both climbers and trellis when the shed needs another coat of preservative.

All-weather shelves

Another solution is to put your goods on show. Garden pots can be very attractive and, displayed on all-weather shelves, can become part of the decorative appeal of the garden. This is an excellent solution for very small gardens and patios, all of which still need space for practical elements.

Instead of buying ready-made garden shelving, you could build your own from timber and treat it with exterior-quality paint. Old metal shelves can be given a new life using car spray paint or specially manufactured metal paint, which can even be sprayed straight over rust.

All shelves should be fixed firmly to the garden wall – avoid fixing to the house wall as this could lead to damp (moisture) problems. Once fitted, use shelves for displays, to store tools, or for bringing on young seedlings, which can look delightful potted up in ranks of terracotta.

RIGHT: *Every available space should be utilized in a small garden. Here, a box on a shelf has been used to grow a few vegetables.*

BELOW RIGHT: *These well-filled borders help to draw the attention away from a storage shed hidden in the corner of the garden.*

BELOW: *French baker's shelves against a house wall make a garden nursery for growing seedlings on – and do not take up much room.*

BASIC PATTERNS

Having decided on the *style* of garden that you want, and the *features* that you need to incorporate, it is time to tackle the much more difficult task of applying them to your own garden. The chances are that your garden will be the wrong size or shape, or the situation or outlook is inappropriate to the style of garden that you have admired. The way round this impasse is to keep in mind a style without attempting to recreate it closely.

If you can't visualize the whole of your back or front garden as, say, a stone or Japanese garden, it may be possible to include the feature as an element within a more general design.

STARTING POINTS

If you analyse successful garden designs, most fall into one of the three basic patterns described below, though clever planting and variations on the themes almost always result in individual designs.

Circular theme

Circular themes are very effective at disguising the predictable shape of a rectangular garden. Circular lawns, circular patios, and circular beds are all options, and you only need to overlap and interlock a few circles to create a stylish garden. Plants fill the gaps between the curved areas and the straight edges.

Using a compass, try various combinations of circles to see whether you can create an attractive pattern. Be prepared to vary the radii and to overlap the circles if necessary.

Diagonal theme

This device creates a sense of space by taking the eye along and across the garden. Start by drawing grid lines at 45 degrees to the house or main fence. Then draw in the design, using the grid as a guide.

Rectangular theme

Most people design using a rectangular theme – even though they may not make a conscious effort to do so. The device is effective if you want to create a formal look, or wish to divide a long, narrow garden up into smaller sections.

Circular theme

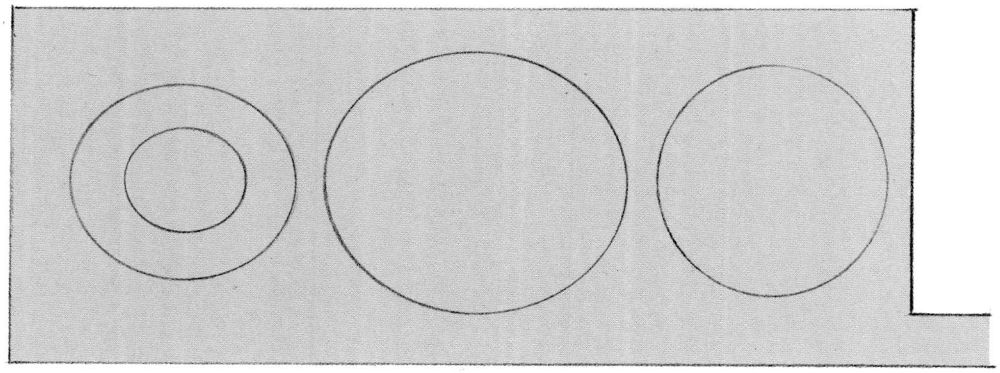

Diagonal theme

Rectangular theme

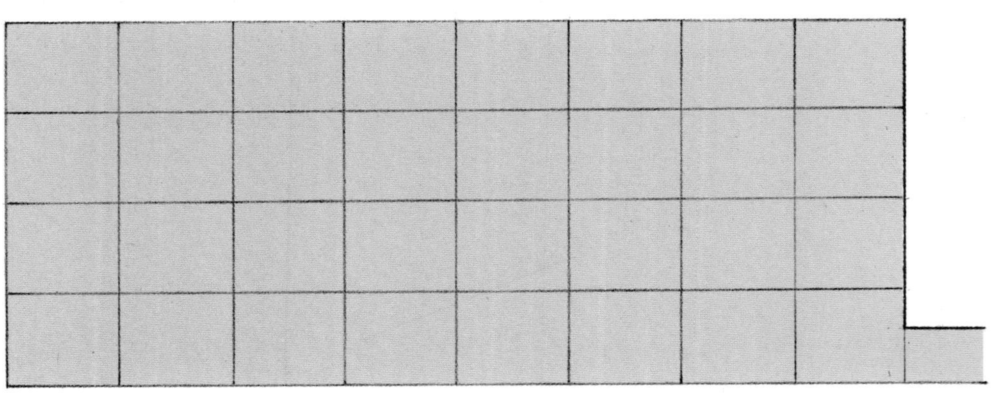

Circular theme

Diagonal theme

Rectangular theme

MEASURING UP

Whether designing a garden from scratch or simply modifying what you already have, you need to draw a plan of the garden as it is. A drawn plan will enable you to see the overall design clearly, and to experiment with different ideas before committing yourself to a definite option.

HOW TO MEASURE THE SITE

YOU WILL NEED:

- One, or ideally two, 30m (100ft) tape measures (unless your garden is very short). Plasticized fabric is the best material as linen stretches and steel is difficult to manipulate.
- A steel rule about 1.8m (6ft) long (to measure short distances).
- Pegs to mark out positions, and meat skewers to hold one end of the tape in position if working alone.
- Clip-board and pad or graph paper.
- A couple of pencils, sharpener and an eraser.

1 Make a rough visual sketch by eye. It does not have to be accurate, but try to keep existing important features roughly in proportion. Leave plenty of space on the plan for adding dimensions. If necessary, use several sheets of paper, and indicate where they join.

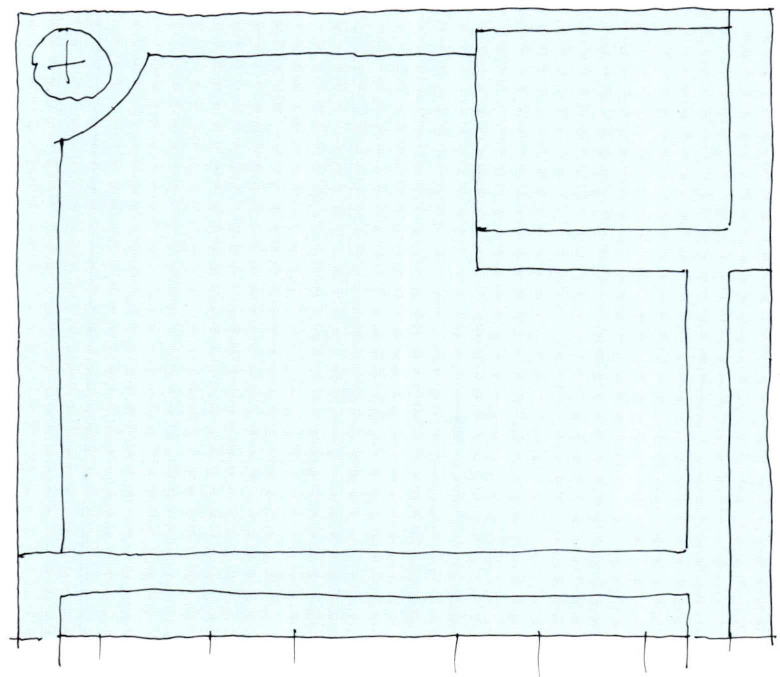

2 Choose a base line from which to start measuring. Make it a long, straight edge from which the majority of other points can be measured. A long fence or a house wall are often convenient starting points. From the straight edge or base line, measure off key points, such as the positions of windows, doors, any outbuildings, and so on. Measure out at right angles to establish the distances from the base line to the important features so that you can build the outline plan. Most key points on your plan can be established by measuring again at right angles from these right angles if necessary.

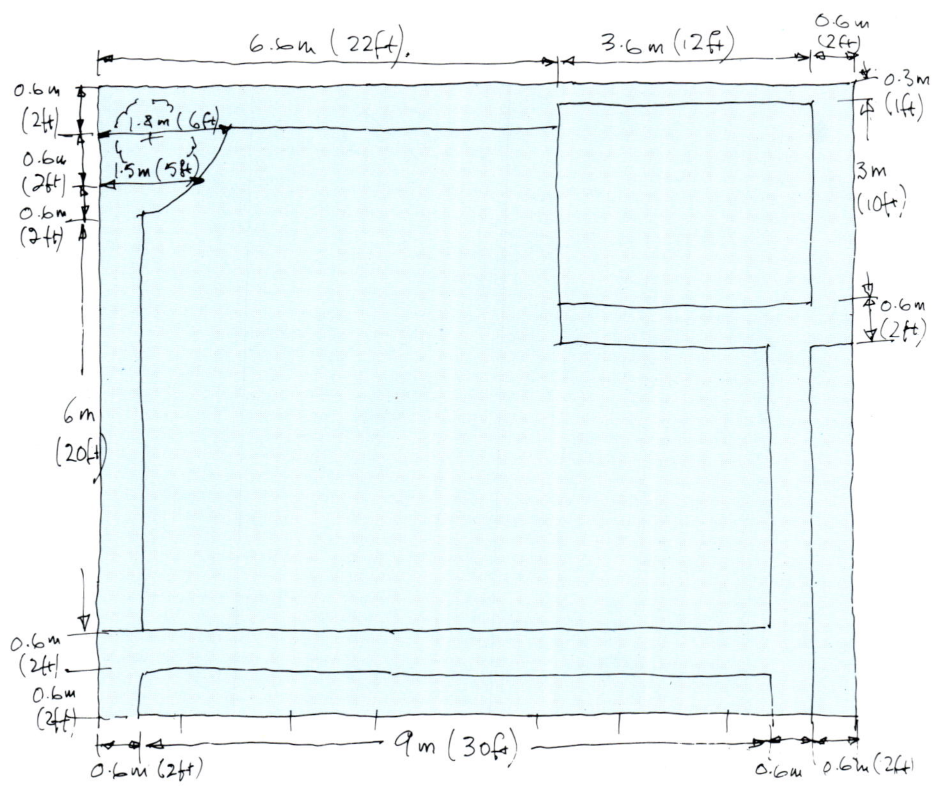

HOW TO MAKE A SCALE DRAWING

1 To make a scale drawing, choose a scale that enables you to fit the garden (or at least a self-contained section of it) onto the one sheet of graph paper. Buy large sheets of graph paper if necessary. For most small gardens, a scale of 1:50 (2cm to a metre or ¼in to 1ft) is about right. If your garden is large, try a scale of 1:100. Draw your base line in first, then transfer the scale measurements. When the right-angle measurements have been transferred, draw in the relevant outlines.

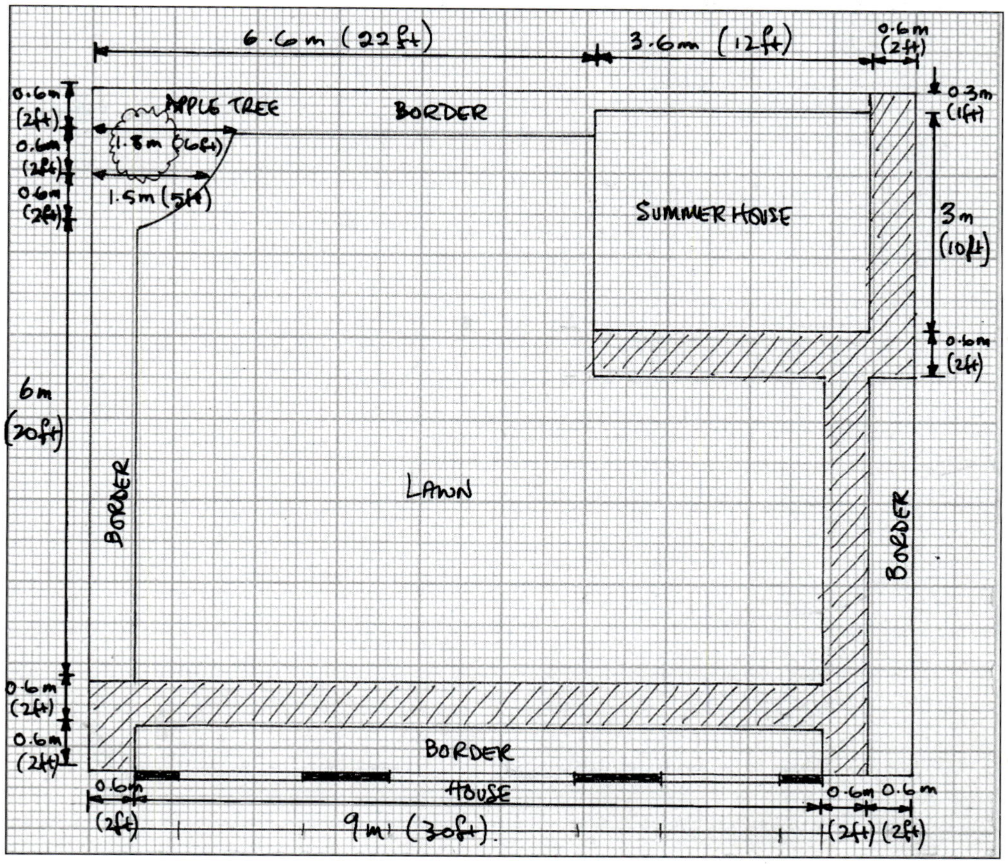

DON'T MAKE WORK

When measuring your plot, don't waste time measuring and plotting the position of features that you have no intention of retaining in your replanned garden. If you intend to remove an unsightly tree or large shrub, or to pull down a garden shed that has seen better days, leave them off your plan – they will only clutter and confuse.

HOW TO USE TRIANGULATION

It may not be possible to position some features or key points simply by measuring a series of right angles. These are best determined by a process known as triangulation. Using a known base, perhaps the corners of the house, simply measure the distance from two points to the position to be established. By transferring the scale distances from the two known points later, the exact position can be established. To transfer the triangulated measurements, set a compass to each of the scale distances in turn, and scribe an arc in the approximate position. Where the second arc intersects the first one, your point is established.

To fix position of tree, measure to A, then to B. Strike arcs on a scale drawing with compasses set at these measurements. Where the arcs cross shows the position of the tree in relation to the house.

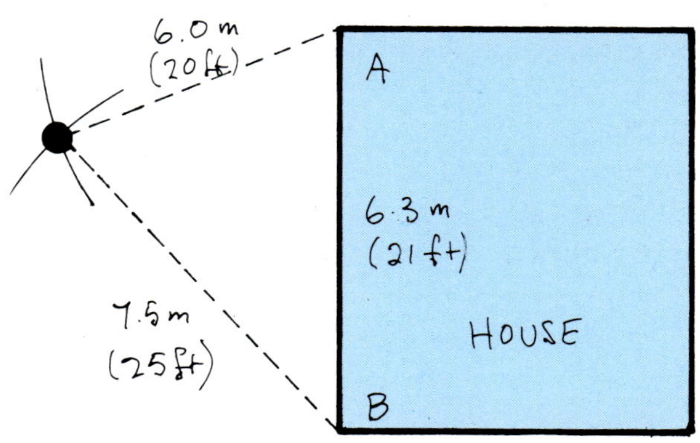

SLOPES AND CONTOURS

In a large garden, slopes are often significant and may have to be taken into account. You can generally ignore gentle slopes in a small garden, or make a mental note of them.

Creating the Design

The most off-putting part of drawing up the design is the blank sheet of paper. Once this is overcome, producing alternative plans becomes fun, and there is the satisfaction of marking out the space to see the final effect in the garden. Just follow the stages below.

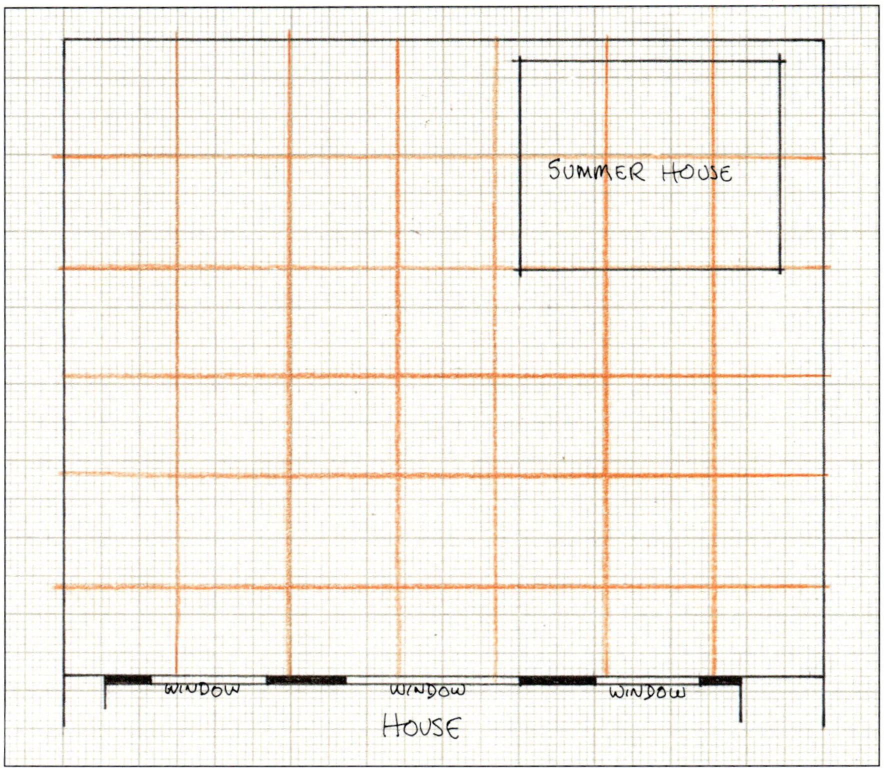

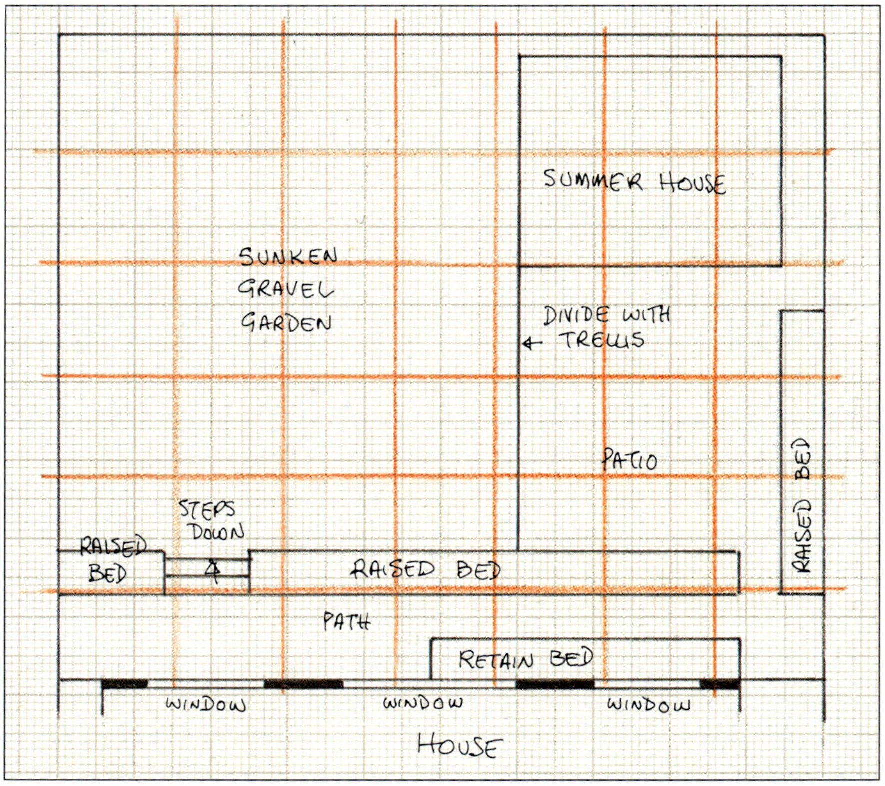

Stage 1: the basic grid

With the measurements transferred to graph paper you should already have a plan of your garden, showing any permanent structures and features that you want to retain.

Now superimpose onto this grid the type of design you have in mind – one based on circles, rectangles or diagonals, for example. If you are sure of the type of layout you want, draw these directly onto your plan in a second colour. If you think you might change your mind, draw the grid on a transparent overlay. For most small gardens, grid lines 1.8–2.4m (6–8ft) apart are about right.

Using an overlay, or a photocopy of your plan complete with grid, mark on the new features that you would like to include, in their approximate positions. You might find it helpful to cut out pieces of paper to an appropriate size and shape so that you can move them around.

Stage 2: the rough

Using an overlay or a photocopy, start sketching in your plan. If you can visualize an overall design, sketch this in first, then move around your features to fit into it. If you have not reached this stage, start by sketching in the features you have provisionally positioned – but be prepared to adjust them as the design evolves.

You will need to make many attempts. Don't be satisfied with the first one – it may be the best, but you won't know this unless you explore other options.

Don't worry about planting details at this stage, except perhaps for a few important plants that form focal points in the design.

Stage 3: the detailed drawing
Details such as the type of paving should be decided now – not only because it will help you to see the final effect, but also because you need to work to areas that use multiples of full blocks, slabs or bricks if possible. Draw in key plants, especially large trees and shrubs, but omit detailed planting plans at this stage.

Trying it out
Before ordering materials or starting construction, mark out as much of the design as possible in the garden. Use string and pegs to indicate the areas, then walk around them. If possible take a look from an upstairs window. This will give a much better idea of the overall design and whether paths and sitting areas are large enough.

Use tall canes to indicate the positions of important plants and new trees. This will show how much screening they are likely to offer, and whether they may become a problem in time. By observing the shadow cast at various parts of the day, you'll also know whether shade will be a problem – for other plants or for a sitting-out area.

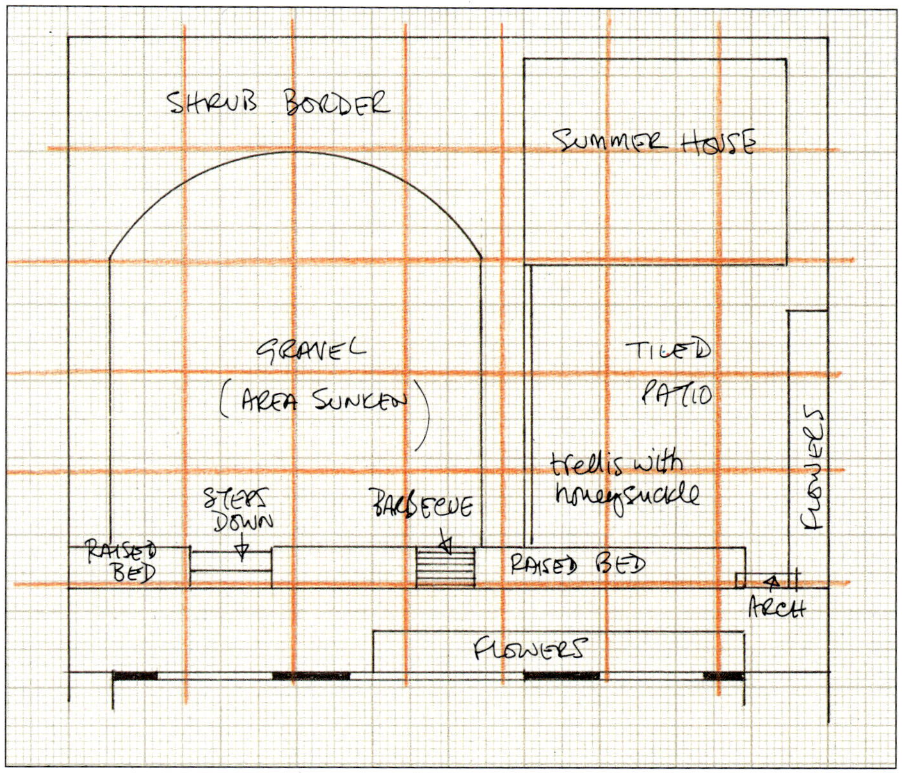

CONSTRUCTION

You can employ a contractor to construct the garden for you, but many gardeners prefer to get help with the main structural features, such as patios and raised beds, and do the rest of the work themselves to keep the cost down. Even the 'heavy' jobs are well within the ability of most gardeners with modest DIY skills. For more information see the next section.

Difficult Sites

Difficult sites and problem shapes can be a challenge, but one that can be met with a little determination and a touch of inspiration. Some ways to tackle a selection of special areas are suggested in the following pages.

If your garden is little more than a roof or a balcony, or your house has been wedged in on a building plot that is perhaps L-shaped, or even triangular, traditional garden design techniques might seem difficult to apply.

Many of the design ideas outlined in the previous chapter can still be applied, however, although you may require an alternative design strategy for specific areas.

Patios usually feature as an element in a larger overall design, but in turn have to be designed themselves. Difficult sites like slopes, windy

ABOVE: *When your front garden is as tiny as this, compensate by making the most of vertical space with climbers and windowboxes.*

LEFT: *High walls, which would otherwise have dominated this garden, are balanced by strong vertical lines. Even the tops of the walls have been put to good use!*

alleys and passageways between houses demand thoughtful planning and appropriate plants.

Front gardens present a special problem, not because of size or shape, but because a large portion of the garden is usually dedicated to the car – often there is a broad drive to the garage or a hard standing area where the vehicle is left for long periods. Legal restrictions about what you can do with your front garden can be another potential problem – especially on estates where the developers or local authority want to maintain an 'open plan' style.

If conditions really are too inhospitable for permanent plants, or the space too limited for a 'proper' garden, containers can provide the answer. Use them creatively, and be prepared to replant or rotate frequently so that they always look good, whatever the time of year.

Unpromising backyards and basements can be transformed as much by a coat of masonry paint, a few choice plants, and some elegant garden furniture and tubs, as by an extensive – and expensive – redesign. Imagination and inspiration are the keynotes for this type of garden design.

In this chapter you will find many solutions to specific problems like these, and even if your particular difficulty is not covered exactly, you should be able to find useful ideas to adapt.

ABOVE: *This long, narrow plot has been broken up into sections, with an angled path so that you don't walk along the garden in a straight line.*

LEFT: *Roof gardens are always cramped, but by keeping most of the pots around the edge it is possible to create a sense of space in the centre.*

UNUSUAL SHAPES

Turn a problem shape to your advantage by using its unusual outline to create a garden that stands out from others in your street. What was once a difficult area to fill will soon become the object of other gardeners' envy because of its originality.

Long and narrow – based on a circular theme
This plan shows a design based on a circular theme. The paved area near the house can be used as a patio, and the one at the far end for drying the washing, largely out of sight from the house. Alternatively, if the end of the garden receives more sun, change the roles of the patios.

Taking the connecting path across the garden at an angle, and using small trees or large shrubs to prevent the eye going straight along the sides, creates the impression of a garden to be explored.

Long and narrow – based on diagonal lines
This garden uses diagonals to divide the garden into sections, but the objective is the same as the circular design. It avoids a straight path from one end of the garden to the other, and brings beds towards the centre to produce a series of mini-gardens.

Long and tapered to a point
If the garden is long as well as pointed, consider screening off the main area, leaving a gateway or arch to create the impression of more beyond while not revealing the actual shape. In this plan the narrowing area has been used as an orchard, but it could be a vegetable garden.

Staggering the three paved areas, with small changes of level too, adds interest and prevents the garden looking too long and boring. At the same time, a long view has been retained to give the impression of size.

Corner sites

Corner sites are often larger than other plots in the road, and offer scope for some interesting designs. This one has been planned to make the most of the extra space at the side of the house, which has become the main feature rather than the more usual back or front areas.

Curved corner sites

Curved corner gardens are more difficult to design effectively. In this plan the house is surrounded by a patio on the left-hand side, and a low wall partitions the patio from the rest of the garden, making it more private. For additional interest, the drive is separated from the gravel garden by a path. Gravel and boulders, punctuated by striking plants such as phormiums and yuccas, effectively marry the straight edges with the bold curve created by the corner site.

Square and squat

A small square site like this offers little scope for elaborate design, so keep to a few simple elements. To give the impression of greater space the viewpoint has been angled diagonally across the garden. For additional interest, the timber decking is slightly raised creating a change of level. In a tiny garden a small lawn can be difficult to cut, but you could try an alternative to grass, such as chamomile, which only needs mowing infrequently.

A variety of styles have been used in this plan, a combination of diagonals and circles – both of which counter the basic rectangle of the garden itself.

L-shaped

L-shaped gardens offer plenty of scope. Even in a small garden, the opportunity to walk around and explore an area that cannot be seen from one place is a considerable plus-point. This plan shows the clever use of focal points – a tree seat and a seat at the far end – to create a reason to explore the garden. The patio area is partially covered with overhead beams and separated from the rest of the garden by raised flowerbeds.

Planning Patios

The majority of small garden patios are little more than a paved area adjoining the back of the house, usually with little sense of design and often boring for most of the year. Your patio can be a key focal point that looks good in all seasons. A patio needs careful designing. It should be an attractive feature in its own right yet still form an integrated part of the total garden design.

Siting a patio

The natural choice for a sitting-out area is close to the house, especially if you plan a lot of outdoor eating. It's convenient, and forms an extra 'room', a kind of extension to the home, with a good view of the rest of the garden.

However, this spot may be shady for much of the day, in a wind tunnel created by adjacent buildings, or simply not fit in with your overall garden design.

Be prepared to move the patio away from the main building to gain shelter or sun or if it suits your design. Using a position at one side of the garden, or even at the end, may give you more privacy from neighbours or a better view of the garden.

ABOVE: *Consider alternatives to paving slabs – bricks, clay and concrete pavers.*
BELOW: *The clever patio overhead makes this area function like an extra room.*

Choosing a shape

Most patios are rectangular – the logical shape for most gardens – but feel free to express yourself in a way that suits the overall design. A circular or semi-circular patio can form part of a circular theme. However, a round patio in a small garden designed around rectangles is likely to look incongruous.

Setting the patio at an angle to the house retains the convenience of straight lines, yet creates a strong sense of design. Consider using this shape on a corner of the house.

Patio boundaries

A clearly defined boundary will emphasize the lines of a design based on a rectangular grid. A low wall, designed with a planting cavity, will soften the hard line between paving and lawn.

High walls should be used with caution as a patio boundary, but occasionally they can be useful on one or perhaps two sides of the patio as a windbreak or privacy screen. A screen block wall will break up the space less than a solid wall, blocks or bricks. Planting suitable shrubs in front of the wall will soften the impact and help to filter the wind.

Changes of level

If the garden slopes towards the house a change of level helps to make a feature of a patio. Use a few shallow

LEFT: *Patios don't have to be by the house. A cosy corner of the garden can even be more appealing.*

BELOW: *A patio at its best where plants and people meet. The use of bricks instead of large slabs gives the illusion of size.*

steps to act like a 'doorway' to the rest of the garden.

A raised patio is a practical solution if your garden slopes away from the house. This creates a vantage point, a terrace from which you can overlook the rest of the garden. On a flat site, simply raising the level by perhaps 15cm (6in) can be enough to give the patio another dimension.

Paving materials

The choice of paving sets the tone of the patio: brash and colourful, muted but tasteful, integrated or otherwise. Do not be afraid to mix materials. Single rows of bricks will break up a large area of slabs. Choose any combination of materials that is appropriate for the setting.

If the patio is close to the house, choose bricks or pavers that match the house bricks closely. The facing bricks used for the house may be unsuitable for paving, but you should be able to achieve a close match.

FINISHING TOUCHES TO PATIOS

It is the finishing touches such as collections of containers and pergolas that turn a patio from a hard, flat and rather uninteresting area into a spot where you can enjoy relaxing.

RIGHT: *If you can position your patio away from the house, it may be necessary to construct a free-standing overhead feature.*

Patio pergola

The overhead beams of a pergola help to give the patio an enclosed, integrated appearance that effectively extends the home. They provide excellent support for climbers that can bring useful shade as well as beauty. Avoid covering the whole patio with a thick canopy of climbers, however, as you will be searching for the sun, and spattered in drips after a summer shower.

Grape vines are good climbers for an overhead support, particularly as they lose their leaves in autumn, so you will get full winter sun. A relative with larger leaves and lovely autumn colour is *Vitis coignetiae.*

Floor joists are ideal for overhead beams, but they will need to be securely fixed to the house or garden wall using joist hangers. Use a cold chisel to remove some of the mortar between the bricks, to make room for the joist hanger. Insert the hanger and mortar it into position. Once set, you can position the beam and nail it into place through the holes in the hanger.

Depending on the span of the pergola, you will need at least one cross-beam supported on posts. Use sturdy posts, together with ground anchors and supports to keep the timber out of contact with damp ground and prolong its life.

If you want permanent shade, or always to be screened from overlooking windows, you can fix reed or rush matting to the overhead beams. First you will need to nail timber battens on top of the beams, arranging them at right-angles. Then lay lengths of reed or rush matting,

ABOVE: *Joist hangers are used to secure sawn timber to the house for a patio overhead.*

GETTING THE HEIGHT RIGHT

Patio beams should always be high enough to give plenty of clearance beneath them when clothed with plants. Even plants trained and tied in regularly may have shoots that cascade downwards, and this is especially hazardous with thorny plants such as climbing roses. If the beams are used as hanging basket supports in an area where you will be walking, make sure the bottom of the basket will be above head height. As a guide, a clearance of about 2.4m (8ft) should be the minimum in most instances.

or pieces of bamboo screen, across the battens. Use carpet tacks or small nails to fix the shading into position.

ABOVE: *Even on a tiny patio, there is room to create levels. Here, raised beds are built in white-painted brick to match the garden walls.*

BELOW: *This irregularly paved area is softened by the addition of a collection of container-grown, largely pink and white plants.*

Built-in features

A built-in barbecue blends with the garden in a way that a free-standing one cannot, and it will probably be used more often. Build it from bricks or blocks, depending on the material used in nearby buildings; include a sheet of mild steel, on which to burn the charcoal, and a grill on which to place the food.

It is not essential to cement the bricks or blocks in place, but do prepare the site before you begin, making sure it is both flat and firm. Lay a flat bed of bricks on the ground, then position the metal sheet. Lay two layers of bricks around three sides, leaving the front open. Be sure to stack the bricks so that the joints are staggered between the layers. Position the grill, then top with another two or three layers of bricks to provide some protection from the wind.

Built-in seats not only save space, they also give the patio a well-designed, sophisticated look. A few bright cushions give hard bench seats comfort and colour.

Planting spaces

Most people fill the space in their patio with plant containers, partly for convenience, but planting directly into the ground makes watering less of a chore. Permanent plants such as shrubs and small trees are best grown in the ground whenever possible. Some manufacturers make paving slabs that are designed to form a series of planting holes.

Raised beds

Building a raised bed, either against the house wall, or to form the patio boundary, enables you to bring far more plants into the patio area, especially useful in very small plots, where the patio is the garden. Build the bed from bricks, concrete blocks, or old railway sleepers, but be sure to provide a solid foundation. Place a layer of rubble then one of gravel in the bed, to provide good drainage, then fill with a suitable potting compost (soil mix), depending on the plants you want to grow.

FRONT GARDENS

Front gardens greet visitors and can give delight to passers-by. Unfortunately they are difficult to design well if you have to accommodate a driveway for the car, and possibly a separate path to the front door. Even enthusiastic gardeners with delightful back gardens are often let down by an uninspired front garden. We have taken four typical front gardens and shown how they can be improved. Pick ideas from any of these that you think could enhance your own space.

EXAMPLE ONE

This is a typical design for a front garden: a rectangular lawn is edged with a flower border used mainly for seasonal bedding, and bordered by a hedge. The redesigned garden concentrates on softening the harsh demarcation between drive and ornamental section. Plants now play a more prominent role, and the emphasis is on informality instead of angular lines.

Problems

- The drive isn't part of the garden design, and this makes the area left for plants and grass look even smaller.
- The soil close to the base of a hedge is often dry and impoverished, so bedding plants don't thrive.

Solutions

- Most of the lawn has been dispensed with, and the flower beds enlarged and planted with low-maintenance shrubs. Plenty of evergreens have been used to provide year-round interest.
- Gravel has been used for the drive, and extended to form a broad and informal sweep to the front door. Not everyone likes gravel as a surface to walk on, however, and pavers could have been used instead. If plenty of plants cascade over the edge, the widening sweep would still look soft and attractive.

EXAMPLE TWO

Tall conifers along the drive dominate the garden and will continue to do so even after redesigning it. Remove trees that are too large rather than attempt to design around them.

Problems

- Tall hedges offer privacy, but here the scale is out of proportion, and depending on the aspect may keep out too much light.
- Rose beds are popular, but the small circular bed in the lawn looks incongruous with the rectangular design and can be difficult to mow around.
- Narrow, straight-edged beds around the edges make the lawn seem even smaller.

Solutions

- The concrete drive has been paved with bricks or brick-like pavers.
- A central planting strip has been left to break up the expanse of paving.
- The tall, dark hedge has been replaced with an attractive white ranch fence. The gravelled area beneath is planted with alpines.
- Climbing roses are planted by the house walls instead of a central weeping rose. They provide a fragrant welcome in summer.
- Existing borders remain to minimize the reconstruction.
- Small shrubs such as hebes and lavenders have been used, along with low-growing perennials like *Stachys lanata* (syn. *S. byzantina* or *S. olympica*) and *Bergenia cordifolia*, instead of seasonal bedding plants.
- A small deciduous tree, a crab apple, replaces the large conifer in the bottom corner. The area beneath can be planted with spring-flowering bulbs such as crocuses and snowdrops.
- The small circular bed has been enlarged and filled with gravel, as a base on which to stand pots.
- The narrow bed has been filled in with grass removed when the new paving in front of the house was laid. Bricks or blocks form a crisp edge.

FRONT GARDENS

EXAMPLE THREE

Gardens don't come much more boring than this: a concrete drive, small narrow flower bed in front of the window and along the edge of the garden, and a single flowering cherry tree.

The solution for this garden was a simple one, as the redesigned garden shows. The cottage-garden style includes plants of all kinds which grow and mingle happily together with minimum intervention.

Besides being a short cut to the front door, the stepping stones encourage exploration of the garden and its plants. You actually walk through the planting, which cascades and tumbles around the paving slabs. The garden design has been reversed, with plants forming the heart of the garden rather than peripherals around the edge.

Problems

- Although the cherry is spectacular in flower, and provides a show of autumn colour, it is only attractive for a few weeks of the year. Its present position precludes any major redesign and so it is best removed.
- Unclothed wooden fences add to the drab appearance.
- Small flower beds like these lack impact, and are too small for the imaginative use of shrubs or herbaceous perennials.

Solutions

- The lawn and tree have been removed, and the whole area planted with a mixture of dwarf shrubs, herbaceous perennials, hardy annuals, and lots of bulbs for spring interest.
- Stepping-stones have been provided for those who want to take a short-cut (they also make access for weeding easier).
- The fences have been replaced with low walls so that the garden seems less confined.

EXAMPLE FOUR

This garden is a jumble of shapes and angles, and lacks any sense of design. With its new look, the old curved path has been retained because its thick concrete base and the drain inspection covers within it would have made it difficult to move, but all the other lines have been simplified and more appropriate plants used.

Problems

- Rock gardens are seldom successful on a flat site, and although small rock beds in a lawn can be made to resemble a natural rock outcrop, in this position the rocks can never look convincing.
- The tree here is young but will grow large and eventually cast considerable shade and dominate the garden.
- Small beds like this, used for seasonal bedding, are colourful in summer but can lack interest in winter. This curve sits uneasily with the straight edge at one end and the curve of the path at the other.

Solutions

- The rock garden has been paved so that the cultivated area is not separated by the drive.
- Gravel replaces the lawn. This needs minimal maintenance and acts as a good foil for the plants.
- Dwarf and medium-sized conifers create height and cover. By using species and varieties in many shades of green and gold, and choosing a range of shapes, this part of the garden now looks interesting throughout the year.
- Stepping-stones add further interest. Because it isn't possible to see where the stepping stones lead to from either end (the conifers hide the route), a sense of mystery is added and this tempts the visitor to explore.
- The existing path has been retained but covered with slate crazy-paving it looks more interesting.
- A pond creates a water feature.
- The awkward, narrow curving strip has been turned into a 'stream', with circulating water flowing over a cascade into the pond at one end.

Basement Gardens and Backyards

Some gardens are not just small, they are gloomy too because they are below street level, or hemmed in by tall walls. Because there is little that can be done to alter this sort of garden structurally, it is best to direct any efforts towards improving the environment and devising a strategy that helps plants survive, or at least ensure lots of lush-looking plants to flourish despite the handicaps. Not all of the techniques shown here will be applicable to your own garden, but most of them can be adapted to suit even the most unpromising site.

Using lighting
Garden lights can extend the hours of enjoyment you derive from your garden, and you don't need many of them for a lot of impact in a small area. You can illuminate most of the space – useful if you often entertain in the evening – or use just one or two spotlights to pick out dramatic elements in the design. Some can be swivelled so that you can highlight different features. For subtle lighting, a cheaper and pretty option is to use lanterns which hold candles.

Painting the walls
In a garden enclosed by walls or fences, you need to do everything possible to reflect light and make the background bright and cheerful. Painting the walls a pale colour will improve things dramatically.

Using trellis
Trellis can be used as a decorative feature in its own right, or as a plant support. If you want to make a feature of it, paint it white, but if it is used primarily as a plant support, make sure it has been treated with a non-toxic preservative. Enclose unsightly downpipes in a trellis 'box' over which you can grow an evergreen climber such as ivy.

Adding water features
The sound of running water is refreshing on a summer's day, and in a small area you only need a trickle to do the job. A wall spout (with a tiny pool at ground level, from which the water is recirculated) or a self-contained wall fountain is ideal.

ABOVE: *Ferns thrive in shady positions where many other plants would languish. If you can provide moisture from a water feature, so much the better.*
RIGHT: *Even the tiniest basement garden or backyard has space for a water feature.*

Introducing wind chimes
Wind chimes both look and sound good. Choose one primarily for the sound it makes.

Training wall shrubs
Cover some of the walls with climbers, but try espalier or fan-trained fruit trees or espalier pyracanthas too.

Furnishing in style
White-painted furniture looks bright in a small, enclosed garden, but don't add too much furniture or the area will look cluttered rather than elegant.

Using containers with character
If the area is small, make everything work for its space. Instead of plastic containers, use interesting old kitchen utensils, or other unexpected holders, but be sure to add drainage holes to prevent waterlogging.

Focal points in shade
Basement areas and enclosed backyards are often inhospitable for plants – the light is poor and the walls keep off much of the rain. If, in addition, you have a tree that casts shade, even the shade-loving plants will struggle. Use these positions for ornaments or make them into focal points.

Planting ferns
Ferns do well in a cool, shady spot, so use them freely in those areas too dull for bright summer flowers. Try a collection of hardy ferns – they won't look dull if you nestle an attractive ornament among them, or include white flowers, perhaps backed by a white wall. On a hot summer's day the space will be an oasis of coolness and tranquillity.

Growing white-flowered plants
Use pale flowers if the area lacks direct sun. You won't be able to use plants that need strong sun light, but fortunately some of the best white-flowering plants are shade-tolerant. Try white varieties of impatiens and white nicotianas, for example. White flowers will show up more brilliantly than coloured ones in a dull spot.

Introducing exotics
Gardens enclosed by walls can be hot and sunny too, and being sheltered provides the ideal environment for many exotic plants to grow successfully. Try a few bold houseplants to create a tropical effect.

LEFT: *Use wall pots and half baskets to make a dominant wall more interesting. They will be more effective staggered rather than in straight rows.*

LEFT BELOW: *White flowers, like this, nicotiana, show up well in darker corners.*

Making the most of steps
Open railings can be used as supports for attractive climbers, planted in pots at the base of the steps, but always keep them trimmed so that slippery leaves do not trail across the steps or obstruct the hand-rail. If the steps are very wide, place pots of bright flowers on the steps themselves to produce a ribbon of colour. Do not obstruct the steps. If there is no space on the steps, use a group of containers filled with flowers at the top and bottom of the stairway.

Fixing windowboxes and wall baskets
Use windowboxes lavishly – not only beneath windows but fixed to walls too. Windowboxes, wall pots and half-baskets can all bring cascades of colour to a bare wall. Stagger the rows instead of placing them in neat and tidy lines.

Capturing the scents
An enclosed garden is an ideal place in which to grow scented plants – the fragrances are held in the air instead of being carried off on the wind. Use plenty of aromatic plants, especially big and bold plants like daturas, and those with a heavy perfume such as evening-scented nicotianas and night-scented stocks.

Roof Gardens

Despite the obvious handicaps, many people manage to create verdant planted areas on the top of roofs and tall buildings. If they are not overlooked, roof gardens can prove to be very private. However, there are potential structural limitations that must be checked out before you progress with any construction or planting plans. Never construct a roof garden without seeking professional advice from a structural engineer on whether the roof is able to take the weight.

You might be advised that it is safe, or told to keep the weight to certain areas – perhaps to the parapet wall – but you should abandon any idea of a roof garden if advised that it would be unsafe. Sometimes additional strengthening can be added, but this is a major and potentially expensive job.

RIGHT: Euonymus *fortunei 'Emerald 'n Gold', provides thick, vividly coloured cover, perfect for adding brightness to a roof garden.*

BELOW: *Mock orange (*Philadelphus*) is one of the most popular of fragrant shrubs. The combination of pure white flowers and the sweet perfume suggest purity and innocence.*

WIND-TOLERANT PLANTS

Calluna vulgaris (Scotch heather)
Cornus alba (red-barked dogwood)
Cotinus coggygria (smoke bush)
Erica carnea (Alpine heath, winter heath)
Euonymus fortunei varieties
Hippophäe rhamnoides (sea buckthorn)
Hydrangea macrophylla
Hydrangea paniculata 'Grandiflora'
Lavatera olbia (tree mallow)
Lonicera pileata (honeysuckle)
Mahonia aquifolium (Oregon grape)
Olearia × haastii
Pachysandra terminalis
Pernettya mucronata
Philadelphus (mock orange)
Spiraea japonica
Tamarix tetrandra (tamarisk)

The shape of the roof will largely determine your design. Usually raised beds are built around the edge, with a sitting area in the centre. Pots can be used to provide variety within the paved area.

The roof is one place where artificial grass does have a place in the garden. Paving is heavy, artificial grass light. And it adds a touch of much-needed colour.

ABOVE: *A roof garden can be quite spectacular, especially if the building is strong enough to take structural features such as those shown here.*

RIGHT: *Trellises provide privacy and shelter from the wind and can be fairly light which avoids increasing the weight.*

Keeping weight down

Do everything possible to keep down the weight. Avoid thick, heavy paving stones – if you do use paving, choose the thinnest. Use lightweight, loam-free potting composts (soil mixes), and plastic or glass-fibre containers rather than terracotta or wood.

Watering

Plants in containers need frequent watering in warm or windy weather. Carrying water to the rooftop is unappealing, and getting out a hosepipe (garden hose) to connect to a tap indoors is also cumbersome. Give some thought to installing an automatic watering system.

Using windbreak screens

A windbreak of some kind is likely to be an essential feature of a roof garden, since gusting wind and turbulence can play havoc with plants – and people. A windbreak screen can also be invaluable in providing privacy and in masking many of the unattractive features that a rooftop presents.

A structure that is partly permeable to the wind is much more effective than a solid one, where localized turbulence is created as the wind hits it and is deflected. Black windbreak netting becomes almost invisible if it is strung between two posts and then hidden behind a painted trellis, especially if plants are then grown up the trellis.

This form of windbreak is both effective and does not take up much room – an important consideration when space is at a premium.

Using plants for protection

Where more room is available, a screen of tall, wind-tolerant shrubs installed along the most vulnerable side will act to shelter the area behind them. Many plants will tolerate this kind of exposure, while still providing colour and interest throughout the year. For a permanent screen, it is important to use mainly evergreen plants, although some of the tough deciduous shrubs can be included to add variety.

With this barrier in place, the effect of the wind should be considerably reduced, allowing you to complete a decorative planting scheme. As far as the space will allow, plan for a staggered effect, using tall plants or small shrubs at the back, next to the windbreak screen, and moving through to ever smaller perennials and annuals. At the front, you should end up with a relatively warm, sheltered space, which is ideal for less resilient plants – delicate spring bulbs, for example.

BALCONIES AND VERANDAS

For someone without a garden, a balcony may be their entire 'outdoor room', a 'garden' to enjoy from indoors when the weather is inclement. Even more than a patio, the balcony or veranda is an outdoor extension of the home.

The area is usually small, so the money you are prepared to spend on gardening will go a long way. Splash out on quality flooring and furniture, and ornate containers, which will create a classy setting for your plants.

Choosing flooring
The floor will help to set the tone and style, and it can make or mar a tiny 'garden' like this.

Paving slabs are best avoided: they are heavy, frequently lack the kind of refinement that you can achieve with tiles, and the size of individual slabs may be too large to look 'in scale' for the small area being covered.

Think of the veranda or balcony floor as you might the kitchen or conservatory floor – and use materials that you might use indoors. Quarry tiles and decorative ceramic tiles work well, and produce a good visual link with the house. Make sure ceramic tiles are frostproof however. Tiles are relatively light in weight, and their small size is in proportion to the area.

Timber decking is another good choice for a veranda.

The problem of aspect
Aspect is an important consideration. Unlike a normal garden, or even a roof garden, the light may be strong and intense all day, or there may be constant shade, depending on position. Balconies above may also cast shade.

If the aspect is sunny, some shade from above can be helpful. Consider installing an adjustable awning that you can pull down to provide shade for a hot spot. Choose sun-loving plants adapted to dry conditions for this situation – your indoor cacti and

RIGHT: *Roof gardens and balconies are often improved if you lay a wooden floor and create a timber overhead.*

succulents will be happy to go outside for the summer.

If the aspect is shady for most of the day a lot of flowering plants won't thrive. You may have to concentrate on foliage plants, though some bright flowers, such as impatiens and nicotiana, do well in shade.

Countering the wind

Like roof gardens, balconies are often exposed to cold and damaging winds. The higher a balcony the greater problem wind is likely to be.

To grow tender and exotic plants, provide a screen that will filter the wind without causing turbulent eddies. A trellis clothed with a tough evergreen such as an ivy is useful, or use screens of woven bamboo or reeds on the windiest side – these not only provide useful shelter and privacy, but make an attractive backdrop for plants in containers.

Adding colour round the year

Create a framework of tough evergreens to clothe the balcony or veranda throughout the year, and provide a backdrop for the more colourful seasonal flowers.

Use plenty of bright seasonal flowers in windowboxes or troughs along the edge, with trailers that cascade down over the edge.

In the more sheltered positions, grow lots of exotic-looking plants, and don't be afraid to give lots of your tough-leaved houseplants a summer holiday outside.

Pots of spring-flowering bulbs extend the season of bright flowers, but choose compact varieties – tall daffodils, for example, will almost certainly be bent forward as wind bounces back off the walls.

Add splashes of colour with cut flowers. In summer choose long-lasting 'exotics' such as strelitzias and anthuriums.

ABOVE: *In mild areas or a sheltered position, you can turn your balcony into a tropical garden.*

RIGHT: *Turn your balcony into an outdoor room where many indoor plants thrive in summer.*

FEATURES *and* STRUCTURES

Overall garden design is important, but it is individual features that make a garden special. Major structural decisions, such as the type of paving to use, the shape of the lawn, or how to define the boundaries, have a significant impact, but even small details like ornaments and garden lights can lift a small garden above the ordinary. The use of containers is especially important in a small garden – on a tiny balcony they may be *the garden. Use them imaginatively, choosing containers that are decorative, and grouping them for added interest.*

ABOVE: *Create the urge to explore with small paths that lead to features such as seats and ornaments.*

OPPOSITE: *The garden floor is important, whether paving or a lawn, but it is features, like this arbour and its seat, that give the garden character.*

the GARDEN FLOOR

THE GARDEN FLOOR – LAWN, PAVING, PATHS, even areas of gravel or ground cover plants – can make or mar your garden. These surfaces are likely to account for more area than the beds and borders. Although they recede in importance when the garden is in full bloom, for much of the year they probably hold centre stage.

Removing existing paths and paved areas presents a practical problem. If they are laid on a thick bed of concrete you will probably have to hire equipment to break up the surface. Provided these areas do not compromise your design too much, it is much easier to leave as many as you can in position. Consider paving over the top with a more sympathetic material. It should be relatively easy to extend the area if you want to.

Lawns are more easily modified than paths and paved areas. At worst you can dig them up and resow or relay them. If you simply want to change the shape, you can trim off surplus grass or lift and relay just part of the lawn.

ABOVE: *Paths can be both functional and attractive, often giving the garden shape and form.*

OPPOSITE: *Hard land-scaping, such as bricks, combined with soft landscaping, such as lawns, can look very harmonious if designed with integration in mind.*

OPPOSITE ABOVE: *A brick edging marks the boundary between lawn and border, and serves the practical purpose of making mowing easier.*

LEFT: *Areas like this would soon become weedy if not densely planted. Here hostas suppress the weeds, and* Soleirolia soleirolii *spills over onto the path.*

Timber decking is very popular in some countries, seldom used in others. Much depends on the price of timber locally, and to some extent the climate, but decking should always be on your list of options.

There are useful alternatives to grass for areas that are not used for recreation or are seldom trodden on. Ground cover plants not only suppress weeds in flower beds, but can replace a lawn where the surface does not have to take the wear and tear of trampling feet. Inset stepping-stones to protect the plants. Where the garden is *very* small, low-growing ground cover may be much more practical than a lawn that is almost too tiny to cut with a mower.

LAWNS

The lawn is often the centrepiece of a small garden, the canvas against which the rest of the garden is painted. For many gardeners this makes it worth all the mowing, feeding and grooming that a good lawn demands. If your lawn has to serve as a play area too, be realistic and sow tough grasses, and settle for a hard-wearing lawn rather than a showpiece. It can still look green and lush – the important consideration from a design viewpoint. Instead of aiming for a bowling-green finish, the shape of the lawn or a striking edging could be its strong visual message.

Working with circles
Circular lawns can be very effective. Several circular lawns, linked by areas of paving, such as cobbles, work well in a long, narrow garden.

If the garden is very small, all you will have space for is a single circular lawn. If you make it the centrepoint with beds around it that become deeper towards the corner of the garden, you will be able to combine small trees and tall shrubs at the back with smaller shrubs and herbaceous plants in front. To add interest, include a couple of stepping-stone paths that lead to a hidden corner.

Using rectangles
Rectangular lawns can look boring, but sometimes they can be made more interesting by extending another garden feature – such as a patio or flower bed – into them to produce an L-shaped lawn.

Alternatively, include an interesting feature such as a birdbath or sundial (often better towards one side or end of the lawn than in the middle). A water feature is another good way to break up a boring rectangle of grass.

An angled lawn
If you have chosen a diagonal theme for your design, you will probably want to set your lawn at an angle to the house so that it fits in with the

ABOVE RIGHT: *A sweeping lawn can help to create a sense of perspective.*
RIGHT: *This lawn would look boring with straight edges. The curves add style.*

other features. The same rectangle of lawn becomes much more interesting when set at an angle of about 45 degrees. By lifting and patching the lawn, you may be able to achieve this without having to start from scratch.

Creating curves

A sweeping lawn with bays and curves where the flower borders ebb and flow is very attractive. It is difficult to achieve in a small garden. However, you can bring out a border in a large curve so the grass disappears around the back. You may be able to do this by extending the border into an existing rectangular lawn.

Changing height

If you have to create an impression in a small space, try a raised or sunken lawn. The step does not have to be large – 15–23cm (6–9in) is often enough. If making a sunken lawn, always include a mowing edge so that you can use the mower right up to the edge of the grass.

ABOVE: *Sunken lawns make a bold feature.*

KEEPING A TRIM EDGE

Circular lawns must be edged properly. Nothing looks worse than a circle that isn't circular, and of course constant trimming back will eat into the lawn over the years. To avoid this, incorporate a firm edging, such as bricks placed on end and mortared into position, when you make the lawn.

Where the edges are straight use proprietary lawn edging strips.

HOW TO CREATE A MOWING EDGE

If flowers tumble out of your borders, or there is a steep edge that makes mowing difficult, lay a mowing edge of bricks or paving slabs.

1 Mark out the area of grass to be lifted using the paving as a guide. Lift the grass where you want to lay the paved edge. To keep the new edge straight, use a half-moon edger against the paving slab. Then lift the grass to be removed by slicing it off with a spade.

2 Make a firm base by compacting gravel or a mixture of sand and gravel where the paving is to be laid. Use a plank of wood to ensure it is level. Allow for the thickness of the paving and a few blobs of mortar.

3 It is best to bed the edging on mortar for stability, but as it will not be taking a heavy weight just press the slabs onto blobs of mortar and tap level (use a spirit-level to double-check).

MAKING A NEW LAWN

You can make a new lawn using either seed or turf (sod). Each method has its advantages and disadvantages. Your choice will depend largely on how long you – and your family – can bear to wait before you use the lawn, and how much money you are prepared to spend.

SOWING A NEW LAWN

The advantage of growing a lawn from seed is that it is usually less expensive than laying turf (sod) and you can choose the grass seed mixture to suit your own particular needs. Seed companies usually offer a range of mixtures for specific purposes, such as play areas or under shade, but they can be expensive. The main disadvantage of using seed is that it can take the best part of a year for the lawn to established.

Thorough ground preparation is essential for a quality lawn, and this should start several weeks before sowing. You can sow in either spring or autumn, as long as the ground is warm and not too dry.

1 Dig the ground well, and remove any difficult or deep-rooted perennial weeds. Rake the soil level. Use pegs marked with lines 5cm (2in) down from the top as a guide.

2 Allow the soil to settle for a week, then consolidate it further by treading evenly to remove air pockets. Shuffle your feet over the area, first in one direction then at right angles.

3 Rake the soil to produce a fine soil for sowing seeds. Allow weed seeds to germinate. Hoe them off or use a weedkiller that leaves the ground safe for replanting within days.

4 Use string to divide the site into strips 1m (1yd) wide, and use a pair of canes to mark off a 1m (1yd) length. Move the canes along the strips as you sow.

5 Use a small container that holds enough seed for a square metre or square yard (make a mark on it if the amount only partly fills it). Scatter the seeds as evenly as possible.

6 For a large area, it is worth hiring a seed distributor. Check the seed delivery rate on paper first. Rake the seed into the soil surface and use a water sprinkler to keep the soil moist.

LAYING A LAWN FROM TURF (SOD)

Turf (sod) provides the best method of creating a lawn quickly – you can use it within a few months – and soil preparation is a little less demanding. You will usually find that it is a more expensive option than growing a lawn from seed, but many gardeners are happy to pay a premium for the convenience.

1 You should dig and consolidate the soil as described for seed, but there is no need to wait a few weeks to allow weeds to emerge – the turf (sod) will prevent weed seeds germinating. Start by laying the turf (sod) along a straight edge.

2 Use a plank to stand on while you lay the next row, as this will help to distribute your weight. Stagger the joints from row to row, to create a bond as if you were laying bricks. If using a long roll of turf (sod), there will be fewer joints. Make sure that these do not align.

3 Tamp down each row of turf (sod) (you can use the head of a rake as shown), then roll the plank forwards to lay the next row.

4 Brush sieved sandy soil, or a mixture of peat and sand, into the joints. This will help to bind the turves (pieces of sods) together

5 Shape edges when the lawn is laid. Lay a hose or rope to form the shape for a curved edge, or use a straight-edged piece of wood for a straight edge, and trim with a half-moon edger.

Weed-free Paths and Lawns

A weed-filled lawn will spoil your garden, but with modern weedkillers it is quite easy to eliminate weeds to leave your grass looking like a lawn rather than a mown wildflower meadow. It's easy, too, to clear garden paths of unsightly weeds – and to keep them that way.

Killing weeds in lawns and paths
The only place where weeds are really acceptable is in a specially designated wildlife corner, although some people find daisies and other so-called weeds in the lawn a very attractive feature. Generally, however, weeds have to be controlled, and pulling them up by hand is a time-consuming job that few of us enjoy. It is even more frustrating if they grow back again within a few days.

The method on the opposite page shows how easily you can deal with weeds in the lawn. Paths can also be kept weed-free for a season using one of the products sold for the purpose. Most of these contain a cocktail of chemicals which act quickly to kill existing weeds and others that prevent the growth of new ones for many months. A single application should be enough to keep the path clear of weeds for a long time. It is a good idea to use an improvised shield to prevent the weedkiller being blown by the wind onto the flowerbeds while you are applying it to the paths.

ABOVE: *This garden illustrates the beauty of a well-maintained lawn that is free of weeds. The lawn in this garden is the perfect spot for a bird house, which will attract many local birds, and possibly squirrels, all year round. The addition of a couple of rose bushes adds elegance and interest to this very pretty garden.*

LEFT: *The most beautiful and expensive of paths can be marred by weeds. Either make sure they are mortared between the joints, or use a path weedkiller to keep them smart.*

KILLING WEEDS IN LAWNS

This method ensures a weed-free lawn with as little as one application a year.

1 Weeds in lawns are best controlled by a selective hormone weed-killer, ideally in mid- or late spring. These are usually applied as a liquid, using a dribble bar attached to a watering-can. To ensure even application, you should mark out the lawn with string lines, spacing them the width of the dribble bar apart.

2 Always mix and apply the weedkiller as recommended on the packet by the manufacturer. There are a number of different plant hormones used, some killing certain weeds better than others, so always check that the product is recommended for the weeds you most want to control. When mixed, simply walk along each strip slowly enough for the droplets from the dribble bar to cover the area evenly.

3 If your lawn also needs feeding, you can save time by using a combined weed and feed. The most efficient way to apply these products – which are likely to be granular rather than liquid – is with a fertilizer spreader.

4 If you only have a few trouble-some weeds in a small area, it is a waste of time and money treating the whole lawn. For this job a spot weeder that you dab or wipe onto the offending weed should work very well.

WORDS OF WARNING

Weedkillers are extremely useful aids, but they can be disastrous if you use the wrong ones, or are careless in their application.

- Always check to see whether it is a total or selective weedkiller.
- If selective, make sure it will kill your problem weeds – and make sure it is suitable for applying to the area you have in mind. Lawn weedkillers should be used only on lawns.
- Don't apply liquid weed-killers on a windy day.
- For greater control, use a dribble bar rather than an ordinary rose on watering-cans.
- Keep a watering-can specially for applying weed-killers, otherwise residues may harm your plants.
- Avoid run-off into flowerbeds, and if necessary use a shield while applying a weedkiller.

Caring for Lawns in Autumn

Autumn is a good time to prepare your lawn for the year ahead, and the best time to tackle any long-term improvements. Tasks such as raking out lawn debris as well as feeding and aerating will improve the quality of your lawn greatly if they are carried out every year.

1 Over the years, grass clippings and debris form a 'thatch' on the surface of your lawn. This affects growth of the grass and should be removed with a lawn rake.

2 If grass growth is poor, the soil beneath may have become compacted, preventing oxygen reaching the plant roots. You can aerate the lawn by pushing the prongs of a garden fork about 15cm (6in) into the ground.

3 Brush a soil improver into the holes made by the fork. Use sand or a mixture of fine soil and sand if the ground is poorly drained. Alternatively, use peat or a peat-substitute, or very fine, well-rotted garden compost if the ground is sandy.

4 If your lawn is in poor condition and needs reviving, apply an autumn lawn feed. It is essential that you use one formulated for autumn use, as spring and summer feeds will contain too much nitrogen.

5 You can tidy an uneven lawn edge at any time, but doing it in autumn will mean one less job to do at busier times of year. Use a half-moon edger against a board held in position with your feet. This is not an annual job.

MECHANICAL AIDS

Working on large areas such as lawns can be exhausting and back-breaking work. Raking out thatch is a particularly tiring job. If you have a fairly large lawn area, it is definitely worth investing in a powered lawn rake. This will remove the thatch both rapidly and efficiently for you.

You can also take the sheer drudgery out of aerating your lawn by using a hollow-tined aerator that removes a core of soil effortlessly and efficiently.

If you need to remove a large quantity of leaves from your lawn in the autumn, you also might prefer to invest in a special leaf sweeper or blower.

Collecting and Composting Leaves

Never waste the leaves that accumulate in your garden. They will make excellent garden compost if you collect them and allow them to rot down. In addition, if they are left on the ground, they can damage areas of grass as well as smother other small plants on the edges of beds and borders.

1 Don't let leaves lie for long on your lawn. The grass beneath them will turn yellow and be prone to disease. On a small lawn, rake them up with a lawn rake.

2 The leaves that build up on paths and drives are best brushed up with a broom or besom.

3 You can buy special tools to lift the leaves without too much bending, but using two pieces of wood is also an effective method of lifting them once they have been brushed into a heap.

4 Leaves can be added to the compost heap, but some leaves rot down slowly, so it is best to compost large quantities on their own. Rotted leaves are also a useful addition to potting composts (soil mixes).

DON'T LET LEAVES SMOTHER SMALL PLANTS

If you let leaves lie for long on small plants such as alpines, they may begin to rot due to the lack of light and free movement of air. The leaves will also provide a haven for slugs and other pests that may eat your plants. Wait until most of the leaves have fallen from the trees, then go around and pick them off vulnerable plants.

NATURALIZING BULBS

Many spring- and autumn-flowering bulbs look delightful naturalized in a lawn. Planted at random among the grass and left undisturbed, they soon form large colonies, and will flower year after year. One possible drawback is that you won't be able to cut the lawn for several weeks after flowering, until the leaves have died down – although some people may see this as an advantage.

What to plant?
If you are lucky enough to have space in your garden to naturalize bulbs in lawn or an area of longer grass, then choose those bulbs that will multiply and flower freely. These include an array of spring-flowering bulbs such as crocuses, daffodils (*Narcissus*), snowdrops (*Galanthus*), small fritillaries (*Fritillaria*) and winter aconites (*Eranthis hyemalis*). Even planting just a few early-flowering tulips can create a spectacular swathe of bright colour. Although tulips look spectacular growing within the lawn, avoid planting them too close together because their broad leaves can smother the grass beneath.

Naturalizing is also an ideal way of growing colchicums: these are leafless at flowering time in autumn (the leaves appear later in the spring) and the grass will help to disguise the bare stems. Despite this these delightful plants are well worth growing for their large goblet-shaped, usually pink or white, flowers.

You can use a number of different bulbs, or grow just one type, and choose flowers all of the same colour, or an eye-catching mixture. Even if you decide to limit yourself to the familiar daffodils and crocuses, there are many different kinds of these bulbs to choose from, so you will have plenty of choice.

A variety of methods
There are several different ways of naturalizing bulbs. You can dig individual planting holes in the grass (satisfactory for just a few bulbs), or lift strips of turf (sod) to expose a larger area of soil for planting. Alternatively, if you have a lot of bulbs to plant over a wide area, then individual planting holes may be more appropriate than creating larger excavations to take a group of bulbs.

For more delicate bulbs, which won't be able to compete with strong-growing turf (sod), the best method is to plant them in bare but well-cultivated ground and sow a fine grass seed over the top.

HOW TO NATURALIZE SMALL BULBS IN GRASS

1 If you have a lot of small bulbs, such as crocuses and winter aconites, to plant in a limited area, it is best to lift sections of turf (sod) and plant the bulbs underneath. Use a spade to slice beneath the grass, then roll it back for planting.

2 Loosen the soil with a fork first as it will be very compacted, and work in a slow-acting fertilizer such as bonemeal.

3 Scatter the bulbs randomly. Very small ones can be left on the surface; larger ones are best buried slightly. Cover the bulbs with twice their own depth of soil. Roll back the grass, firm it well, and water.

DIVIDING ESTABLISHED CLUMPS

1 Naturalized bulbs and those left in borders for years will eventually need dividing to stop overcrowding, which will lead to deteriorating results. Lift very large clumps when the leaves have just died back, or any time when the bulbs are dormant.

2 Separate the clump into smaller pieces and then replant. You do not have to separate the clump into individual bulbs.

WHICH WAY UP

It is of great importance to check that a bulb is the right way up when planted, with the growing point upwards. Most bulbs have a very obvious top and bottom and present no problem. Others, especially corms and tubers, can cause confusion because they lack an obvious growing point. If you are in any doubt, it is best to plant them on their side – the shoot will grow upwards and the roots down.

A few bulbs that do have an obvious top are planted on their side because the base tends to rot in wet soil – although these are rare exceptions. *Fritillaria imperialis* is sometimes planted this way, and it is always worth planting vulnerable bulbs on a bed of grit or coarse sand to encourage good drainage around the base.

HOW TO NATURALIZE LARGE BULBS IN GRASS

1 Large bulbs such as daffodils are easier to plant using a bulb planter, which takes out a core of soil. Scatter the bulbs randomly over the surface so that the display will look natural.

2 Push the bulb planter into the soil, twisting it a little if the ground is hard, then pull it out with the core of soil. Place the bulb at the bottom of the hole.

3 Crumble some soil from the bottom of the core. Drop some of this into the hole to fall around the bulb and make sure it is not suspended in a pocket of air. Then press the core back into position.

GRASS SUBSTITUTES

Grass is still the best form of living carpet for a large lawn subject to wear, but small areas are ideal for experimenting with those alternatives to grass that will give your garden a highly individual touch.

RIGHT: *For an attractive-looking lawn in a small area not subject to heavy wear, chamomile is ideal.*

BELOW: *Thyme is tough enough to grow between paving, where it is often crushed underfoot.*

None of the plants described will form such a hard-wearing lawn as grass, but they have their own attractions. Bear in mind that you can't use a normal selective lawn weedkiller on these broad-leaved plants, so be prepared for some hand weeding. On a small-scale, however, this is manageable, and a price worth paying if you fancy a lawn with a difference.

Scent with chamomile

This classic grass substitute has been used for centuries to make an attractive, pale green lawn. The fact that it is aromatic when walked on combined with an ability to tolerate a reasonable amount of wear, makes it an excellent choice for a small, ornamental area. But, like the other plants suggested here, chamomile is not a practical proposition for a children's play area.

What it looks like Chamomile has small, feathery, aromatic leaves and white daisy flowers, though the non-flowering 'Treneague' is preferable as flowers spoil the close carpeted effect. It spreads rapidly by creeping stems, which is one reason that it makes such a good substitute for grass.

How to sow or plant You can sow seed, but the best lawns are established from young offshoots or cuttings of a non-flowering variety. If you buy seed, start them off in seed trays to produce young plants to put out later. If you buy young plants or offshoots by post they will probably arrive in a plastic bag – larger specimens from a garden centre will be pot-grown but you will pay more.

Plant 23cm (9in) apart – closer if you have a lot of seed-raised plants or cuttings of your own. Close spacing will achieve quicker cover, but the final result is unlikely to be any better. If you are growing from seed, start off under glass in early spring, and plant out in late spring, rather than sow directly in the open ground like grass.

Trim with the mower set high to encourage the development of sideshoots if the plants do not seem to be making enough bushy side growth. You will have to mow flowering forms occasionally to keep the plants compact.

You may find chamomile under one of its two widely used Latin names *Chamaemelum nobile* or *Anthemis nobilis*.

Thyme

Thyme is another popular alternative to grass for a small area, but be sure to choose the right kind of thyme. The culinary species is too tall and bushy for this purpose. Choose the more prostrate *Thymus serpyllum*.

Thymes are good for dry soils, and do well in alkaline (chalky) areas. Unfortunately they tend to become woody and straggly after about four or five years. Cuttings are easy to root, however, so periodic replanting should not be an expensive task.

What it looks like Thymes have small, aromatic leaves, and *T. serpyllum* has low, spreading growth 5cm (2in) high. Clusters of tiny purple, white, pink, red, or lavender flowers appear in summer.

How to sow or plant Plant about 23cm (9in) apart. You can raise your own plants from seed (sow in trays, not directly into the soil).

HOW TO PLANT A THYME LAWN

1 Prepare the ground thoroughly by digging over the area and levelling it at least a month before planting. Dig out any weeds that appear. Hoe off seedlings. Rake level.

2 Water the plants in their pots, then set them out about 20cm (8in) apart, in staggered rows (a little closer for quicker cover, a little further apart for economy but slower cover).

3 Knock the plant from its pot and carefully tease out a few of the roots if they are running tightly around the edge of the pot.

4 Plant at their original depth, and firm the soil around the roots before planting the next one.

5 Water the ground thoroughly and keep well watered for the first season.

ABOVE: *Clover – in this case wild white – makes a novel lawn, as gardeners usually spend so much time trying to eliminate it.*

Clover

If clovers seem to thrive better than the grass in your existing lawn, eliminate the grass and try a clover lawn – it will probably look greener than grass in dry weather! You will, of course, still have to weed, to remove non-clover seedlings.

What it looks like The three-lobed leaves of the clover are well known. The white or purple flowers should not be a feature of a clover lawn – mow the plants before they are tall enough to flower.

How to sow or plant Clover is sown in-situ, on ground cleared of weeds, ideally in spring. You can sometimes buy clover seed from companies specializing in wild flower seeds. White clover (*Trifolium repens*) is a good one to sow for a lawn.

Cotula

There are several low-growing species of cotula that can be used for a lawn. In some countries they are regarded as lawn weeds, in others lawns are sometimes created for them. They are worth a try if you are prepared for a rampant plant that may need curtailing.

What it looks like Cotulas are low-growing plants, with divided, fern-like leaves. The creeping stems root as they grow. Masses of small yellow flowers are produced in mid summer.

How to sow or plant Plant about 10–15cm (4–6in) apart. *Cotula coronopifolia* is the one usually used as a grass substitute. The cheapest way is to sow seed, but this is only likely to be available from suppliers dealing in the less common plants.

IMAGINATIVE PAVING

Most small gardens have a patio or at least a paved area close to the house. Often it is the main feature around which the remainder of the back garden is arranged. It can be the link that integrates home and garden. At its worst, paving can be boring and off-putting; at its best it can make a real contribution to the overall impact of the garden.

On the following pages you will find a selection of popular paving materials, with suggestions for use, and their advantanges and disadvantages. Always shop around because the availability and price of natural stones vary enormously, not only from country to country, but also from area to area.

Even the availability of man-made paving will vary from one area to another. Choosing the material is only part of the secret of successful paving – how you use it, alone or combined with other materials, is what can make an area of paving mundane or something special.

LEFT: *Bricks and pavers often look more attractive if laid to a pattern such as this herringbone style.*

Colour combinations

Your liking for bright and brash colour combinations will depend on the effect you want to create. Be wary of bright colours though – they can detract from the plants, although they will mellow with age.

Sizing up the problem

In a small garden, large-sized paving units can destroy the sense of scale. Try small-sized paving slabs (which are also easier to handle), or go for bricks, pavers, or cobbles.

Mix and match

Mixing different paving materials can work well, even in a small space. Try areas or rows of bricks or clay pavers with paving slabs, railway sleepers with bricks, in fact any combination that looks good together and blends with the setting. Avoid using more than three different materials, however, as this can look too fussy in a small garden.

Paving patterns

You can go for a completely random pattern – crazy-paving is a perfect example – but most paving is laid to a pre-planned pattern using rectangular paving slabs or bricks. Look at the brochures for paving slabs. These usually suggest a variety of ways in which the slabs can be laid.

Although a large area laid with slabs of the same size can look boring, avoid too many different sizes, or complex patterns in a small space. Simplicity is often more effective.

Bricks and clay pavers are often the best choice for a small area, because their small size is more likely to be in harmony with the scale of the garden. The way they are laid makes a significant visual difference, however, so choose carefully.

The stretcher bond is usually most effective for a small area, and for paths. The herringbone pattern is suitable for both large and small areas, but the basket weave needs a reasonably large expanse for the pattern to be appreciated.

Stretcher bond

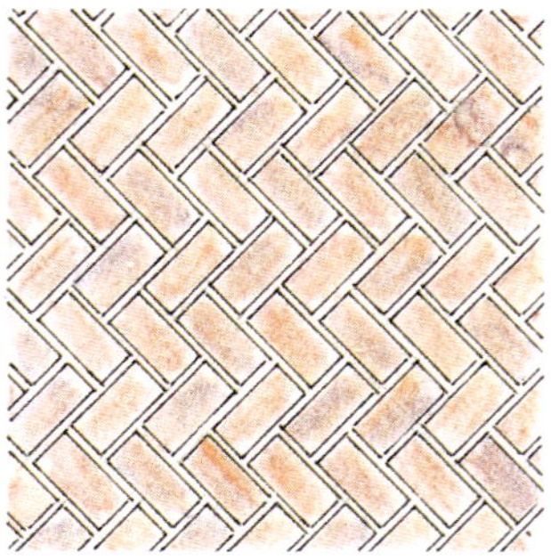

Herringbone

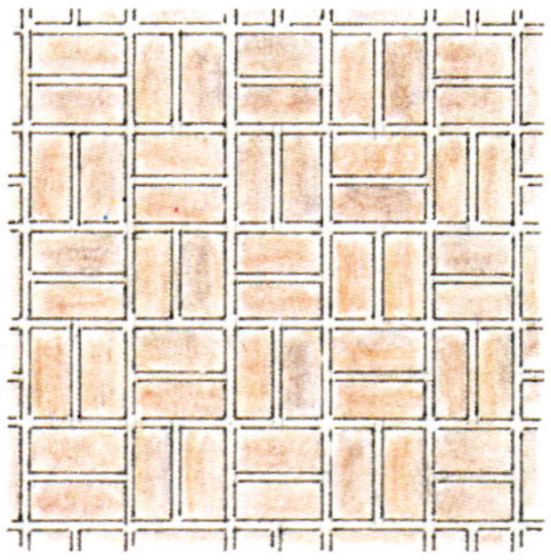

Basket weave

HOW TO LAY PAVING

1 Excavate the area to a depth that will allow for about 5cm (2in) of compacted hardcore topped with about 3–5cm (1–2in) of ballast, plus the thickness of the paving and mortar. As an alternative to hardcore topped with ballast, you can use 5cm (2in) of scalpings. Check the depth of the foundation before laying the paving. If adjoining the house, make sure that the paving will end up below the damp-proof course.

2 Put five blobs of mortar where the slab is to be placed – one at each corner, and the other in the middle.

3 Alternatively, cover the area where the paving is to be laid with mortar, then level.

4 Position the slab carefully, bedding it on the mortar.

5 Use a spirit-level to ensure that the slab is level, but use a small wedge of wood under one end to create a slight slope over a large area of paving so that rainwater runs off freely. Tap the slab down further, or raise it by lifting and packing in a little more mortar. Position the level over more than one slab (place it on a straight-edged piece of wood if necessary).

6 Use spacers of an even thickness to ensure regular spacing. Remove these later, before the joints are filled with mortar.

7 A day or two after laying the paving, go over it again to fill in the joints. Use a small pointing trowel and a dryish mortar mix to do this. Finish off with a smooth stroke that leaves the mortar slightly recessed. This produces an attractive, crisp look. Wash any surplus mortar off the slabs before it dries.

Paving Materials

There are plenty of paving materials from which to choose, so spend time looking through brochures and visit garden centres and builders' merchants before you come to a decision.

RIGHT: *Bricks, unlike clay pavers, are laid with mortared joints. This can emphasize the design.*

PAVING SLABS

Rectangular paving slabs

The majority of paving slabs are based on a full-sized slab 45 × 45cm (18 × 18in) or 45 × 60cm (18 × 24in). Half and quarter slabs may be a little smaller in proportion to allow for mortar joints. Thickness may vary according to make, but provided you mix only those made by the same manufacturer this won't matter.

A *smooth* surface can be boring, slippery, and a little too much like public paving, but many have a *textured* finish. Textures vary. A riven finish usually looks like natural stone, an exposed aggregate finish has exposed gravel to give a natural-looking non-slip finish.

Slabs imprinted with a section of a larger pattern are usually unsatisfactory in a small area. As quite a large area of paving is usually required to complete the pattern, they only emphasize the space limitations.

Shaped paving slabs

Use shaped slabs with caution. Circular slabs are useful for stepping-stones, but are difficult to design into a small patio. Hexagonal slabs also need a fairly large area to be appreciated. Special half-block edging pieces are usually available to produce a straight edge.

Paved and cobbled finish slabs

Some designs are stamped with an impression to resemble groups of pavers or bricks, some containing as many as eight basket-weave 'bricks' within the one slab. They create the illusion of smaller paving units, and are very effective in a small area.

TOP LEFT: *Slabs like this are particularly useful for a small area because they give the illusion of smaller paving units.*
TOP RIGHT: *Paving slabs with a riven finish look convincingly like real weathered stone.*
MIDDLE LEFT: *Paving slabs will always weather. Pale colours like this will soon look darker, while bright colours will become muted.*
MIDDLE RIGHT: *Hexagonal paving slabs can be attractive, but are not usually satisfactory in a very small area.*
BOTTOM: *Rectangular shapes like this can be used alone, or integrated with other sizes to build up an attractive design.*

Planting circles

A few manufacturers produce paving slabs with an arc taken out of one corner. Four of these placed together leave a circular planting area for a tree or other specimen plant.

BRICKS AND PAVERS

Bricks and pavers are especially useful for a small garden. You can create an attractive design even in a small area, and you may be able to obtain them in a colour and finish that matches your home, which will produce a more integrated effect.

Always check that the bricks are suitable for paving, however, as some intended for house building will not withstand the frequent saturation and freezing that paths and patios are subjected to. After a few seasons they will begin to crumble. Clay pavers, on the other hand, have been fired in a way that makes them suitable for paving. Concrete pavers and blocks are another option, though these are usually more suitable for a drive than a small patio.

Rectangular pavers

Clay pavers look superficially like bricks but are designed to lock together without mortar. They are also thinner than most bricks, though this is not obvious once they have been laid. Concrete pavers or paving blocks are laid in a similar way and are more attractive than concrete laid in-situ for a drive. They can look a little 'municipal'.

Interlocking pavers and blocks

Concrete pavers or blocks are often shaped so that they interlock. Interlocking clay pavers may also be available.

Bricks

Bricks require mortar joints – they won't interlock snugly like clay pavers. On the other hand you may be able to use the same bricks for raised beds and low walls, giving the whole design a more planned and well-integrated appearance.

To use bricks economically, lay them with their largest surface exposed, not on edge. This excludes the use of pierced bricks (which have holes through them). It does not matter if they have a frog (depression) on one side, provided this is placed face-down.

Setts and cobbles

Imitation granite setts, which are made from reconstituted stone, and cobbles, which are natural, large, rounded stones shaped by the sea or glaciers, are both excellent for small areas of irregular shape. Their size makes them much easier to lay to a curve. Bed them into a mortar mix on a firm base.

Tiles

Quarry and ceramic tiles are appropriate for small areas near the house, or to create a patio that looks just that little bit different. Always make sure ceramic tiles are frostproof. Lay them on a concrete base that has been allowed to set, and fix them with an adhesive recommended by the supplier or manufacturer.

LEFT: *Hard paving comes in many forms. The top row shows (from left to right) natural stone sett, clay paver, clay brick, artificial sett. The centre row shows a typical range of concrete paving blocks. The bottom row illustrates some of the colours available in concrete paving slabs.*

Paths and Path Materials

As with any other garden structure, paths should be designed to suit the purpose they are to serve. There are a wide range of materials on the market to suit every need so shop around before deciding which you require.

RIGHT: *Although the gaps between these paving slabs have been filled with chipped bark in this example, you could also use gravel.*

Practical paths should be functional first and attractive second. Drives for cars and paths to the front door must be firmly laid on proper foundations. And don't skimp on width – it is extremely frustrating for visitors if they have to approach your door in single file. It might be better for the route to take a detour, perhaps forming an L-shape with the drive, if there isn't enough space for a wide path directly to the door.

Internal paths, used to connect one part of the garden to another, can be more lightly constructed, and are softened with plants.

Casual paths, which often lead nowhere and are created for effect, such as stepping-stones through a flower bed, can be lightly constructed and much less formal in style.

BELOW: *Paving can reflect artistic ambitions.*

BELOW RIGHT: *Victorian-style rope edging.*

Bricks and pavers

These are ideal materials for internal garden paths that have to be both practical and pretty. Complex bonding patterns are best avoided unless the path is very wide.

Paving slabs

By mixing them with other materials the look of paving slabs can be much improved. A narrow gravel strip either side can look smart, and the gravel can be extended between the joints to space out the slabs. The slab-and-gravel combination is ideal if you need a curved path.

A straight path can be broken up with strips of beach pebbles mortared between the slabs. Tamp them in so that they are flush with the surrounding paving.

Crazy-paving

Use this with caution. In the right place, and using a natural stone, the effect can be mellow, and harmonize well with the plants. Be more wary of using broken paving slabs – even though they are cheap. Coloured ones can look garish, and even neutral slabs still look angular and lack the softness of natural stone.

Path edgings

Paths always make a smarter feature with a neat or interesting edging. If you have an older-style property, try a Victorian-style edging. If it is a country cottage, try something both subtle and unusual, like green glass bottles sunk into the ground so that just the bottoms are visible. Or use bricks: on their sides, on end, or set at an angle of about 45 degrees.

CREVICE PLANTS

Plants look attractive and soften the harsh outline of a rigid or straight path. They are easy to use with crazy-paving or any path edged with gravel. It may be necessary to excavate small holes. Fill them with a good potting mixture. Sow or plant into these prepared pockets.

Some of the best plants to use for areas likely to be trodden on are chamomile, *Thymus serpyllum* and *Cotula squalida*. For areas not likely to be trodden there are many more good candidates, such as *Ajuga reptans* and *Armeria maritima*.

HOW TO LAY CLAY OR CONCRETE PAVERS

The method of laying clay or concrete pavers described in the following steps can be used for a drive or a patio as well as a path.

1 Excavate the area and prepare a sub-base of about 5cm (2in) of compacted hardcore or sand and gravel mix. Set an edging along one end and side first, mortaring into position, before laying the pavers.

2 Lay a 5cm (2in) bed of sharp sand over the area, then use a straight-edged piece of wood stretched between two height gauges (battens fixed at the height of the sand bed) to strike off surplus sand and provide a level surface.

3 Position the pavers, laying 2m (6½ft) at a time. Make sure they butt up to each other, and are firm against the edging. Mortar further edging strips into place as you proceed.

4 Hire a flat-plate vibrator to consolidate the sand. Alternatively, tamp the pavers down with a club hammer over a piece of wood. Do not go too close to an unsupported edge with the vibrator.

5 Brush more sand into the joints, then vibrate or tamp again. It may be necessary to repeat this once more.

Decorative Floors

A single surface of one kind of paving is likely to look flat and dull in anything but the smallest of patios. To create a much more interesting view, you might like to introduce some variation and texture – either with different decorative paving materials, or by using plants.

Often, it simply is not practical to go for major change, and you may feel you are stuck with a stretch of uniform concrete slabs. But there are ways to improve the situation – perhaps by removing some of the slabs to increase the planting areas around the perimeter and within the main paving areas. Or you could use decorative detailing to disguise parts of a less than pretty surface.

Ornamental paving

Coloured tiles have been used to create decorative floors down the centuries. It is likely that tiles laid in an intricate mosaic pattern over the whole patio will be overpowering, especially in a very small garden, and put up fierce competition with the plants. However, you can turn an ordinary paved area into something quite distinctive by replacing one or two of the paving slabs with panels of different coloured ceramic tiles. Arrange them in geometric patterns, forming squares, oblongs, or triangles, depending on the layout of the rest of the space. If you have the room you could extend the paved area by adding two rows of tiles around the perimeter; lay them diagonally in alternating colours – perhaps one row in terracotta, the other in cream, again depending on the design of the rest of the paving.

Pebbles

Pebbles are another decorative material with a centuries-old tradition. Their natural colours and smoothly rounded forms can be used to make exquisite textural panels within concrete or brick paving. Again, geometric shapes are most commonly seen but, in the hands of an artist given enough space, they can become elaborate works of art.

Floor planting

One way of softening uninspired areas of large concrete paving is to replace some of the slabs with mini-gardens. Try planting a miniature herb lawn that releases its aroma as you brush past. Chamomile (the non-flowering variety 'Treneague') and thyme are particularly effective. Or you can plant with larger herbs, such as lavender or sage. Low-growing flowers, such as alyssum, violets, pinks or any of the alpines, can offer a subtle but effective splash of floor-level colour.

If the ground allows, you can encourage small plants to grow between the paving stones, but you will need to be selective. While self-seeded violas can look enchanting, thistles are not so appealing.

ABOVE: *This ceramic sun makes an original floor feature. Planted with low-growing plants, it looks like a rich green tapestry.*

BELOW: *The clay-tiled floor and brick retaining walls make an evocative home for a herb garden and a focal point within the garden.*

MAKING A MINIATURE PEBBLE CIRCLE

This very simple mosaic, which is made from pieces of slate and old terracotta as well as a few beach pebbles and stones, can be used as an eye-catching, decorative detail anywhere in the garden.

1 Prepare a smooth circular area to the size you want the pebble circle to be. Mark out the area for the finished circle using a simple pair of compasses. These can be made from two small pieces of wood linked by a piece of string the length of the radius of the circle.

2 Add sufficient water to a sand and cement mix in order to achieve a crumbly consistency. Using a mortar trowel, smooth the cement over the circle.

3 Working quickly before the cement sets, press in the vertical border of slates.

4 Working in concentric rings, add a circle of old terracotta and another of slates, then a 'wheel' of pebbles and terracotta.

RIGHT: *Tessellated tiles rescued from a crumbling city pathway, which were destined for a builder's skip, make an enchanting detail in a flowerbed.*

TIMBER DECKING

Timber decking creates a distinctive effect, and will make a refreshing change from ordinary paving for the patio area. As with paving, the material used should be in proportion to the size of the garden, so the width of the planks is important. Wide planks look best in a large garden, but in a small, enclosed area narrower planks are usually preferable.

Different designs can be achieved by using planks of different widths and fixing them in different directions, as illustrated here, but on the whole it is best to keep any pattern fairly simple. Leave a small gap between each plank, but not so large that high-heeled shoes can slip into it.

The construction method and timber sizes must reflect the size of the overall structure and its design – especially if built up over sloping ground. In some countries there are building codes and regulations that may have to be met. If in doubt, seek professional help with the design, even if you construct it yourself.

All timber used for decking must be thoroughly treated with a wood preservative. Some preservatives and wood stains are available in a range of colours, and this provides the opportunity for a little creativity. Dark browns and black always look good and weather well, but if you want to be more adventurous choose from reds, greens and greys.

If you want your decking to have a long life, special pressure-treated timber is the best choice. However, the range of colours available is bound to be less extensive.

Parquet decking

The easiest way to use timber as a surface is to make or buy parquet decking. Provided the ground is flat panels are easy to lay and can look very pleasing. Bed them on about 5cm (2in) of sand over a layer of gravel, to ensure free drainage beneath. If you already have a suitable concrete base to use, you can lay them directly onto this.

LEFT: *Timber decking makes a refreshing change from paving slabs or bricks, and can give the garden a touch of class.*

Patterns of Timber Decking

Ground Cover with Plants

If you want to cover an area of ground with a living carpet simply for texture, and don't expect to walk on the area, suitable ground cover plants are the answer.

To use ground cover plants like this, rather than simply as a means to suppress weeds in a flower bed, they must be evergreen, compact, and grow to a low, even height.

HOW TO PLANT CLUMP-FORMING GROUND COVER

1 Clear the ground of weeds first, and be especially careful to remove any deep-rooted or difficult perennial weeds.

2 Add plenty of garden compost or rotted manure, then rake in a controlled-release fertilizer. Add these before laying a mulching sheet.

3 Cover the area with a weed-suppressing mulching sheet. You can use a polythene sheet, but a special woven mulching sheet is much better.

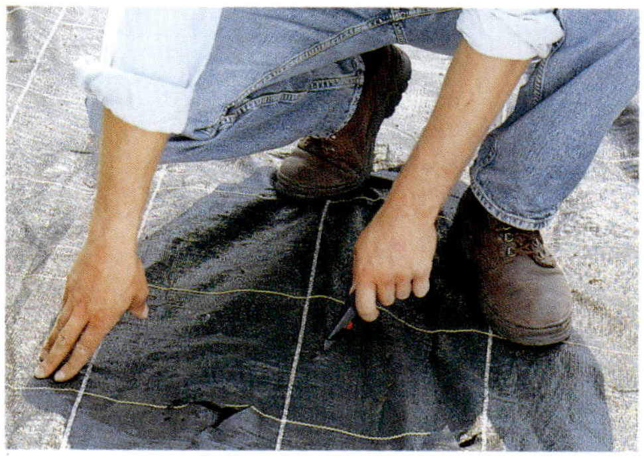

4 Make crossed slits through the sheet where you want to plant. Avoid making the slits too large.

5 Excavate planting holes and firm in the plants. If necessary tease a few of the roots apart first.

6 Water thoroughly, and keep well watered. Remove the sheet once the plants are well established.

GROUND COVER PLANTS

Some of the best plants for the job are *Armeria maritima*, bergenias, *Cotoneaster dammeri*, *Euonymus fortunei* varieties, *Hypericum calycinum*, and *Pachysandra terminalis*. If you want flowers as the main feature, heathers are difficult to better.

HOW TO PLANT CREEPING GROUND COVER

The mulching sheet method is a good way to get clump-forming plants such as heathers off to a good start, but don't use it for those that creep and root, such as ajugas and *Hypericum calycinum*. Plant these normally but apply a loose mulch about 5cm (2in) thick to cover the soil.

Gravel Gardens

Gravel is an inexpensive and flexible alternative to paving or a lawn, although it is not suitable for a patio. It blends beautifully with plants, needs little maintenance, and can be used in both formal and informal designs. It is also a useful 'filler' material to use among other hard surfaces, or in irregularly shaped areas where paving will not easily fit and a lawn would be difficult to mow.

LEFT: *Gravels naturally vary considerably in colour.*

Types of gravel

Gravel comes in many different shapes, sizes and colours. Some types are angular, others rounded, some are white, others assorted shades of green or red. All of them will look different in sun or shade, when wet or dry. The subtle change of colour and mood is one of the appeals of gravel. The gravels available will depend on where you live, and which ones can be transported economically from further afield. Shop around first going to garden centres and builders merchants to see what is available in your area before making your choice.

Gravel paths

Gravel is often used for drives, but it is also a good choice for informal paths within the garden. It conforms to any shape so is useful for paths that meander. However, it is not a good choice for paths where you will have to wheel the mower.

HOW TO LAY A GRAVEL PATH

1 Excavate the area to a depth of about 15cm (6in), and ram the base firm.

2 Provide a stout edge to retain the gravel. For a straight path, battens secured by pegs about 1m (3ft) apart is an easy and inexpensive method.

3 First place a layer of compacted hardcore. Add a mixture of sand and coarse gravel (you can use sand and gravel mixture sold as ballast). Rake level and tamp or roll until firm.

4 Top up to the required height with the final grade of gravel. In small gardens, the size often known as pea gravel looks good and is easy to walk on. Rake and roll repeatedly until the surface is firm and stable.

If the path is wide, it is a good idea to build the gravel up towards the centre slightly so that puddles do not form after heavy rain.

Gravel beds

Gravel can be used as a straight substitute for grass and requires much less maintenance. You can even convert an existing lawn very simply by applying a weedkiller to the grass, laying edging blocks around the edge, then topping up with gravel.

Informal gravel beds still require some kind of edging restraint to prevent the gravel from spreading. If the bed is surrounded by a lawn, simply make sure that the gravelled area is about 5cm (2in) below the surrounding grass.

Other practical ways to prevent the gravel from scattering onto beds and other unwanted areas are to create a slightly sunken garden or to raise the surround slightly with a suitable edging.

Informal gravel areas often look especially effective if some plants are grown through the gravel – either in beds with seamless edges where the gravel goes over them, or as individual specimen plants.

HOW TO LAY A GRAVEL BED

1 Excavate the area to the required depth – about 5cm (2in) of gravel is sufficient in most cases.

2 Level the ground. Lay heavy-duty black polythene or a mulching sheet over the area. Overlap strips by about 5cm (2in).

3 Then tip the gravel on top and rake level.

4 To plant through the gravel, draw it back from the planting area and make a slit in the polythene. Plant normally, enriching the soil beneath if necessary.

5 Firm in and pull back the polythene before re-covering with gravel.

FORMING BOUNDARIES

MOST OF US HAVE AN INSTINCTIVE DESIRE TO mark our territory with a very visible boundary. It gives us a sense of privacy and the illusion of security, but above all it marks out our plot of land, the area in which we create our own very special paradise.

The problem with a small garden is that the boundary forms a large part of the garden, and the chances are that you will see it from whichever direction you look. In a large garden the boundary often merges into the background, but in a small one it can easily dominate.

Tall walls can be an asset – the walled town garden has many of the treasured attributes of an old walled country garden – but drab wooden fences and large overgrown hedges pose real problems if you want to make your garden look smart and stylish.

Don't take your boundary for granted, and never assume it can't be improved. Replacing a fence or grubbing up a long-established hedge are not projects to be tackled lightly – they can be expensive or labour-intensive. Never make changes until you have consulted neighbours that

LEFT: *This is an excellent example of a combination boundary – a wooden picket fence supported on a low wall, with an escallonia flowering hedge growing through it.*

OPPOSITE ABOVE: *Walls make secure boundaries, but to prevent them looking oppressive cover with climbers, and if possible create a view beyond, as this attractive gate has done.*

OPPOSITE: *A wall as tall as this can easily dominate a small garden, but by treating it boldly and using it as a feature it becomes an asset.*

are affected. The boundary may belong to them, in which case it is not yours to change unilaterally. Even if it is legally yours to replace, the courtesy of discussing changes with others affected will go a long way to helping you remain on good terms with your neighbours.

Although you are unlikely to want to exceed them in a small garden, there may be legal limitations on boundary height, perhaps laid down in the terms of the contract when you bought the property. In some countries there may be restrictions placed by the highways authority on road safety grounds.

Restrictions are most likely in front gardens – some 'open plan' estates, for example, may have limitations on anything that might infringe the integrated structure of the gardens.

None of these restrictions need inhibit good garden design, but it is always worth checking whether any restrictions exist before erecting or planting a new boundary.

Hedges for Small Gardens

Many of the classic hedges, like beech, yew, and tall conifers like × *Cupressocyparis leylandii*, and even the privet (*Ligustrum ovalifolium*) have strictly limited use in a small garden. In small gardens the emphasis should be on plants that have much to offer or compact growth. The hedges suggested here are just some of the plants that could be used to mark your boundary without being dull or oppressive. Be prepared to experiment with others.

Clipped formality

The classic box hedge (*Buxus sempervirens*) is still one of the best. It clips well and can be kept compact, but choose the variety 'Suffruticosa' if you want a really dwarf hedge like those seen in knot gardens. A quick-growing substitute is *Lonicera nitida*, and there's a golden form that always looks bright – but be prepared to cut frequently. Some of the dwarf berberis stand close clipping – try the red-leaved *Berberis thunbergii* 'Atropurpurea Nana'. Yew (*Taxus baccata*) is also excellent for formal clipping, and it can be kept compact enough for a small garden.

Colourful informal hedges

If you want to cut down on clipping, and want something brighter and more colourful than most foliage hedges, try the grey-leaved *Senecio* 'Sunshine' or the golden *Philadelphus coronarius* 'Aureus' (unfortunately sheds its leaves in winter). *Viburnum tinus* can also be kept to a reasonable height, and provided you avoid pruning out the new flowers it will bloom in winter. Many of the flowering and foliage berberis also make good 'shrubby' hedges. These will lack a neatly clipped profile, but pruning and shaping is normally only an annual job.

ABOVE: *Although* Lonicera nitida *needs frequent clipping, it makes a neat formal hedge.*

LEFT: *Many shrub roses can make an attractive flowering hedge in summer, but do not plant them too close to the edge of a path otherwise their thorny stems may be a nuisance.*

Using roses

Roses make delightful – and often fragrant – boundaries, but they have shortcomings. Their summer beauty is matched by winter ugliness, and they are not a good choice for a boundary where passers-by may be scratched by thorns. You can use a row of floribunda (cluster-flowered) roses, but the shrubby type are usually preferred for this job.

Old-fashioned lavender and rosemary dividers

Both these herbs make excellent informal flowering hedges, with the merit of being evergreen too. You could try the shorter lavender in front of the taller rosemary. Both become untidy with age, so replace the plants when it becomes necessary.

Other flowering hedges

Forsythia is one of the most popular flowering hedges, but careful pruning is required to achieve consistent flowering on a compact hedge. There are plenty of alternatives, including the shrubby potentillas, berberis like *B. × stenophylla*, with bold flowers, though this one can take up a lot of space, and even tall varieties of heathers if you just want a boundary marker rather than a barrier.

ABOVE: *Box is one of the classic plants to use for clipped formality. This is a glaucous form.*

HOW TO PLANT A NEW HEDGE

1 Prepare the ground very thoroughly. Excavate a trench – ideally about 60cm (2ft) wide – and fork in plenty of rotten manure or garden compost.

2 Add a balanced fertilizer at the rate recommended by the manufacturer. Use a controlled-release fertilizer if planting in the autumn.

3 Use a garden line, stretched along the centre of the trench, as a positioning guide. If the area is windy or you need a particularly dense hedge, plant a double row of trees. Bare-root plants are cheaper than container-grown plants, but only separate them and expose the roots once you are ready to plant. Only the most popular hedging plants are likely to be available bare-root, and for many of the plants suggested you will have to plant a single row of container-grown plants.

4 Use a piece of wood or a cane cut to the appropriate length as a guide for even spacing. Make sure the roots are well spread out. If planting container-grown plants, tease out some of the roots that are running around the edge of the root-ball.

5 Firm the plants in well and water thoroughly. Be prepared to water the hedge regularly in dry weather for the first season. Keep down weeds until the hedge is well established, then it should suppress the weeds naturally.

Garden Walls

Except for special cases, such as basement flats and the need for privacy or screening in a difficult neighbourhood, high walls are inappropriate for a small garden. However, low walls up to about 1–1.2m (3–4ft) are a useful alternative to a hedge, particularly if you want to avoid regular trimming. Although the rain shadow and shade problems remain the same for a wall as a hedge, a wall will not impoverish the soil in the same way as a hedge.

Low walls

A low wall, say 30–60cm (1–2ft) tall, will serve the same demarcation function as a taller one, but in more appropriate scale for a small garden, and shrubs planted behind it are more likely to thrive. Modest garden walls like this are much easier to construct than tall ones, which may need substantial reinforcing piers, and are well within the scope of a competent garden handyman to build.

Brick walls

Plain brick walls can harmonize with the house, but generally look dull from a design viewpoint. A skilled bricklayer can often add interest by laying panels or strips to a different pattern. The choice of brick and the capping will also alter the appearance. Some are capped with bricks, others have special coping tiles. These all add to the subtle variety of brick walls.

Block walls

Many manufacturers of concrete paving slabs also produce walling blocks made from the same material. These are especially useful for internal garden walls and raised beds. They are often coloured to resemble natural stone, but brighter colours are available if you want to match the colour scheme used for the paving. Bear in mind that colours will weather and become much more muted within a couple of years.

ABOVE: *An interesting brick wall.*
RIGHT: *A wall like this makes a solid and secure boundary without making the garden appear too enclosed.*

Screen block walls

Screen block walls (sometimes called pierced block) are most frequently used for internal walls, perhaps around the patio or to divide one part of the garden from another, but they can also be used to create a striking boundary wall too.

These blocks have to be used with special piers and topped with the appropriate coping. They are useful if you want to create a modern image, or perhaps the atmosphere of a Mediterranean garden.

Mixing materials

Some of the smartest boundary walls are made from more than one material. Screen blocks look good as panels within a concrete walling block framework. Screen blocks can also be incorporated into a brick wall, and help to let light through and to filter some of the wind. Panels of flint or other stone can be set into an otherwise boring tall brick wall.

ABOVE: *Dry stone walls are not difficult to build provided you keep them low, and you can plant into the sides for extra interest.*

BELOW: *Walls can be colourful . . . if you create planting areas. The summer bedding plants used here are replaced at the end of the season with bulbs and spring bedding plants to use the planting areas to their full advantage.*

Cavity walls

Low cavity walls that can be lined with plants soon become an eye-catching feature. Pack them with colourful summer flowers, or plant with permanent perennials such as dwarf conifers, which maintain interest throughout the year (but be sure to choose truly dwarf conifers for this). If you plant cascading forms such as nasturtium or trailing lobelia, the effect can be really stunning. For a spring display, try aubrietia and the yellow *Alyssum saxatile*, with a few dwarf spring-flowering bulbs.

Dry stone walling

Dry stone walls are more often used for retaining banks or as internal dividers, but in an appropriate setting this kind of wall makes an attractive boundary. This type of wall looks best where dry stone walls are part of the natural landscape.

The great advantage of a dry stone wall – which is assembled without mortar – is the ability to plant in the sides. This can provide a home for many kinds of alpines.

Walls with a difference

The larger and taller the wall, the more imaginative you should be when designing it. Try incorporating an alcove for an ornament, or a panel into which you can set an artistic piece of wrought-iron that can be viewed against the green of a neighbouring field or garden.

WALL BUILDING MATERIALS

Most builders' merchants stock a good range of bricks, the majority are suitable for garden walls, but if you need a lot of bricks – enough to justify ordering direct – get in touch with a few brick companies. Their expertise can be invaluable, and most will be able to offer you a wide choice.

Buying bricks is something most of us do only rarely, so professional advice is especially useful. The author's experience, however, suggests that you can't always depend on the advice of a builder's merchant. Shop around until you find someone who really appears to have a knowledgeable passion for bricks – they will tell you about all the different finishes and colours available, and most importantly will know whether a particular brick is suitable for the job you have in mind. *Always* explain what you want your bricks for: a building, a garden wall, wall of a raised bed, or for paving. Some bricks which are perfectly suitable for house walls may be very unsuitable for paths or garden walls.

If you need a lot of bricks (many hundreds), it may be better, and cheaper, to buy direct from a brick manufacturer if they will deal with the general public.

ABOVE: *Bricks come in many colours and finishes, and these are just a small selection from the many kinds available. Names of bricks vary from country to country, but whatever names are used you are likely to have a good choice.*

MASONRY MORTAR

A suitable mortar for bricklaying can be made from 1 part cement to 3 parts soft sand. Parts are by volume and not weight. Cement dyes can be added to create special effects, but use coloured mortar cautiously.

Common bonds

Expert brick-layers may use more complicated bonds, but for ordinary garden walls – and especially those that you are likely to lay yourself, perhaps for a low boundary wall or for a raised bed within the garden – it is best to choose one of the three bonds illustrated below.

Running bond or stretcher bond This is the simplest form of bonding, and is used for walls a single brick wide – or where you want to create a cavity, such as a low wall with a planting space.

Flemish bond This is another way to create a strong bond in a wall two bricks wide. The bricks are laid both lengthways and across the wall within the same course.

English bond This is used for a thick wall the width of two bricks laid side by side – useful where strength is needed for a high wall. Alternate courses are laid lengthways then across the wall.

HOW TO LAY BRICKS AND BLOCKS

Although bricks are being laid here, the same principles apply to laying walling blocks.

1 All walls require a footing. The one shown here is a for a low wall just one brick wide: for larger and thicker walls the dimensions of the footing will have to be increased.

Excavate a trench about 30cm (12in) deep, and place about 13cm (5in) of consolidated hardcore in the bottom. Drive pegs in so that the tops are at the final height of the base. Use a spirit-level to check levels.

2 Fill with a concrete mix of 1 part cement, 2½ parts sharp sand and 3½ parts 2cm(¾in) aggregate, and level it off with the peg tops.

3 When the concrete has hardened for a few days, lay the bricks on a bed of mortar, also place a wedge of mortar at one end of each brick to be laid. For stability, always make a pier at each end, and at intervals of about 1.8–2.4m (6–8ft) if the wall is long. Here two bricks have been laid crossways for this purpose.

4 For subsequent courses, lay a ribbon of mortar on top of the previous row, then 'butter' one end of the brick to be laid.

5 Tap level, checking constantly with a spirit-level.

6 The wall must be finished off with a coping of suitable bricks or with special coping sold for the purpose.

BOUNDARY FENCES

Fences have the great merit of being more instant than hedges and less expensive than walls. That is the reason they are so often chosen by builders for new properties, and why they are frequently chosen again when the original fences come to the end of their useful life.

Closeboard and panel fences are popular, but predictable and a little boring. There are plenty of styles to choose from, however, so select a fence appropriate to your garden design yet practical for the purposes you have in mind.

If you want privacy or animal-proofing, you will have to opt for one of the solid styles, but if it is just a boundary-marker that is needed there are many attractive fences that look stylish and won't appear oppressive in a small garden.

The names of particular fence types can vary from country to country. If you do not recognize any of the names here check with the illustrations.

ABOVE: *Closeboard fencing well covered with climbing roses.*

ABOVE: *Wattle or woven fences make an attractive background for plants.*

ABOVE: *A low wooden fence is not obtrusive and can look very attractive.*

Closeboard

Closeboard fencing is erected on site by nailing overlapping feather-edged boards to horizontal rails already secured to stout upright posts. It is a strong, secure fence, but not particularly attractive – especially viewed from the side with the rails.

Panels

Prefabricated panels are quick and easy to erect and a popular choice for that reason. Panels are usually about 1.8m (6ft) long and range in height from about 60cm (2ft) to 1.8m (6ft), generally in 30cm (1ft) steps. The interwoven or overlapping boards are sandwiched between a frame of sawn timber. The woven style is not as peep-proof as overlapping boards.

Interlap or hit-and-miss

This combines strength and a solid appearance with better wind-filtering than a solid fence (which can create turbulent eddies that can be damaging to plants). It is constructed from square-edged boards that are nailed to the horizontal rails on alternate sides. Overlapping the edges gives more privacy, while spacing them further apart can look more decorative.

Picket

Picket fences look good in country gardens, but can also be a smart choice for a small town garden. Narrow, vertical pales are nailed to horizontal timbers, spaced about 5cm (2in) apart. You can make them yourself or buy kits with some of the laborious work done for you. The simplest shape for the top of each pale is a point, but you can make them rounded or choose a more ornate finial shape. A picket fence can be left in natural wood colour, but they look particularly smart painted white. Because they are usually relatively low, and you can see plenty of garden through the well-spaced pales, they don't dominate the garden in the same way as a tall, solid fence.

Ranch-style

Ranch-style fences consist of broad horizontal rails fixed to stout upright posts. They are usually quite low, and frequently consist of just two or three rails. White-painted wood is a popular material, but wipe-down plastic equivalents are very convincing and easy to maintain. For a small garden they provide a clear boundary without becoming a visual obstruction. Also, rain and sun shadows are not created in the way that occurs with more solid fences.

Post and chain

This is the least obtrusive of all fences. Purely a boundary marker, it will do nothing to deter animals or children, or keep balls out of the garden, but it is a good choice if you want a fence that is hardly noticeable. You can use wooden, concrete or plastic posts and metal or plastic chains. Choose a white plastic chain if you want to make a feature of the fence, black if you want the chain to recede and blend into the background.

Chain link

Chain link is not an aesthetic choice, but it is highly practical and an effective barrier for animals. It is probably best to have a contractor erect a chain link fence, as it needs to be tensioned properly. You may like the fact that you can see through it, especially if the view beyond is attractive, but you may prefer to plant climbers beside it to provide a better screen. Choose tough evergreens such as ivy if you want year-round screening.

Bamboo

Bamboo is a natural choice if you've created an oriental-style garden, but don't be afraid to use this type of fence for any garden style if it looks right. Bamboo fences come in many shapes and sizes, and the one you adopt will depend partly on the availability and cost of the material and partly on your creativity and skill in building this kind of fence.

ABOVE: *A fence like this just needs a supply of bamboo and skill at tying knots!*

LEFT: *A white picket fence can make the boundary a feature of the garden.*

How to Erect a Fence

Many gardeners prefer to employ a contractor to erect or replace a fence. They will certainly make lighter work of it with their professional tools for excavating post holes, and a speed that comes with expertise, but some fences are very easy to erect yourself. Two of the easiest are panel and ranch-type fences, which are illustrated in simple steps below.

HOW TO ERECT A PANEL FENCE

1 Post spikes are an easier option than excavating holes and concreting the post in position. The cost saving on using a shorter post and no concrete will go some way towards the cost of the spike.

Use a special tool to protect the spike top, then drive it in with a sledge-hammer. Check periodically with a spirit-level to ensure it is absolutely vertical.

2 Once the spike has been driven in, insert the post and check the vertical again.

3 Lay the panel in position on the ground and mark the position of the next post. Drive in the next spike, testing for the vertical again.

4 There are various ways to fix the panels to the posts, but panel brackets are easy to use.

5 Insert the panel and nail in position, through the brackets. Insert the post at the other end and nail the panel in position at that end.

6 Check the horizontal level both before and after nailing, and make any necessary adjustments before moving on to the next panel.

7 Finish off by nailing a post cap to the top of each post. This will keep water out of the end grain of the timber and extend its life.

HOW TO ERECT A RANCH-STYLE FENCE

1 Although ranch-style fences are easy to erect the posts must be well secured in the ground. For a wooden fence, use 12.5 × 10cm (5 × 4in) posts, set at about 2m (6½ft) intervals. For additional strength add intermediate posts. A size of 9cm (3½in) square is adequate for these.

Make sure the posts go at least 45cm (18in) into the ground.

2 Concrete the posts into position, then screw or nail the planks in position, making sure fixings are rust-proof. Use a spirit-level to make sure the planks are horizontal. Butt-join the planks in the centre of a post, but try to stagger the joints on each row so that there is not a weak point in the fence.

3 Fit a post cap. This improves the appearance and also protects the posts. Paint with a good quality paint recommended for outdoor use.

ABOVE LEFT: *Panel fences are easily erected and provide a peep-proof barrier, but are best clothed with plants to soften the effect.*
ABOVE: *Ranch-style fences make an unobtrusive barrier – ideal where the garden merges into the countryside.*

THE PLASTIC ALTERNATIVE

There are many plastic ranch-style fences. They will vary slightly in the way they are assembled. Detailed instructions should come with them, however, and you should have no difficulty.

The 'planks' are sometimes available in different widths – 10cm (4in) and 15cm (6in) for example – and these help to create different visual appearances. Gates made from the same material are also available from some manufacturers.

Posts are usually concreted into the ground, and the cellular plastic planks are push-fitted into slots or special fittings. Special union pieces are used to join lengths, and post caps are usually glued and pushed into position.

White ranch fencing needs to be kept clean to look good, and plastic can simply be washed when it looks grubby.

TRELLISWORK

Trellis usually makes a much more decorative boundary than a fence. It is not so solid, allowing glimpses of what lies on the other side, and provides a framework for all but the most tender climbers and ramblers. Trellis can also lend height to boundary walls where extra privacy is needed and it can be used to decorate the walls themselves. The decorative aspect is especially valuable where the walls or fences are less than beautiful, or where you would like to add a little extra texture.

Shapes and sizes

Trellis is wonderfully versatile garden feature and comes in a wide variety of panel shapes and sizes. As well as the basic rectangular panels, there are also panels with pointed, convex or concave tops, and even with integral 'windows', all of which should provide you with plenty of scope for being creative. To finish off the supporting posts, there is also an extensive choice of attractive finials in shapes such as globes, acorns, pineapples and obelisks. A coat or two of exterior-quality paint or coloured wood stain – applied to the posts and panels – will immediately give a more finished and highly individual appearance that can also be enjoyed during the winter.

Improvised trellis

The trellis, of course, does not have to be ready-made. Old gates, an old window frame, metal panels or panels made from vines or other organic materials can serve the same purpose as ordinary trelliswork. These also look good in themselves, before being dressed up with climbing plants.

ABOVE: *Ready-made trellis panels in a variety of shapes and sizes can be used to create trellis fencing and even a trellis arbour.*

HOW TO ERECT A TRELLIS FENCE

The key to erecting a trellis fence is to make certain that it is firmly planted in the ground. In all but the most sheltered positions, it will come under enormous pressure from the wind and will work loose unless you have ensured the posts are firmly bedded in the concrete.

1 Start by digging a hole for the first supporting post. Make it at least 60cm (2ft) deep, deeper in light soils.

2 Put the post into the prepared hole and partly fill the hole with dry-mix concrete. Use a spirit-level to check that the post is upright and not sloping. Adjust the position if necessary and then continue filling the hole, tamping the concrete mix down firmly as you work, to hold the post still.

3 Continue filling the hole with concrete, ramming it down well. Frequently check that the post is still upright. It should now be firm enough in the ground so that you can work on it and, once the concrete has set or 'cured', will be permanently secure.

4 Lay the trellis panel on the ground first of all, so that you can work out where the next post hole should be dug. Dig the hole for the post, again to a depth of at least 60cm (2ft).

5 Nail the panel to the first post. You will need to ask someone to support the free end for you.

6 Place the second post in its hole and nail the panel to it, checking that the tops of the two posts are level and the panel is horizontal. Fill the second hole with dry-mix concrete, tamping down as you proceed. Check that the post is upright and adjust its position if necessary.

7 Repeat the steps by digging the third post hole, nailing on the second panel, positioning and nailing the third post, and so on, until the length of trellising is complete. This is more accurate than putting in all the posts and then fixing all the panels, when, inevitably, some gaps will be too large and some too small.

FIXING TRELLIS TO WALLS

Wooden trellis clothed with colourful climbers is an attractive method of decorating an expanse of plain brick or plastered wall. If the trellis itself is pleasing to look at, perhaps with a painted or stained finish, you may want to make it into a feature in itself. If this is the case, it is best to use only a few plants in order to avoid covering it over completely.

Securing trellis

It is essential that the trellis is fixed securely to the wall, preferably with screws. It should be held a short distance from the brickwork or masonry, so that the stems of the climbing plants can easily pass up behind it. This can be simply achieved by using spacers – wooden battens (wooden laths) will do – between the trellis and the wall.

Easy access

If the wall is a painted one, or might need future attention for other reasons, it is sensible to make the trellis detachable. The best method is to fix hinges along the bottom edge of the trellis panel, and a catch to the top edge. This allows the framework to be gently eased away from the wall, bringing the climber with it, so that any maintenance work can take place. Alternatively, the trellis can be held in position by a series of clips or catches, although it will not be as easy to manipulate as one that is held on hinges.

TRELLIS SCREENS

Free-standing trellis panels also offer an effective method of screening or dividing one part of the garden from another. Or you can use them simply as a means of supporting climbers, perhaps in a bed or border, or throughout the garden to define its major routes. Erect the panels as described for a trellis fence, making sure they are bedded firmly in the ground.

ABOVE: Rosa *'Dublin Bay' here climbs up a wooden trellis secured to the wall. The rose is fragrant and flowers over a very long period.*

HOW TO FIX TRELLIS TO A WALL

If you want to fix a series of trellis panels to a boundary wall, simply fit them close together, one butting up to the other. This method is equally suitable for fixing a single panel, to the front wall of the house for example.

1 Mark the position of the trellis. Drill holes in the wall for fixing the spacer battens (laths) and insert plastic or wooden plugs. On a low wall, you will need two battens (laths) at the top and base. For trellis more than 1.2m (4ft) high, allow for an additional batten (lath) halfway up.

2 Drill corresponding holes in the spacer battens (laths) and secure each to the wall with screws, checking with a spirit-level that it is horizontal. Use battens (laths) that hold the trellis at least 2.5cm (1in) from the wall.

3 Drill and screw the trellis to the battens (laths), first fixing the top and then working downwards. Check that the trellis is not crooked.

4 The finished trellis should be tightly fixed to the wall, so that the weight of the climber, and any wind that blows on it, will not pull it away from its fixings.

SEE-THROUGH BOUNDARIES

The best boundary of all might be no boundary . . . at least none that you can see. The ha-ha, once popular with the great landscape gardeners of the past, was a successful way of achieving this. The boundary is a deep, wide ditch that can't easily be seen from within the garden, so the garden appears to continue into the rolling countryside beyond.

The ha-ha is not a technique easily adapted to a small modern garden, and totally inappropriate if you overlook a townscape instead of pleasant green fields. However, the principle of being able to blur the margin between your garden and your neighbour's garden, or perhaps open countryside if you are fortunate enough to have the option, is one worth pursuing.

ABOVE: *A window in the wall can immediately transform a potentially boring area of brick into a real focus point.*

Ditches

A ditch sounds an unattractive feature. However, if one happens to run along one of your boundaries it might be possible to make a feature of it, rather than trying to hide it. Try planting it with bog plants, and landscape it into your garden, perhaps with a pond and an extended bog garden linking the two.

Some people even try to create a ditch, using a liner that restricts water loss and flooding it with water periodically. Provided the view of the garden beyond is attractive, this is a sure-fire way to give your small garden an open style only normally associated with larger gardens.

Shared gardens

Like-minded gardening enthusiasts sometimes design their gardens so that they appear to be linked. Usually this is done by taking the lawn through a gap in the boundary and using shrubs or mixed borders that start in one garden and end in the next. This can work surprisingly well, and although each is responsible for his own area the illusion is that the garden goes on beyond.

If this seems too 'communal', the same effect can be achieved by making lawns and borders meet yet still retain an unobtrusive fence, such as a widely spaced post and rail fence, or even a few simple strands of wire – which can be almost invisible from a distance.

Alternatively, consider linking gardens with an attractive gate. You don't have to use it, but it will look as though there is more garden beyond to be explored.

Shrubby solutions

Although a continuous lawn is the best way to link adjoining gardens and make them look larger, you can instead agree to abolish the fence and both plant shrubs in a bed along the boundary. Even if a relatively narrow strip is used in each garden, the impression will be of a much larger and more substantial shrub border with no sign of obtrusive fences.

Claire-voyée

The term means literally 'clear view', and came into use after the lawless Middle Ages in Europe when it became less necessary to enclose one's property with a solid wall, and apertures were cut in walls to allow the countryside beyond to be viewed from within.

If you have a view that is worth framing, you can introduce a claire-voyée 'window' in the wall of even a tiny garden.

BRIGHTENING UP FENCES AND WALLS

If replacing an existing old fence or wall simply isn't practical because of the time and expense involved, consider ways to camouflage or brighten up the old one.

Climbers

Climbers present one of the most pleasing ways to cover an unsightly wall or fence, but always make sure the fence is firm in its foundations first . . . otherwise the extra weight and wind resistance will just bring it down sooner and you will have to untangle the climber and repair the fence anyway.

For year-round cover, tough evergreens such as ivies are justifiably popular. They can be slow to establish, but ultimately provide dense cover and can easily be clipped back once or twice a year to prevent the shoots encroaching beyond their territory.

For summer-only cover, try the vigorous hop (*Humulus lupulus*), especially in its very attractive golden form 'Aureus'. Once established one plant will cover a large area of fence.

For flowers some of the clematis can be very successful, though winter's an unattractive time. Tall-growing species such as *Clematis montana* sound unlikely candidates, but they will run along the fence and cascade down each side instead of climbing, and the pink *C. m. rubens* looks particularly splendid.

Trained trees

Trained fruit trees can transform a tall wall or fence and turn it into a real feature when laden with flowers or fruit. Even in winter the bare stems of a fan or espalier tree can look dramatic, especially if picked out against a white-painted wall.

Training from scratch is difficult and time-consuming, and it is worth buying ready-trained trees.

RIGHT: *Old fences discolour and look drab and shabby with age. This is one way to transform a dull fence.*

BELOW: *Vigorous clematis such as* C. montana *will cover a fence with blooms in late spring and early summer.*

A coat of paint

A drab old wall can be transformed with a coat of masonry paint. White reflects the light well, but any pale colour can look pleasing, particularly when contrasted with greenery.

Grow striking plants like phormiums or yuccas in front so that their strong profiles are picked out against the background, or stand groups of containers so that they are backed by the painted wall.

Framed effects

Fences are more difficult to paint as a backdrop for plants, and you must be careful about paint seeping through to your neighbour's side, but a little localized painting could work well.

Try a large white circle within which you can frame a striking plant as a focal point. Instead of painting the actual fence, try cutting out a large wooden circle and painting that – then pin it to the fence.

Finishing Touches

A SMALL GARDEN SHOULD BE FULL OF SURPRISES, packed with finishing touches that compensate for the lack of scope offered by limited size.

Many of the focal point techniques used in large gardens can be scaled down and applied on a small scale, and even in a small space the garden can express the owner's sense of fun and personality in the little extras that are grafted onto the basic design.

The whole area can be made to work, every corner can be exploited with devices if not plants, and a degree of flexibility can be built in that makes variety a real possibility.

ABOVE: *A seat like this suggests a gardener with a strong sense of design.*

OPPOSITE ABOVE: *Ornaments have been used to excellent effect here. A sundial commands centre stage and the eye is taken across the garden to a figure which adds light and life.*

OPPOSITE BELOW: *Figures usually look best framed by plants.*

LEFT: *This quiet corner has been transformed by white-painted trellis and a seat.*

In a large garden most ornaments, furniture and fixtures like garden lights are a static part of the design. In a small garden a slight rearrangement of the furniture, the changed position of a light, or the simple exchange of one ornament for another according to mood and season means that the garden need never be predictable despite limitations of size.

Ornaments in particular can set a tone for the garden: serious or frivolous, classic or modern. They suggest the owner's taste . . . and even sense of humour. Just as the painting on the living-room wall or the ornaments on the sideboard can tell you a lot about the occupier, so garden ornaments reveal the personality of the garden maker.

Garden lighting can be practical and even a useful security measure, but it also offers scope for artistic interpretation. Experiment with spotlights in various positions and discover the dramatically different effects created by the use of light and shadows from different angles.

Arches and pergolas are a more permanent element of the garden's design, but they don't have to be planned in at the design stage and are easily added to an existing garden.

PERGOLAS AND ARCHES

A sense of height is important even in a small garden. Unless there is vertical use of plants or upright garden features, the centre of the garden will be flat. Attention will pass over the centre and go instead to the edges of the garden: exactly the lifeless effect you want to avoid.

Small trees, wall shrubs and climbers can provide the necessary verticals, but if these are in short supply an arch or pergola may be the answer.

Traditionally, and especially in cottage gardens, they have been made from rustic poles, but where they adjoin the house or link home with patio, sawn timber is a better choice. The various constructions described here are free-standing, and usually used as plant supports. Their visual effect is to take the eye to further down the garden.

If a pergola or arch seems inappropriate, similar construction techniques can be used to create an intimate arbour.

HOW TO ASSEMBLE AN ARCH

The simplest way to make an arch is to use a kit, which only needs assembling.

1 First establish the post positions, allowing 30cm (1ft) between the edge of the path and post, so that plants do not obstruct the path.

2 Fence spikes are the easiest way to fix the posts. Drive them in using a protective dolly. Check frequently with a spirit-level. Insert the posts and tighten the spikes around them. Alternatively, excavate four holes, each to the depth of 60cm (2ft).

3 Position the legs of the arch in the holes. Fill in with the excavated earth, and compact.

4 Lay the halves of the overhead beams on a flat surface, and carefully screw the joint together with rust-proof screws.

5 Fit the overhead beams to the posts – in this example they slot into the tops of the posts and are nailed in place.

HOW TO JOIN RUSTIC POLES

Rustic arches and pergolas look particularly attractive covered with roses or other climbers. You can be creative with the designs, but the same few basic joints shown here are all that you will need.

1 To fix horizontal poles to vertical ones, saw a notch of a suitable size for the horizontal piece to fit snugly.

2 If you have to join two horizontal pieces, saw two opposing and matching notches so that one sits over the other, and secure them.

3 To fix cross-pieces to horizontals or uprights, remove a V-shaped notch using a chisel if necessary to achieve a snug fit, then nail into place with rust-proof nails.

4 Use halving joints where two pieces cross. Make two saw cuts half way through the pole, then remove the waste timber with a chisel.

5 Secure the joint with a nail. For extra strength, paint the joint with woodworking adhesive first.

6 Bird's mouth joints are useful for connecting horizontal or diagonal pieces to uprights. Cut out a V-shaped notch about 3cm (1in) deep, and saw the other piece to match. Use a chisel to achieve a good fit.

7 Try out the assembly on the ground, then insert the uprights in prepared holes and make sure these are secure before adding any horizontal or top pieces. Most pieces can be nailed together, but screw any sections subject to stress.

ABOVE: *Rustic poles are an appropriate choice for a feature such as this.*

Temporary Supports for Climbers

When trying to add height to your garden, it is not always desirable to have fixed screens or supports. Growing climbers against temporary structures allows a much more flexible garden design, letting you easily ring the changes from year to year, even from one season to the next. While this is not really practical with most perennial climbers, especially those that might take several years to establish themselves, it is entirely possible with annuals.

Temporary supports can often serve two functions at once: to provide an attractive screen as well as a support for vegetables. Thus, peas and beans make good traditional subjects, while more novel ideas include climbing marrows (squash), courgettes (zucchini), gourds and cucumbers.

Choosing materials

Temporary supports are easy to make and a variety of materials can be used. Many are rustic in nature, such as pea-sticks simply pushed into the ground or traditional bean poles tied together in a row or wigwam (tepee). More modern materials include plastic netting held on poles or a metal frame. However, do try to make the supports as attractive as you can: they will often be fully in view until the early summer, when the plants start growing strongly, and won't be completely covered until midsummer.

Supporting perennials

Temporary structures can also be used for a few perennials that are cut to the ground each year, such as the everlasting pea (*Lathyrus latifolius*) or some of the clematis that are either herbaceous or are pruned back almost to ground level each year. Since the latter can grow quite tall, they can be supported by large branches stuck in the ground, to imitate small trees.

LEFT: *A typical bean row, with the scarlet-flowered runner beans climbing up poles that have been tied together for support. The poles can be kept for several seasons before replacing.*

ABOVE: *Climbing plants can be grown more horizontally than usual. It is an ideal way to utilize space after the spring flowers have faded.*

ABOVE RIGHT: *A framework of hazel sticks have been woven into an attractive dome. The burgundy clematis that is growing over it is resplendent with flowers.*

RIGHT: *Sweet peas growing up a temporary screen of pea-sticks. Hazel (*Corylus avellana*) is one of the best types of wood, but any finely branched sticks will do.*

ANNUAL CLIMBERS

Asarina
Cobaea scandens (cup-and-saucer vine, cathedral bells)
Eccremocarpus scaber (Chilean glory flower)
Ipomoea (morning glory)
Lablab purpureus (syn. *Dolichos lablab*)
Lagenaria (gourds)
Lathyrus odoratus (sweet peas)
Mina lobata (syn. *Ipomoea lobata*)
Rhodochiton atrosanguineum
Thunbergia alata (black-eyed Susan)
Tropaeolum majus (nasturtium – climbing varieties)
Tropaeolum peregrinum (syn. *T. canariense*) (canary creeper)

Growing Climbers Through Trees

Trees and shrubs make wonderful natural supports for climbers, often providing conditions that are similar to those in the plant's natural habitat. In the wild, particularly in dense woodland or forests, many climbers may grow to 50m (160ft) or more as they grow ever upwards in their search for light, but in the garden supports of this height are rarely necessary – or even available. If they were, the flowers of the climbers using them would be out of sight.

Good partners

Smaller supports are required for cultivated climbers in the garden, and a large apple tree is usually the highest used. Clematis and roses will scramble through its branches, creating huge fountains of flowers. On a more modest scale, even dwarf shrubs can be used to support some low-growing climbers.

Two in one

One of the advantages of growing climbers through shrubs is that it is possible to obtain two focuses of interest in one area. This is particularly valuable for shrubs that flower early, as these tend to be fairly boring for the rest of the year. Through these it is possible to train a later-flowering climber to enliven the area further on in the season. Clematis are particularly good for this, especially the late-flowering forms, such as the viticellas. These can be cut nearly to the ground during winter, so that when the shrub itself is in flower early in the next season, it is relatively uncluttered with the climber.

Roses and fruit

A fruit tree that has come to the end of its fruiting life can be given new appeal if you grow a rose through it. However, it is important to remember that old trees may be weak and the extra burden of a large rose, especially in a high wind, may be too much for it to bear.

BELOW: *Scrambling plants can provide vertical interest through the summer. Here,* Euonymus fortunei *'Emerald Gaiety' scrambles up a tree with* Geranium × oxonianum *below.*

CLIMBERS FOR GROWING THROUGH TREES

Clematis (vigorous kinds)
Hydrangea petiolaris (climbing hydrangea)
Humulus (hop)
Lonicera (honeyuckle)
Polygonum baldschuanicum (syn. *Fallopia baldschuanica*) (Russian vine)
Rosa (roses – vigorous varieties)
Vitis coignetiae (crimson glory vine)

HOW TO GROW A CLIMBER THROUGH A TREE OR SHRUB

1 Any healthy shrub or tree can be chosen. It should preferably be one that flowers at a different time to the climber. Choose companions that will not swamp each other. Here, a low *Salix helvetica* is to be planted with a small form of *Clematis alpina*. The two will make a delicate mix, especially the blue clematis flowers against the silver foliage.

2 Dig the planting area at a point on the perimeter of the shrub and prepare the soil by adding well-rotted organic material. For clematis, choose a position on the shady side of the plant, so that its roots are in shade but the flowers will be up in the sun. Dig a hole that is bigger than the climber's rootball and plant it. Most plants should be planted at the same depth as they were in their pots but clematis should be 5cm (2in) or so deeper.

3 Using a cane, train the clematis into the bush. Once the clematis has become established, you can remove the cane. Spread the shoots of the climber out so that the it spreads evenly through the shrub, not just in one area.

4 If possible, put the climber outside the canopy of the shrub or tree, so that it receives rain. However, it is still important to water in the new plant and, should the weather be dry, continue watering until the plant has become established.

CLIMBERS SUITABLE FOR GROWING THROUGH SHRUBS

Clematis (small varieties)
Cobaea scandens (cup-and-saucer vine, cathedral bells)
Eccremocarpus scaber (Chilean glory flower)
Hedera (ivy)
Ipomoea (morning glory)
Jasminum (jasmine - climbing species)
Lathyrus odoratus (sweet pea)
Lonicera (honeysuckle - climbing species)
Passiflora (passion flower)
Stephanotis floribunda (Madagascar jasmine)
Tropaeolum majus (nasturtium – climbing varieties)
Tropaeolum peregrinum (syn. *T. canariense*) (canary creeper)

SIMPLE PILLARS

A very effective way of creating vertical emphasis in a border or a small garden is to grow a climber up a single pole, which is usually called a pillar. Whether solitary or in groups, these can look very elegant and also make it possible to grow a large number of climbers in a relatively small space.

Using pillars
A surprising number of climbers are suited to growing up pillars. Most climbing roses, for example, look particularly good in this situation, although it is probably best to avoid vigorous climbers or rambling roses.

Temporary or permanent
An advantage of using pillars is that they are both inexpensive and simple to erect as well as to take down. They can be permanently positioned in a border, but if you want to be able to remove them in winter, when the plants have died down, set each post in a collar of concrete or a metal tube, so you can simply lift it out when the time comes.

Pillared walkway
If space is available, a very attractive walkway can be created by using a series of pillars along a path. Enhance this further by connecting the tops with rope, along which swags of climbers can grow. This is a delightful way of growing roses and creates a romantic, fragrance-filled route through the garden. The effect is suitable for formal designs, but is so soft and flowing that it gives a very relaxing feel.

CLIMBERS FOR PILLARS

Clematis
Eccremocarpus scaber (Chilean glory flower)
Humulus (hop)
Lonicera (honeysuckle)
Rosa (roses)
Solanum jasminoides (potato vine)
Tropaeolum (nasturtium)

RIGHT: *Single-post pillars help to break up what would, otherwise, be a dull, rather two-dimensional border. Although it is only a thin structure, when clothed with a climber it becomes a well-filled out, irregular shape, as this* Rosa *'American Pillar' shows.*

OPPOSITE: *Although single-post pillars are rather slim, they can accommodate more than one climber. Here, there are two roses,* Rosa *'American Pillar' and* R. *'Kew Rambler'.*

HOW TO ERECT A SIMPLE PILLAR

1 Dig a hole at least 60cm (2ft) deep. Put in the post and check that it is upright. Backfill with earth, ramming it firmly down as the hole is filled. In exposed gardens, fill the hole with concrete to give the pillar a more solid fixing.

2 Plants can be tied directly to the pillar, but a more natural support is provided using wire netting, secured with nails or staples. Plants such as clematis will then be able to climb by themselves, with little attention from you other than tying in wayward stems.

3 Plant the climber a little way out from the pole, to avoid the compacted area. Lead the stems to the wire netting and tie them in, to get them started. Self-clingers will now make their own way, but plants such as roses will need to be tied in as they climb. Twining plants such as hops can be grown up the pole without the wire.

TRIPODS AND HOOPS

Tripods and hoops can provide a means of raising the level of the planting in a small garden, without creating an imposing barrier. They also provide a useful opportunity for growing climbers – even edible climbers – in beds and borders or other areas where space is limited.

Using tripods

Tripods can be formal, made to a classic design, or they can be made from more natural-looking rustic poles. The former are better where they are still partly on show when the climber is in full growth. The latter, in spite of their informal charm, are more suitable for carrying heavy, rampant climbers that will eventually cover them completely.

More formal designs can be bought complete, ready to be installed in the garden. A rustic-pole tripod is much more basic and can easily be constructed by most gardeners. Tripods can be made to any height, to suit the eventual height of the plants and the visual aspects of the site.

Climbers for tripods

Although any type of climber can be grown up a tripod, self-clingers would not be so good because there is not enough flat surface to which they can attach themselves. Tripods are ideal for carrying two or more climbers at once. If possible, choose plants that flower at different times. Alternatively you could choose two that flower at the same time but look particularly well together.

Using hoops

Training a climber over hoops allows you to direct the growth of the plant, thus helping to keep its final height in proportion to the border in which it is growing. Most climbers are suitable for this purpose, although very vigorous plants are best avoided; they will soon outgrow their allotted space, no matter however much training you do.

1 Position three posts in the ground. The distance apart will depend on the height: balance the two to get a good shape. You can drive the posts into the ground, but the tripod will be more secure if you dig holes at least 60cm (2ft) deep, insert the posts and ram the earth back in. Fill the holes with dry-mix concrete.

2 Nail cross-pieces between the posts. These will not only help support the plants but also give the structure rigidity. Rails 40–45cm (15–18in) apart should be sufficient for tying in stems. If you want more support for self-clingers, wrap a layer of wire netting around the structure. The plants will soon hide it.

3 Nail the pieces on first and then cut them to the right length. Alternatively, cut to length and then drill holes in the appropriate places before nailing to the poles.

4 Plant the climbers in and around the tripod. Avoid the area close to the poles as the earth here may be hard or replaced with concrete. Dig in well-rotted organic matter first.

5 Water all the plant in well. If the weather continues dry, keep watering until the plants have become established.

6 The finished tripod will look raw at first, but will soon weather and become covered in plants.

TRAINING A CLIMBER OVER HOOPS

Bending the new young growth of a climber into curving arches encourages flowering buds to form along the whole length of the stem, rather than just at the tip, as happens if the branch grows upwards.

1 In early spring, use lengths of a pliable wood (hazel is ideal) to make a series of hoops around the climber. Bend each length carefully so that it does not crack, and push both ends of each one into the ground.

2 Allow each hoop to overlap the previous one.

3 Sort out the long shoots of the climber and carefully bend them over and then tie them to a convenient point on the hoop. In some cases it may be easier to tie the shoot to a stem that has already been tied down.

4 Initially the overall effect will look rather untidy, but gradually the leaves will turn to face the light and the plant will produce new buds all along the upper edges of the curved stems. Each year, remove a few of the older stems and tie in all the new ones. After a few years, you will need to replace the hoops with new ones.

USING ORNAMENTS

Ornaments can be used around the garden in much the same way as around the house. Choose them simply because you like them, because they will look good in a particular position, or as a device for attracting attention and admiration.

RIGHT: *A bird bath is a better choice than a sundial for a position often in shade.*

In a small garden their use as a focal point is paramount. Large focal points are impractical or can only ever be few in number, but small ornaments, birdbaths, sundials, and attractive urns can be used liberally. The only 'rule' is not to have more than a couple in view at once, as they will then compete for attention rather than taking centre stage. There is no limit to the number you can use in a small garden provided they form part of a journey of discovery. Use them among plants that you only discover from a particular viewpoint, or around a corner that is not visible from where you viewed the previous focal point.

Never let ornaments detract from major focal points that form part of the basic design, and don't allow the garden to look cluttered. Aim for simplicity with surprises.

Sundials

Whole books are written about sundials, and purists expect them to be functional. Setting them up accurately not only demands a sunny spot but quite a lot of calculations too, with compensation for geographical position. Most of us, using the sundial simply as an ornament, are happy to go out at noon on a sunny day in summer and align the gnomon to give the appropriate reading. It won't be accurate as the seasons change, but then you are unlikely to be using it to decide when it is time to leave for the office.

Accuracy may not be important, but a sunny position is. The whole object of a sundial is lost in a shady spot, where a birdbath would serve a similar design function without looking incongruous.

BELOW: *A chimney pot makes an unusual plinth for a sundial.*

Choose the plinth carefully – they vary in style and height (you could even build your own from bricks) and go for a fairly low plinth if the area available is quite small.

The best place for a sundial is as a centrepiece for a formal garden, perhaps in the centre of a herb garden with paths radiating out from the centre. The lawn is another practical choice, but if the lawn is small, consider placing the sundial to one side rather than in the centre.

Birdbaths

The positions suggested for a sundial are also appropriate for a birdbath, but birdbaths are much more useful for shady positions – though not too close to trees, otherwise they become filled with leaves and debris. A birdbath can even look effective in a flower border, with much of the plinth covered by flowers, or try it as a patio ornament if you want the pleasures of watching the birds drinking from it and bathing.

Sculptures
The use of sculptures and artistic objects demands confidence. Few people react adversely to a sundial or birdbath, but sculptures or artistic ornaments that generate admiration in one person can be abhorrent to another. This should never deter anyone from using ornaments that please them, but they are bound to be somewhat more difficult to place in a small garden.

Human figures
Busts sound unlikely ornaments for a small garden, but provided they aren't too large they can look great in an alcove or on a plinth in a dull corner. Small figures can sometimes work well if surrounded by clever planting.

Animal figures
Animal figures are always a safe bet, especially if set among the plants, or even on the lawn.

Abstract ornaments
Abstract ornaments should be used with restraint – they make a considerable impact. Too many will tend to make the area look more like an art gallery than a garden.

Wall masks, plaques and gargoyles
These are great for relieving a dull wall, but are almost always best set amid the leaves of a climber such as ivy. The foliage frames the feature, and emphasizes its roles as an unusual focal point.

Gnomes
You probably love them or hate them, and that is the problem with using gnomes. One or two little people cleverly used with restraint can be very effective and add a sense of fun, but usually either they are banished from the garden or there is a whole army of them. The problem with the latter approach is that the garden will simply appear as a setting for a gnome collection.

Plinths and pedestals
Plinths are essential for raising a sundial, birdbath or bust to an appropriate height, but they can look stark in a small garden. Make more of a feature of a plinth by planting some low-growing plants around the base, and then use a few tall ground cover plants that can gradually stretch up around the base.

A plinth can look severe on a lawn and mowing around it can be difficult. Try setting one in a gravel bed with alpines around the base, or leave the bed as soil and plant thymes or other low-growing aromatic herbs.

ABOVE: *Small animal figures creeping out from the plants add a sense of fun.*

ABOVE: *This kind of ornament needs careful placing in a small garden – always take time to consider position.*

RIGHT: *Figures are often more exciting when they are discovered among the plants.*

GARDEN LIGHTING

Garden lights not only make your garden look more dramatic as dusk falls, they also extend the hours during which you can enjoy it. If you like entertaining in the garden on summer evenings, or just want to sit and relax, lights will add another dimension to the space.

When illuminating your garden you are not attempting to fill the garden with floodlights, but rather to use spotlights to pick out a particular tree, highlight an ornament, or bring to life the droplets of a cascade or fountain.

You don't even need elaborate mains lighting. Low-voltage lighting supplied from a transformer indoors is perfectly adequate for most lighting jobs in a small garden.

Lighting beds

Summer bedding looks good with pools of light thrown downwards onto the beds. If you find the lights obtrusive during the day, choose a low-voltage type that is easy to move around. Simply push the spiked supports into the bed when you want to use the garden in the evening.

Picking out plants

Use a spotlight to pick out one or two striking plants that will form focal points in the evening. The white bark of a birch tree, perhaps underplanted with white impatiens, the tall ramrod spikes of red hot pokers (kniphofias), or a spiky yucca, make excellent focal points picked out in a spotlight. Tall feathery plants, such as fennel, also illuminate well.

Spotlighting ornaments

Ornaments and containers full of plants also make striking features to pick out in a spotlight.

Before highlighting an ornament, try moving the beam around. Quite different effects can be achieved by directing it upwards or downwards, and side lighting creates a very different effect to straight-on illumination.

ABOVE: *An illuminated garden can become magical as dusk falls, and you will derive many more hours of pleasure from being able to sit out in the evening.*

Illuminating water

Underwater lighting is popular and you can buy special sealed lamps designed to be submerged or to float, but the effect can be disappointing if the water is murky or if algae grows thickly on the lenses. A simple white spotlight playing on moving water is often the most effective.

THINKING OF THE NEIGHBOURS

There is a problem with using garden lights in a small garden: you have to consider neighbours. It is unsociable to fix a spotlight where the beam not only illuminates your favourite tree but also falls on the windows of your neighbour's house. If you direct beams downwards rather than upwards, the pools of light should not obtrude.

WHEN PROFESSIONAL ADVICE IS NEEDED...

Low voltage lighting is designed for DIY installation, but 110–120 AC/DC demands special care. If you are going to wire your garden, use special outdoor fittings, and be aware of any regulations concerning the depth cables have to be buried and the protection required; you may be able to do the wiring yourself. But if in the slightest doubt use a professional electrician. If you want to keep the cost down, offer to do the labouring, such as digging trenches, yourself.

LEFT: *The best garden lighting is not obtrusive or unattractive during the day, and throws off white light when illuminated.*

HOW TO INSTALL LOW-VOLTAGE LIGHTING

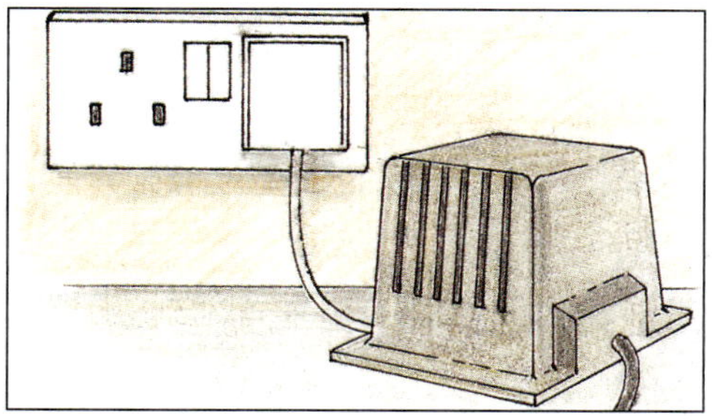

1 A low-voltage lighting kit will come with a transformer. This must always be positioned in a dry place indoors or in a garage or outbuilding.

2 Drill a hole through the window frame or wall, just wide enough to take the cable. Fill in any gaps afterwards, using a mastic or other waterproof filler.

3 Although the cable carries a low voltage and you will not be electrocuted, it is still a potential hazard if left lying on the surface where someone might trip over it. Unless the lights are to be positioned close to where the cable emerges from indoors, run it underground in a conduit

4 Most low-voltage lighting systems are designed so that the lamps are easy to position and to move around. Many of them can just be pushed into the ground wherever you choose to place them.

Candle Power

Candles must surely offer the most romantic outdoor lighting. The light they cast is soft, natural and flattering. Sitting near candles in the garden evokes campfires. They are also very practical for outside as they are eminently portable and they don't rely on electricity, so avoiding the problem of trailing cables. Candlelight is perfect for the table but, in various forms, can also provide subtle illumination throughout the garden itself, while flares can add that extra sparkle.

Candles

There are many forms of candlelight. Ordinary indoor candles can simply be taken outside, candelabra and all, for a candle-lit dinner. Ones containing beeswax burn more slowly than those made solely of paraffin wax, and they give off a lovely honey scent.

Lanterns

If the weather is a touch breezy, use a lantern or some other holder that protects the flame from the elements. Choose lanterns that can take a substantial size candle, otherwise you will be forever jumping up and down to light yet another. Also, check that the metalwork is robust, as some aluminium (aluminum) lanterns collapse once the lit candle melts the solder holding it together.

ABOVE: *Garden flares, 'planted' around the garden, provide a surprising amount of light. Many are also scented to discourage insects, which is of benefit when eating outdoors.*

LEFT: *A large, glass, hanging lantern makes enchanting lighting for dinner* al fresco. *Lotus-like flower candles float above a bed of shells, looking like an exotic lily pond.*

As well as lanterns, you could also try Victorian nightlights, tumbler-like glass containers that hang on wires, huge glass hanging lanterns, and candles in garden pots or galvanized buckets, which – once they burn down below the rim – have the added advantage of being protected from the wind.

Garden flares

Candles that are specially designed to cope with the outside elements are garden flares, which produce a huge flame and can burn for up to three hours. The light they give off is surprisingly bright, which makes them ideal for general lighting around the entertainment area or for lighting the route along pathways. This is particularly useful for any guests that do not know the garden as well as you do.

Position with care

The main danger from outdoor candles and garden flares is that the wind blows the flames, so it is important to position them well away from any furniture or foliage.

GILDED POTS

Ordinary terracotta pots, gilded and filled with candle wax, offer the most enchanting outdoor lighting. Make several pots in assorted sizes to group on tables, patios, walls and outdoor shelves.

1 Prime each pot with red oxide primer. Allow to dry for three to four hours.

2 Apply a coat of water-based gold size and allow to dry for about 30 minutes or until the size becomes transparent.

3 Lay pieces of gold Dutch metal leaf carefully onto the size, smoothing each one with a cloth or soft-bristled brush. Brush off any excess leaf.

4 Apply a coat of amber shellac to seal the metal leaf and allow to dry for 30 minutes.

5 To age the pots, tint a little white acrylic paint with aqua acrylic. Thin with water and brush on and rub off with a cloth. Allow to dry. For the candle, suspend the wick in the pot by tying it to a stick laid across the pot, ensuring it reaches the bottom. Melt the wax in a double boiler. Pour into the pot. Allow to set overnight.

Illuminate a warm summer night in your garden with candlelight. These pretty gilded pots will add a sparkle to the evening.

FURNISHING THE GARDEN

A few seats and a table make the garden an inviting place to eat, or to sit and relax. Unfortunately where space is at a premium every item has to be chosen and placed with care. Built-in seats, and especially tree seats, are a good choice for a small garden.

Portable furniture
Furniture that can be moved is useful for a quick scene change and helps to prevent your garden becoming predictable. It is surprising how effective a canvas 'director's chair' can look on a summer's day, and it is quick and easy to fold up and store when not in use.

Built-in
Built-in furniture saves space and helps prevent a small garden looking cluttered. The best place for built-in seating is the patio, where it can often be designed along with the rest of the structure. White-painted planks look smart, and can quickly be transformed with cushions to look elegant as well as feel comfortable.

Built-round
A tree seat makes an eye-catching garden feature, and this is one occasion when the advice not to have a seat beneath a tree can be ignored! White paint will help the seat to stand out in the shade of its branches.

Wrought and cast iron
Genuine cast and wrought iron furniture is expensive and very heavy, but alloy imitations are available with all the charm of the original but at a more manageable price and weight. White is again a popular colour, but bear in mind that although this type of furniture can stand outside throughout the year, it will soon become dirty. Cleaning the intricate patterns isn't easy. Colours such as green look smart yet don't show the dirt.

Use cushions to add patches of colour, and to make the chairs less uncomfortable to sit on!

LEFT: *White-painted metal furniture looks tasteful and can help enliven a dull corner of the garden.*

BELOW: *A charming wooden seat.*

BELOW LEFT: *A reconstituted stone seat has a timeless appeal that beckons you to sit and rest.*

Wooden seats and benches
Timber seats can be left in natural wood colour to blend with the background or painted so that they become a focal point. White is popular, but green and even red can look very smart. Yacht paint is weather-resistant.

Plastic
Don't dismiss plastic. Certainly there are plenty of cheap and nasty pieces of garden furniture made from this material, but the better pieces can look very stylish for a patio in the setting of a modern garden.

HOW TO MAKE A TREE SEAT

1 Start by securing the legs in position. Use 3.8cm × 7.5cm (1½in × 3in) softwood, treated with a preservative. You will need eight lengths about 68cm (27in) long. Concrete them into position.

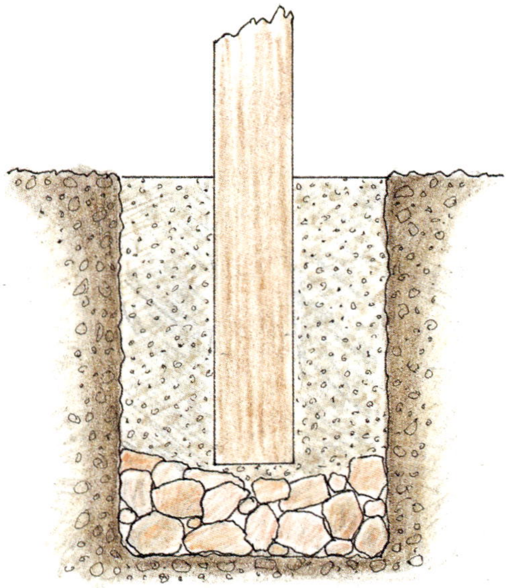

2 Position the legs about 38–45cm (15–18in) apart in two rows about the same distance either side of the trunk.

3 Cut four pieces of 2.5 x 5cm (1 x 2in) softwood for the cross-bars. Allow 7.5cm (3in) overhang at each end. Drill and screw these to the posts.

4 Then, cut slats to the required length (the number will depend on the size of your seat). Allow for a 2.5cm (1in) space between each slat. Paint the slats and cross-bars with white paint (or a wood preservative or stain if you prefer), and allow to dry before final assembly. Test the spacing, using an offcut of wood as a guide, and when satisfied that they are evenly spaced on the cross-bars, mark the positions with a pencil. Then glue and nail into position.

Decorating Garden Furniture

Co-ordinating furniture with its surroundings helps to give the garden a feeling of harmony. By painting or staining furniture, you can also keep the costs down, as you can pick up bargain pieces from junk shops or rejuvenate old kitchen chairs that are due for replacement. Whether you opt for a simple decorative finish or one that is more elaborate, the key to success lies in the preparatory work you do.

Practicality

If garden furniture is to be left outside all year, bear in mind that any decorative finish will have to be able to withstand a lot of beating from the weather – frosts, strong winds, torrential rain, and the blistering sun of high summer. For this reason, it is best to use exterior-quality products: they are less likely to peel and flake, their colours are less likely to fade, and they are specifically designed to protect the surface they are covering. However, you can achieve a reasonably hard-wearing finish using paints made for interior use, then finishing with several coats of a polyurethane varnish.

Compatibility counts

Whatever you plan to paint or stain, it is important to use compatible primers, undercoats and varnishes, otherwise they may react against each other. So, if you intend to use a water-based product, make sure that you also prime and finish using water-based products; similarly,

ABOVE: *This colourful, plastic-covered chair offers indoor comfort outside. Its bright green framework and pink floral pattern provide a witty contrast to the Louis XIV style.*

LEFT: *An old Lloyd loom chair has been given a fresh look with two vivid shades of blue spray-on car paint.*

ABOVE: *Clashing Caribbean colours in pink and tangerine make for a lively look in a brightly coloured garden.*

ABOVE: *This simply shaped chair has been given a bright, modern finish to team with the painted shed behind.*

ABOVE: *The same chair has been decorated with a traditional Tyrolean design. The colours complement the colours of a summer garden.*

acrylics should be kept together and oil-based products should be kept together.

Also, ideally, you should stick to one manufacturer's products for each job as that will ensure compatibility. When you are not able to do this, it would be wise to test a small, hidden area first to see how the different products behave.

Working outdoors

If you have to paint outdoors, it is a good idea to choose a dry, warm day – preferably after several similar days and with the prospect of more to come. The reasons for this carefulness are clear. If the surface is damp, the paint will not adhere properly. If the surface is hot, from baking sun, it will blister. If frost is about, it will 'lift' the paint.

Preparatory work

It really is important to make sure the surface you are working on is properly prepared first, following the instructions given by the manufacturer of the product you are using.

Smooth wood

Most garden furniture is made from smooth-planed wood. There are three types of product you can use to paint these: exterior gloss, exterior woodstain, and exterior varnish, which comes in a clear, matt or gloss finish as well as in a wide selection of colours. Most woodstains – as the name implies – come in wood colours, although some specialist manufacturers produce coloured stains too. Garden furniture is usually bought ready-treated with a preservative that you can simply paint over. However, check this is the case before you buy.

Wash the surface with a proprietary paint cleaner or a mild detergent, then rinse thoroughly. Rub down with wet and dry paper. Allow to dry out completely, then paint on a coat of exterior primer. Allow to dry, then rub down and apply an undercoat. Allow to dry, then rub down and apply exterior gloss paint. Always allow plenty of drying time between each stage, taking the manufacturer's specified time as the minimum.

If you would prefer a finish that allows the grain of the wood to show through, you can choose either a woodstain or a varnish. The colour in woodstains penetrates the wood; varnish, even if it is a stained varnish, sits on top. These products are usually applied directly to the clean, dry wood.

Metal

Metal tables and chairs (as well as gates and railings) can be painted with exterior-quality gloss paint. Brush previously painted metal with a wire brush to clean it and remove any loose paint and metal badly eroded by rust. Then dust off. Treat rust with a rust cure and prime any new or bare metal with the appropriate metal primer, then allow to dry before applying the top coat. There are also special metal paints available in aerosol and brush-on versions that can be applied straight over the metal without priming, even if truly rusty. However, it is worth removing any loose rust first with a wire brush.

Entertaining Outdoors

Entertaining friends in the garden is one of the joys of summer. Pleasant company and beautiful surroundings rarely fail to induce a feeling of well-being and relaxation, and serving food that you have grown yourself brings deep satisfaction. The food can be simple, with freshly picked salads, fruits or vegetables and meat or fish grilled or barbecued with fresh herbs, the aroma complementing the scent of the herbs growing in the nearby beds.

ABOVE: *Lunch taken outside in the summer can be a memorable occasion. Attractive garden furniture and a pretty flower arrangement create a suitably restful ambience for eating outdoors.*

However informal the occasion, your guests will feel more comfortable if the eating area is sheltered, rather than completely in the open. If it is not next to the house, it will need to be screened by hedges or trellis to lend some privacy. You don't need a large space – just think how cramped restaurants can be, yet, once seated, you feel comfortable.

Awnings and umbrellas

Shade and shelter are important, but they needn't be permanent fixtures. You can put up a capacious sun umbrella or a prettily striped awning to provide temporary shade – allowing you to dine outside even in the middle of the day in high summer.

Stimulating the senses

Once the eating area is established, try to incorporate something that stimulates each of the senses. Place a handsome specimen plant within view, or position the chairs to look onto a pleasant vista. Nature will offer plenty to please your ear: summer birdsong, the hum of bees and whisper of trees and shrubs gently stirred by a breeze can be enhanced by the tinkling of wind chimes. A water feature can offer the relaxing sound of a trickling stream.

For fragrance, site plants with richly perfumed blooms near the seating area. Old-fashioned roses are hard to beat or try aromatic lavender and rosemary. Many flowers exude their scent at night. Summer jasmine and tobacco plants (*Nicotiana*) are two favourites. For touch, you can plant a contrast of textures from feathery

CLIMBERS FOR ARBOURS

Clematis (some fragrant)
Hedera (ivy – evergreen)
Humulus (hop – dies back in the winter)
Lonicera (honeysuckle – many fragrant)
Polygonum baldschuanicum (syn. *Fallopia baldschuanica*) (Russian vine – very vigorous)
Rosa (roses – many fragrant)

ABOVE: *In the summer, a couple of potted strawberry plants are transformed into a centrepiece when contained in a wire jug.*

love-in-a-mist (*Nigella*) and shapely ferns to rich succulents. Finally, taste can be stimulated by nearby aromatic herbs or fragrant fruits such as strawberries and blackberries.

ABOVE: *Original Edwardian awnings like this one come with a lightweight metal frame that is easily erected and the awning is slipped over.*

Decorating the table

Decorating the table can be effortless. Outdoor table decorations are the very easiest to put together because they are at their most successful when they complement their surroundings. So plunder the garden and then combine the ingredients with flair. You may cut a few flowers, adding foliage or even fruit and vegetables. Or you may simply gather together some of the smaller pots from around the garden. For an evening meal, add soft lighting, such as provided by candles, and the scene will be enticingly set.

Arbours

An arbour – a simple framework over which climbers are trained to create a shady outdoor room – can provide the perfect setting for entertaining friends. It can be just big enough to take a couple of chairs or bench, but best of all is an arbour large enough to accommodate a table and several chairs, where you can sit and linger over *al fresco* meals.

Designing an arbour

The structure can be of metal or wood, or the arbour can have brick or stone piers with a wooden roof. The design may be triangular, semi-circular, rectangular or octagonal – any shape, in fact, that fits the site.

Most climbers are suitable for clothing the arbour; but if you do not like bees, it is best to stick to climbers grown for their foliage rather than their flowers.

Solid construction

An arbour may have to remain in place for many years, so make sure you build it well. Take trouble to use timbers treated with preservative (not creosote, which may kill the climbers) and make certain that it is a strong design, well supported in the ground. As with similar structures that are covered in heavy climbers, the wind can wreak havoc on weak construction.

Container Choices

Many plant containers are purely practical: plain clay pots, unadorned plastic windowboxes, wooden troughs that are functional but not inspiring. There is nothing wrong with any of these if they are to be covered with trailers and cascading blooms, but most plants have an upright habit and an interesting container forms part of the display and becomes an important feature.

Containers are especially useful in a small garden because they bring life and colour, or just subtle shades of green, to corners that might otherwise remain bare. By hanging interesting or colourful containers on bleak walls, by using them alongside the steps to a basement garden, or simply using tubs by the front door, containers make the most of all the available space.

LEFT: *Don't discard the old metal watering-can. It can be painted and pressed into use for plants such as ivies.*

FAR LEFT: *This old copper boiler has found new life as a container for tulips and pansies.*

OPPOSITE ABOVE: *Although a clematis seems an unlikely choice for this old chimney pot, it will eventually cascade down over the edge.*

OPPOSITE BELOW: *Containers are invaluable in a small garden as they can be used to take advantage of any spare space.*

BELOW: *It is surprising how much you can do with a roof garden, by growing a wide range of plants in containers.*

Don't confine your choice of container plants to summer bedding and spring bulbs, however. If you do, your containers will look like monuments to past glories for many months of the year. Plant evergreen shrubs, or groups of evergreen border plants. Use short-term pot plants in the winter and don't be afraid to discard them after a few weeks.

Houseplants can be used in summer to add a touch of the exotic to your patio. Provided they are carefully acclimatized first (placed in a sheltered position, and protected from winds and strong sun, perhaps with a covering of horticultural fleece for the first week), you can use them to create tropical corners. It's best to use only those plants with thick or fleshy leaves.

Be bold. Use kitchen utensils such as pots and pans as containers, old chimney pots, drainpipes, boots and shoes, but always make sure that there are drainage holes.

You can even make large clay pots more interesting by painting on an attractive design with masonry paint. Use a stencil if you are not artistically inclined.

Hanging Gardens

When you want colour high up, the easiest way is to create a hanging garden, either in a basket or in a wall-mounted container. Ready-made hanging baskets are designed so that as the flowers grow, they cascade through the side struts and spill over the edge in a joyous show of colour, soon covering the whole basket. An alternative is to make the basket or container part of the display. Ordinary shopping baskets, buckets, agricultural containers, even kitchen equipment such as colanders, pots and pans, can all be used to create a hanging garden.

Lightening the load
If the containers are large and possibly too heavy to be supported, one trick is to put a layer of broken-up expanded polystyrene/plastic foam (from plant trays or packaging) in the bottom of the container. This is lighter than the equivalent amount of potting compost (soil mix) and provides good drainage.

Providing liners
Containers should have drainage holes and baskets will need lining to stop the compost (soil mix) being washed out when you are watering. Liners can be home-made from a piece of plastic sheet cut to size, with a layer of moss tucked between the basket and plastic for a more decorative look, although it will soon dry out and die unless sprayed frequently. Alternatively, you can use a proprietary liner, made from paper pulp, to fit manufactured hanging baskets, or coconut matting which comes in a variety of shapes and sizes for all kinds of baskets.

ABOVE: *Winter-flowering pansies will flower whenever the weather is not too severe. Use them on their own or with a small-leaved ivy.*

Potting composts (soil mixes)
Whatever type of container you choose, it needs to be filled with a good potting compost (soil mix) to give the plants the best possible conditions for growth. Ones based on peat or peat substitute are lighter and cleaner to use than soil-based mixtures. Add a slow-release fertilizer and water-retaining granules for the most luscious results.

Plants for an early spring basket
* *Crocus*
* Ferns
* *Hedera* (ivy)
* *Myosotis* (forget-me-nots)
* *Narcissus* (miniatures only)
* *Primula* (primroses and polyanthus)
* *Vinca minor* (lesser periwinkle)
* *Viola* × *wittrockiana* (pansies)

Plants for the summer
* *Ageratum*
* *Alyssum*
* *Bacopa* 'Snowflake' (syn. *Sutera cordata* 'Snowflake')
* *Begonia semperflorens*
* *Brachycome*
* *Calendula* (marigold – dwarf)
* *Campanula isophylla*
* *Convolvulus sabatius*
* *Dianthus*
* *Diascia*
* *Felicia*
* *Fragaria*
* *Fuchsia*
* *Hedera* (ivy)
* *Impatiens* (busy Lizzie)
* *Lantana*
* *Lobelia*
* *Pelargonium* (geranium)
* *Petunia*
* *Salvia*
* *Scabiosa* (scabious)
* *Scaevola*
* *Thymus* (thyme)
* *Tropaeolum* (nasturtium)
* *Verbena*
* *Vinca minor* (lesser periwinkle)
* *Viola* (violas)
* *Viola* × *wittrockiana* (pansies)

Plants to last into late autumn
* *Begonia*
* *Felicia*
* *Fuchsia*
* *Impatiens* (busy Lizzie)
* *Pelargonium* (geranium)
* *Helichrysum*
* *Salvia*
* *Scaevola*

Plants for winter hanging baskets
* *Convolvulus cneorum*
* *Hedera* (ivy)
* *Viola* × *wittrockiana* (pansies)
* *Vinca minor* (lesser periwinkle)

HOW TO PLANT A HANGING BASKET

The best hanging baskets are those planted with fairly small plants that are then grown on in a light, frost-free place until it is safe to put them outdoors – perhaps in late spring or early summer. A greenhouse is ideal, but you can also use an enclosed or sheltered porch. Giving the baskets protection for a few weeks enables the plants to recover from the transplanting before they face the winds and drier soil and air outdoors.

1 Stand the basket on a large pot or a bucket to keep it stable while planting. Use a wire basket if you want a traditional display with plenty of plants cascading from the sides as well as the top.

2 Water-retaining crystals can be added to the potting compost (soil mix) to act as a buffer if you are occasionally forgetful about watering your plants. However, these are no substitute for regular, daily watering during dry and hot weather.

3 You can use a proprietary liner and cut slits in it for planting. If you are making a traditional basket, line it with moss to the level of the first row of plants. Fill the basket with potting compost (soil mix) up to that level, then insert the plants.

4 Add more moss and more potting mix and repeat until just below the rim. Use a bold plant for the centre. It may be necessary to remove a little of the potting compost (soil mix) from the root-ball if the plant has been in a large pot.

5 Fill in with plants around the edges. Encourage cascading plants to trail quickly and effectively by planting the root-ball at a slight angle so that the plant tilts slightly towards the edge of the basket.

6 Water thoroughly and keep in a warm, sheltered place until the plants are well established. If you do not have hanging facilities in the greenhouse, keep the basket on the support used for planting it up.

WINDOWBOXES

Windowboxes are ideal for enhancing a beautiful facade and, just as important, for improving or disguising less attractive surroundings. A prettily planted windowbox will divert attention long before any peeling paint or a cracked window pane is even noticed.

Wonderful deep window ledges are not a feature that is often found in many modern houses, and often brackets or other supports will be needed to hold the windowbox in place. In fact, you don't have to have a windowsill at all: a windowbox is just as decorative placed on a doorstep, on the ground under a window, on a balcony, or on top of a wall.

Nowadays there are almost as many different styles of container available as there are plants and you will find there is something to suit every taste and budget – from a simple rustic wooden box through stylish, although expensive, terracotta to the grandest stone trough. Whichever style you choose, a windowbox allows you to create a miniature garden, which is easily reduced to bare earth for you to experiment again and again, without great expenditure of time or money.

LEFT: *These nasturtium leaves look as if they have been splattered with cream paint. They are planted with snapdragons (*Antirrhinum*) and* Brachycome *'Lemon Mist'.*

SPRING-FLOWERING BULBS

Anemone coronaria
Crocus
Cyclamen repandum
Fritillaria meleagris (snake's head fritillary)
Hyacinthoides hispanica (syn. *Scilla hispanica* and *S. campanulata*) (Spanish bluebell)
Hyacinthus (hyacinth)
Muscari armeniacum
Muscari latifolium (grape hyacinth)
Narcissus (daffodil)
Ornithogalum umbellatum (star of Bethlehem)
Puschkinia scilloides (syn. *P. libanotica*) (striped squill)
Scilla siberica (Siberian squill)
Tulipa (tulip)

PLANTING UP A SPRING WINDOWBOX WITH BULBS

Spring bulb displays are less predictable than summer flowers, and it can be especially disappointing when different bulbs planted in the same windowbox flower at different times. The consolation is that this does at least extend the planting interest beyond the time you originally anticipated. A good alternative is to plant single-subject displays which, although often brief, are frequently bolder.

1 Make sure that there are drainage holes, and cover these with a layer of material such as broken pots or pieces of chipped bark (usually sold for mulching).

2 Add enough potting compost to cover the bottom couple of centimetres (about an inch). As the bulbs do not need a lot of nutrients during the winter, you can often use some of the potting mixture (soil mix) previously used for summer bedding.

3 You can pack in more bulbs by planting in layers. Place large bulbs such as daffodils or tulips at the lower level.

4 Add more potting compost (soil mix), then position the smaller bulbs such as crocuses and scillas. Try to position them so that they lie between the larger bulbs. Be careful about the bulbs that you mix – for example small crocuses will be swamped by tall daffodils, so choose miniature or dwarf daffodils to keep a suitable balance.

5 Fill with more potting compost (soil mix), but leave 2–3cm (¾–1in) at the top for watering and perhaps a decorative mulch. As the windowbox will look bare for some months, you could include winter pansies to add a touch of interest. Don't worry about the bulbs beneath – they will find their own way through the pansies.

ABOVE: *There is nothing quite like the sight of delicate narcissi, elegant tulips and yellow-and-black pansies to herald the end of winter and the beginning of spring.*

HALF-BASKETS AND WALL POTS

Most people love to have a traditional hanging basket, but they can be disappointing unless cared for lovingly. Even though the basket is planted with an all-round view in mind, the side nearest the wall will perform poorly in comparison with the sunny side unless you turn the basket every day or two to even-up growth. A half-basket or wall pot fixed to the wall can be just as effective, and because it is planted to look good from the front only, it can be just as bold and striking as a conventional basket. Some wall pots are also decorative in their own right.

PUTTING OUT WALL BASKETS

Half-baskets and wall pots are difficult to accommodate in the greenhouse or other sheltered or frost-free place, so it is best to wait until frost is very unlikely before planting. If you are able to give them a week or two in a greenhouse or cold frame, however, the plants will suffer less of a check to growth and the display should be much more pleasing.

PLANTING A WALL POT

1 If the wall pot is fairly small, then you may prefer to take it down to plant it. However, drill and plug the fixing holes, insert the hooks or screws, and try it out on the wall before you plant it up.

2 Insert a layer of drainage material, such as broken pots or gravel, then partly fill with a potting mixture (soil mix).

3 Choose more restrained plants for a very ornamental wall pot that you want to display as a feature in its own right.

RIGHT: *This wirework basket is an attractive container for a planting scheme which includes deep pink pansies, a variegated-leaf geranium (*Pelargonium*) with soft pink flowers, a blue* Convolvulus *and deep pink alyssum. Wall baskets look good amongst climbing plants, but you will need to cut and tie back the surrounding foliage if it gets too exuberant.*

OPPOSITE: *Trailing rose-pink petunias provide the main structure of this wall basket and are combined with two colourful verbenas and white alyssum. On their own, the pale petunia flowers could look somewhat insipid but they are enhanced by the deeper tones of the verbenas.*

PLANTING A HALF-BASKET

1 If you are using a wire or metal half-basket, first line it with moss and then fill with compost (soil mix) to the height of the first layer of plants.

2 It is very easy to plant the sides of a half-basket. Simply poke the plants through the metal bars. Add more moss and compost (soil mix) before you add the remainder of the plants at the top of the basket.

3 Plant the top of the basket with bold and spectacular plants for an eye-catching display.

Pots for Doorway Decoration

Always choose an imposing plant in an attractive container to go by the front door, and if possible one that looks good for a long period.

This is the place for a clipped bay in an ornate pot or Versailles tub, or an attractive bamboo in an oriental-style container.

LEFT: *Remember to appeal to the sense of smell as well as sight. Here lavender not only colour co-ordinates, it adds a touch of fragrance as well.*

BELOW LEFT: *Formally clipped box can be expensive to buy, but with patience you can train your own. They are ideal for a formal setting.*

BELOW: *Don't forget that pots can always be used to grow well-trained shrubs.*

If you have chosen imposing plants to go by the front door supplement these with a group of smaller containers that add seasonal colour, and perhaps scent. Don't be afraid to move pots around to maintain interest. Keep a small lilac in a tub or grow pots of hyacinths and move them to the front door as they come into flower to add a heady perfume.

Formal shrubs

If space really is limited and the rest of the garden has a formal style, a couple of clipped or trained evergreens can look elegant throughout the year. Clipped bays are good, but in cold areas are likely to suffer from damaged leaves in winter, but many conifers have a naturally formal outline and remain attractive throughout the year with minimal attention. Box can be bought clipped into topiary shapes, and though expensive to buy will add instant impact. You can easily buy a box plant and clip it into a ball or pyramid shape over the course of a couple of years, if you are happy with a simple geometric shape.

Scented delights

Scent always arouses comment from visitors to the door. In winter you will have to rely on bulbs like hyacinths and *Iris danfordiae*. In spring follow these with daphne and then lilac (both indifferent for the rest of the year, so be prepared to move them to a less conspicuous part of the garden after flowering).

Summer brings the opportunity to use scented bedding plants such as flowering tobacco plants and stocks.

Climbers in pots

A climber round the door always looks attractive, and you can usually erect a trellis for support. If there is a choice, plant directly into the ground, but if that is not possible, pot a climber in a tub. Large-flowered clematis will do well, and even a honeysuckle. You can try a climbing or rambling rose, but these are more demanding in pots.

Grouping Pots and Plants

If isolated pots seem to lack impact, try grouping them together – the mutual support they lend each other gives them a strength that they lack individually. If the pots are rather plain, placing smaller ones in front will mask those behind and bring the display almost to ground level.

Groups in the porch
Make a bold display in a porch by using tall plants, especially evergreen shrubs, at the back and smaller flowering plants in front.

If space is limited, instead of going for a lush effect with lots of foliage and flowers, concentrate on the containers rather than the plants. Decorative pots are often available as matching sets. Grouping these together looks good even if the plants they contain are only mediocre.

Groups in corners
Difficult corners are an ideal place in which to use containers to create colour, filling in a spare piece of ground where nothing much seems to do well. Patios usually have corners that would otherwise remain unused. Group shrubs or tall houseplants at the back and colourful summer bedding plants in front, along with bright-leaved indoor plants for the warmest months.

Alternatively, choose a small group of elegant containers and use the plants in a more restrained way. A trailer growing from a pedestal container with a cluster of distinctive small pots around the base can be as eye-catching as a large group.

In a dull corner, perhaps formed where two wooden fences join, or where house joins fence in a sunless position, try making a bed of small-sized gravel on which to place a group of terracotta pots. Red gravel will help to bring colour. Fill the pots with bright annuals for the summer, and winter-flowering pansies and bulbs for winter and spring. Try spacing the pots out and adding a few interesting pieces of rock among them.

ABOVE LEFT: *Grouping plants in a porch makes a high-impact feature. Replace plants when they have passed their best, to keep it looking good.*

ABOVE: *Feature groups of plants in containers where the garden needs an uplift. The beach pebbles add an individual touch.*

LEFT: *Individually, these containers would not look special, but grouping them makes a focal point.*

Groups on the lawn
Clusters of pots are an ideal means to breaking up a large expanse of lawn. Don't stand them directly on the grass, but use a bed of sand or gravel – this will stand out well from the grass, and make mowing round the containers easier.

PERMANENT PLANTS FOR TUBS

It is easy to have colourful tubs and troughs in summer, but to get the best from containers you need some year-round interest. Sometimes it is worth thinking beyond the traditional summer annuals, and to reserve a few containers for permanent plants.

Small trees and shrubs give height to your patio display, and plantings that provide winter interest mean that your garden never becomes boring. Use small containers and window-boxes to add splashes of seasonal colour, but include a few large tubs or troughs planted up with shrubs and perennials for a more permanent display.

Many shrubs used in troughs and tubs eventually outgrow their containers. Plant these in the border and start off with new ones.

ABOVE: *This Japanese maple will eventually make an attractive small tree. In the meantime the container is an eye-catching feature.*

LEFT: *Few gardeners bother to grow herbaceous perennials in containers, but some, like this* Lychnis coronaria, *are brilliant in flower. If you dead-head the lychnis regularly it will remain colourful for many months.*

RIGHT: *The silver-grey cineraria in this container cannot be permanently planted in cold areas, but is easily replaced each year. Plants like this are useful for filling in the gap around the base of trees and shrubs grown as standards.*

Trees for tubs

Trees are unlikely candidates for containers, and certainly for small gardens. Fortunately the restricted root-run usually keeps them compact and they never reach the proportions of trees planted in the ground. Even in a small garden some height is useful.

Choose trees that are naturally small if possible. Laburnums, crab apples (and some of the upright-growing and compact eating apples on dwarfing roots too), *Prunus* 'Amanogawa' (a flowering cherry with narrow, upright growth), and even trees as potentially large as *Acer platanoides* 'Drummondii' (a variegated maple) will be happy in a large pot or tub for a number of years. Small weeping trees also look good. Try *Salix caprea* 'Pendula', *Cotoneaster* 'Hybridus Pendulus' (cascades of red berries in autumn). Even the pretty

dome-shaped grey-leaved *Pyrus salicifolia* 'Pendula' is a possibility.

These must have a heavy pot with a minimum inside diameter of 38cm (15in), and a loam-based compost (soil mix). Even then they are liable to blow over in strong winds unless you pack some other hefty pots around them, at least in bad weather.

Good shrubs for tubs

Camellias are perfect shrubs for tubs, combining attractive, glossy evergreen foliage with beautiful spring flowers. *Camellia x williamsii* and *C. japonica* hybrids are a good choice. Many rhododendrons and azaleas are also a practical proposition, and if you have a chalky soil this is the best way to grow these plants . . . provided you fill the container with an ericaceous compost.

Many hebes make good container plants (but not for very cold or exposed areas), and there are many attractively variegated varieties. The yellow-leaved *Choisya ternata* 'Sundance' and variegated yuccas such as *Yucca filamentosa* 'Variegata' and *Y. gloriosa* 'Variegata' are also striking shrubs in containers.

For some winter interest, try *Viburnum tinus*.

Border perennials

Few people bother to grow border perennials in containers, but if you have a paved garden, or would like to introduce them to the patio, don't be afraid to experiment. Dicentras, agapanthus, and many ornamental grasses are among the plants that you might want to try, but there are very many more that you should be able to succeed with – and they will cost you nothing if you divide a plant already in the border.

Evergreen perennials

Evergreen non-woody perennials such as ajugas, bergenias and *Carex morrowii* 'Evergold' are always useful for providing colour and foliage cover in the winter, but look best as part of a mixed planting.

HOW TO PLANT A TREE OR SHRUB IN A TUB

1 Choose a large tub or pot with an inside diameter of at least 38cm (15in), except for very small shrubs. Make sure it is heavy (clay or ceramic for instance, not plastic) and place pieces of broken clay pots or chipped bark over the drainage hole.

2 Part-fill with a loam-based compost (potting soil). Do not use lightweight alternatives as the weight is required for stability.

3 Knock the plant from its pot, and if the roots are tightly wound round the root-ball, carefully tease out some of the roots so that they will grow into the surrounding potting soil more readily.

4 Test the plant for size and position. Add or remove soil as necessary, so that the top of the root-ball and soil level will be 2.5–5cm (1–2in) below the rim of the pot to allow for watering.

5 Firm the compost (potting soil) around the roots, as trees and shrubs offer a great deal of wind resistance. Water thoroughly after planting, and never forget to water regularly in dry weather.

YEAR-ROUND CONTAINERS

In a large garden containers are usually used for splashes of summer colour. The voids left in winter when the plants have died are not so noticeable among the many other garden features. In a small garden, and especially on a patio, bare containers in winter look positively off-putting, and only emphasize the lack of year-round plants.

The choice for summer is limitless, so the emphasis here is on autumn and winter – the seasons for which most effort has to be made.

Year-round troughs and boxes

Dwarf evergreen shrubs and dwarf conifers, in their many shapes and colours, will provide year-round interest. But to prevent them becoming so much background greenery, leave space in front to plant a few bulbs or small bedding plants. Allow for a space the size of a small pot for these seasonal plantings, so that you can easily replace the small flowers as they finish. Grow a reserve of them in pots to fit the space.

Autumn highlights

Grow one or two autumn-glory shrubs in tubs that you can bring out of their place of hiding when you need a final burst of colour.

Ceratostigma willmottianum has compact growth and lovely autumn foliage tints while still producing blue flowers. Berries can also be used as a feature, and you can usually buy compact pernettyas already bearing berries in your garden centre.

Winter colour

Some winter-flowering shrubs can be used in tubs, such as *Viburnum tinus* and *Mahonia* 'Charity'. But try being bold with short-term pot plants like Cape heathers (*Erica* x *hiemalis* and *E. gracilis*) and winter cherries (*Solanum capsicastrum*) and similar species and hybrids). You will have to throw them away afterwards, but they will look respectable for a few weeks even in cold and frosty winter weather.

LEFT: Solanum capsicastrum *is widely sold as a houseplant in the winter months, but you can use it as a short-term plant to add a touch of colour to permanent plantings of evergreens in outdoor containers. Those pictured were still happy in late winter. Discard once the berries shrivel.*

BELOW: *The intense blue flowers of ceratostigma last well into autumn, when there is the bonus of rich foliage colour before the leaves fall.*

HOW TO PROTECT PLANTS FROM FROST

Many of the most dramatic summer patio shrubs – like daturas and oleanders – must be taken into a frost-free place for the winter. Others that are frost-tolerant but of borderline hardiness in cold areas, like the bay (*Laurus nobilis*), or that are vulnerable to frost and wind damage to the leaves that is disfiguring even though not fatal (such as *Choisya ternata* 'Sundance') need a degree of winter protection. It is a pity to lose these magnificent patio plants for the sake of a little forethought as autumn draws to a close.

1 Shrubs that are fairly tough and need a little protection from the worst weather, can be covered with horticultural fleece, or bubble polythene. Insert four or five canes around the edge of the pot.

2 Cut the fleece or polythene to size first. If you use fleece, you may be able to buy it as a sleeve (ideal for winter protection for shrubs in tubs). Allow for an overlap over the pot.

3 If in a sleeve, slip it over the canes; if in a sheet, wrap it round the plant, allowing a generous overlap. For particularly vulnerable plants, use more than one layer.

4 Securely tie the protection around the pot. For very delicate plants, it is a good idea to bring the material well down over the pot, to keep the root-ball warm.

5 Tie the top closed if covering with fleece (moisture will be able to penetrate and tying the top will help to conserve warmth). If using polythene, it is best to leave the top open for ventilation and to permit watering if necessary.

A MOVING BUSINESS

Those shrubs that won't tolerate winter outdoors, even with protection, must be taken into a greenhouse or conservatory. Moving a heavy container is difficult, but the following tips are useful.

Try rolling the pot on its edge. Even a heavy container can be moved quite easily like this. Alternatively, 'walk' the container onto a low trolley. If one person pushes the trolley while another holds the container, even large trees and shrubs can be moved.

Scented Planters

Scent gives a lovely extra dimension to container planting schemes, especially for planters that are sited at nose level, such as windowboxes. On warm days the aromas will drift in through open windows. Use plants with scented leaves for a really lasting effect: herbs such as lavender and mint are excellent foils for larger-flowered plants and will fill the air with fragrance. The scented-leaved pelargoniums are perfect container plants and you can choose from a wide variety of lovely variegations and leaf shapes as well as perfumes that range from lemon and mint to rose. Their charming flowers are an added bonus. Put scented plants in containers near paths and doorways, where their rich fragrances will be released each time you brush past them.

An enclosed area with no wind is the perfect place to grow scented container plants as the perfume will hang in the air. You can have anything from marzipan to the smell of melting, rich brown chocolate. Just place the pots around a chair, sit back and relax.

Shrubs and climbers

Daphne odora 'Aureomarginata' is a perfect shrub for a tub. It grows quite slowly to about 1.5m (5ft), and has beautifully scented purplish flowers. Feed it well, place it in the sun, and add plenty of grit to the compost for quick drainage.

PELARGONIUM EXTRA

During the summer, pick and dry the leaves of scented-leaved pelargoniums for use in pot-pourri or in muslin bags in order to scent linen. If you have a greenhouse or conservatory, then move the windowbox inside for the winter and water sparingly until the spring.

LEFT: *A mix of blue flowers works well in this stencilled wooden window box. Petunias twine with* Convolvulus *and* Brachycome *daisies.*

BELOW: *Dianthus and violas are delightful cottage-garden plants and make a pretty display in late spring and early summer.*

Jasminum officinale is a fast, vigorous climber; it will quickly race up the side of a house or, with a restricted root run, can be trained round a large frame. Give it a hot, sunny spot, water well, and inhale.

Lilies galore

Lilies have equally strong scents. The range is huge, running from the highly popular and reliable *Lilium regale* to the various, multi-coloured hybrids like 'Black Dragon' and 'Green Dragon', and the stunning strain called Imperial Crimson, with white flowers speckled red. Good drainage is the secret of success when growing lilies.

Conversation piece

For a talking point, choose the unusual but wonderful *Cosmos atrosanguineus*, which has dark maroon flowers and a whiff of chocolate on hot, sunny days. For marzipan, try an old-fashioned heliotrope like 'Princess Marina'. And for an unusual small, almost black, flower and the scent of summer fruits, plant *Salvia discolor*.

ABOVE: *Scented geranium and verbena are combined with heliotrope and petunias to make a windowbox that is fragrant as well as visually pleasing.*

ABOVE: *This hanging basket is filled with sweet peas (*Lathyrus odoratus*). These have been interplanted with chives to provide a contrasting leaf shape.*

TOP: *Bronze and gold is the theme in this striking and unusual hanging basket of pansies,* Mimulus, *and* Lysimachia, *offset by the dark crimson leaves of* Heuchera.

INDOORS, OUTDOORS

At the end of the summer, pelargoniums can be potted up and kept through the winter as a houseplant. In much warmer climates, with enough sunshine, some may even continue to flower. If you reduce the height of the plant by at least half, it will soon send out new shoots.

BRIGHTENING UP YOUR CONTAINERS

Transforming an ordinary terracotta pot or plastic tub into something special is not difficult. There are so many different materials to choose from that it is easy to find one that suits you. You may prefer paint applied in bold geometric patterns or simple motifs. If you are skilled with the brush, you might try something a little more figurative. Another option is to stick small objects onto your pots – ceramic chips, perhaps, to make a mosaic or shells in a simple, textural pattern.

CREATING A BLACK AND WHITE ARRANGEMENT

Linking the colour of the container with the plants creates a harmony of design – and this is given extra dramatic impact when the colours used are black and white. Red and white would create similar impact.

1 Select a terracotta pot, 30cm (12in) high. First, mark out a checkered pattern onto the pot using masking tape.

2 Apply a coat of matt white paint to the top and bottom rows of squares.

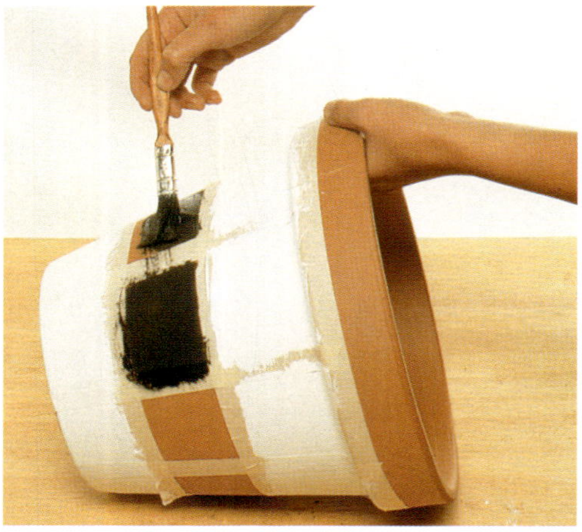

3 For the rim of the pot and the middle row of squares, use matt black paint.

4 When the paint is dry, gently peel off the masking tape.

5 Cover the drainage holes with crocks and half-fill with compost (soil mix). Put a white osteospermum at the back of the container.

6 Plant an *Ophiopogon planiscapus* 'Nigrescens'. Fill with compost (soil mix) and firm in. Plant and firm in three violas. Scatter slow-release plant food granules on the surface.

PAINTING TERRACOTTA POTS FOR A MEDITERRANEAN EFFECT

The brilliant colours of the Mediterranean are always a cheerful and welcome sight. They can be recreated in less sunny climes with these brightly coloured, painted pots. For a very authentic effect, they should be filled with plants that thrive in the Mediterranean climate, such as rosemary (*Rosmarinus*), thyme (*Thymus*) and a host of other herbs as well as the brightest scarlet-red pelargonium you can find.

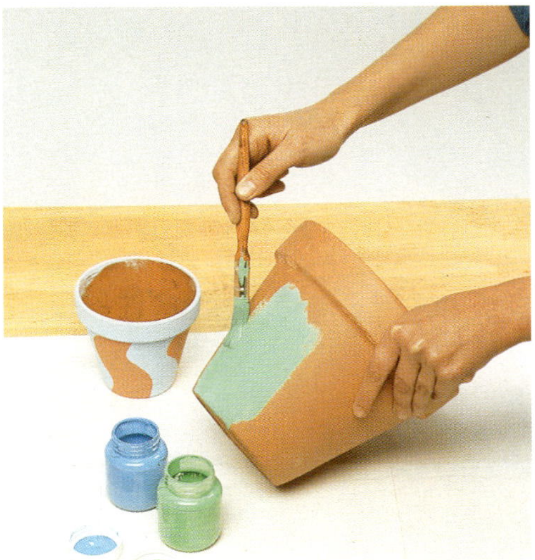

1 Choose a range of terracotta pots in various sizes and decide which you will paint with solid colours and which with patterns. Use brightly coloured emulsion, but bear in mind that terracotta is porous and will absorb the paint, so you may need to apply more than one coat to get the effect you want.

2 Paint the rim of one pot with a contrasting colour. This is a simple technique that creates a simple but elegant effect.

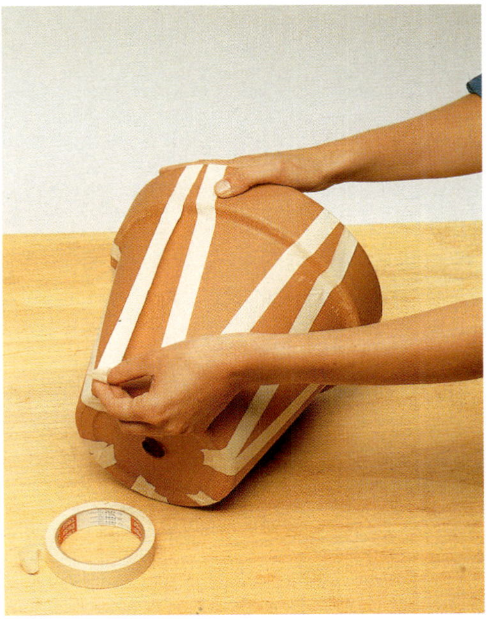

3 Create a pattern using strips of masking tape to block out specific areas.

4 Paint every other section to create a zig-zag effect.

5 The finished pots can then be planted with rosemary, thyme and pelargoniums and placed outside the door for a Mediterrenean effect. They look striking against a white wall.

ABOVE: *This elegantly shaped pot has been painted with striking stripes that match the pink flowers of the* Hebe.

METAL CONTAINERS AND EFFECTS

Metal containers come in all shapes and sizes, and in different textures, from a wirework basket to a beaten copper trough. Many old gardening or cooking implements can be used as containers. You can soon spruce them up with a spray-painted or stencilled finish. Simple paint techniques can also be used to give lighter, cheaper materials, such as plastic, the appearance of metal.

Wire baskets
Hanging baskets made from wrought iron or galvanized wire always look especially attractive, and the delicate tracery of some reproduction antique wirework baskets makes them particularly beautiful – to the extent that they do not even need many plants. Lined with sphagnum moss, free-standing wire-mesh baskets for the kitchen make pretty containers for spring bulbs or other small flowering plants. Woven aluminium baskets add a sleek elegance to any display. Always line the basket before planting or, better still, use simply as a cachepot.

Galvanized tinware
Available both new and secondhand, galvanized metal containers range from small planters to free-standing pots and from small buckets to tin baths.

Aluminium cans
Painted aluminium food tins make cheerful containers for herbs, or for seedlings or cuttings in the nursery. For larger planters in the garden, ask your local restaurant or school for some of the catering-size tins that they normally throw away. Make sure the cans are clean, and remove labels before use.

Practicalities
If you are using any metal container that wasn't originally designed to hold plants, make holes in the base in order to ensure that water can drain freely. If the metal shows signs of rusting, treat it with a suitable rust-killer before adding any decorative finish.

RECREATING VERDIGRIS

The luminous, blue-green tones of verdigris are relatively simple to reproduce on a cheap, galvanized bucket.

1 Sand the surface of the bucket, then prime with metal primer. Allow to dry for two to three hours. Paint with gold paint and allow to dry for two to three hours.

2 Paint with amber shellac and allow to dry for 30 minutes. Mix white acrylic paint with aqua-green and enough water to make a watery consistency.

3 Sponge some aqua verdigris paint on and allow to dry for one or two hours. Apply a coat of polyurethane varnish.

4 The blue-green tones of the final verdigris bucket complement purple violas beautifully. To make the rust bucket shown behind the verdigris one, follow the same steps but use rust-coloured acrylic paint instead of the aqua.

FAKING A LEAD CHIMNEY

Nothing can match the wonderful chalky tones of lead which have made it a popular material for garden containers for centuries. But lead is heavy and expensive, so here is a simple way of faking a lead finish, using a plastic terracotta-coloured chimney and some simple paint effects.

1 Roughen the surface of the chimney with glasspaper (sandpaper). Paint with one coat of acrylic primer and leave to dry for one to two hours.

2 Apply a coat of charcoal grey emulsion and allow to dry for one to two hours.

3 Tint some acrylic scumble glaze with white emulsion thinned with water. Paint over the chimney randomly. Wash over with water and allow to dry.

4 Add more of the white scumble mixture to parts of the chimney for extra colour and 'age'. When dry, varnish with polyurethane varnish.

5 The finished lead chimney could be planted with silver-leaved plants to complement the chalky tones of the fake lead.

ABOVE: *A collection of brightly coloured aluminium (aluminum) tin cans are easy to cut up and mount on a wall for a humorous effect.*

Rock and Water Gardens

Rock and water features add an extra dimension to any garden, but imagination is needed to get the best from them in a small area. The vast majority of rock and water plants thrive best in a sunny position, and it may be difficult to find a suitable site in a small garden. If you can't find a spot that is in the sun for at least half the day – and preferably longer – it might be better to choose a water feature that depends less on plants for its effect, and to grow your rock plants in other ways, such as between paving and in raised beds or a gravel garden.

Very small ponds are much more difficult to 'balance' biologically than large ones, and green water is often a problem for much of the year. If the garden is very tiny choose a bubble fountain, wall spout, or container pond instead.

Rock gardens look best on a natural slope or built to look like a natural outcrop of rocks in a large lawn. Most small gardens offer neither opportunity. Combining a rock feature with the pond is often the most satisfactory solution. You can create the raised ground from the soil excavated for the pond.

Rock plants – or alpines if you prefer the label – offer huge scope for an enthusiastic gardener with a passion for plants but without the space to grow many. You can plant dozens in the space taken by just one medium-sized shrub, and even the tiniest garden can be home for hundreds of plants.

Be careful with the choice of water plants. Some irises and rushes are compact, others are rampant and will soon make a take-over bid. There are waterlilies that need deep water and a large surface area, others that will be happy in 23cm (9in) of water and will make do with a much smaller surface area.

TOP: Sedum spurium *'Atropurpureum'*.
ABOVE: *Campanulas – here growing through* Asplenium scolopendrium *– are popular rock plants.*
RIGHT: *This sink garden contains more than half a dozen different plants in less space than a single shrub would normally occupy.*
OPPOSITE: *Raising the edges of this pond has emphasized its role as the centre of attention.*
OPPOSITE ABOVE: *Various species of dianthus do well in a rock garden and always have a special appeal.*

Ponds and Water Features

Making a pond is very easy nowadays – most flexible liners are strong and long-lasting, and pre-formed pools are as near as you can get to buying an instant pond off the shelf. If you don't have space for a 'proper' pond, make one in a barrel or shrub tub.

If you want to grow plants and keep fish, choose a bright position for your pond, one that receives sun for at least half the day. Avoid overhanging trees, they not only cast shade but shed leaves too, which can pollute the water.

Fountains and cascades

Introduce a cascade if you build a rock garden with your pond. A simple low-voltage submersible pump linking the head of the cascade with a hose is usually adequate for a small cascade with a modest flow of water.

Fountains need a large area of water, otherwise drift will cause a gradual drop in the water level. Be aware that the disturbed surface does not suit waterlilies and some other aquatic plants. A simple bubble or geyser type of jet is often more appropriate than a high, ornate jet in a small garden.

ABOVE: *You don't need a large garden to enjoy the sight and sound of moving water, as this attractive feature shows.*

Wall features

In a courtyard or a basement garden enclosed by walls, a wall fountain is often the best choice. You don't need a great gush of water.

You can fix a spout that pours water into a reservoir at the base of the wall to be recirculated through a hidden pump; alternatively buy one that is self-contained with water simply trickling into an integrated dish beneath the spout.

Miniature ponds

If you've no room for a proper pond, make one in a half-barrel or even a plastic shrub tub. Sink it into the ground, half-sink it into the soil, or have it free-standing, perhaps on a paved area such as the patio. Container ponds are not suitable for fish, but you can grow an interesting small collection of aquatic plants in them, including miniature waterlilies.

HOW TO MAKE A POND USING A LINER

1 Mark out the shape of your pond with a piece of rope, hosepipe or by sprinkling sand. Then remove the grass and excavate the soil to the required depth, leaving a shallow ledge about 23cm (9in) wide at about that depth from the top.

2 Remove the grass or soil around the edge if you plan to pave it. Allow for the thickness of the paving plus a bed of mortar. Check levels and remove extra soil from one side if necessary. The water surface needs to be level to the sides of the pond.

3 Remove sharp stones and large roots, then line the pool with about 1cm (½in) of damp sand – it should stick to the sides if they slope slightly. Use a polyester mat (from water garden specialists) or old carpet instead of sand if the soil is stony.

HOW TO INSTALL A PRE-FORMED POND

1 Transfer the shape of your pool to the ground by inserting canes around the edge. Use a hosepipe or rope to define the shape.

2 Excavate the hole to approximately the right depth, and following the profile of the shelves as accurately as possible.

3 Place a straight-edged piece of wood across the top and check that the edges are level. Measure down to check the depths.

4 Place the pool in the hole and add or remove more soil if it does not sit snugly. Also remove any sharp stones. Check that it is absolutely straight with a spirit-level.

5 Remove the pond and line the shape with sand. Backfill so that the pond shape fits the hole snugly.

6 Run water in from a hose, and backfill and firm again as the water rises. Check the levels frequently as the backfilling often tends to lift the pool slightly.

4 Drape the liner over the hole, anchoring the edges with bricks. Run water into the pool from a hose. As the weight of water takes the liner into the hole, release the bricks occasionally. Some creases will form but are not usually noticeable.

5 Trim the liner, leaving an overlap around the edge of about 15cm (6in), to be covered by the paving.

6 Bed the paving on mortar, covering the edge of the liner. The paving should overlap the edge of the pool by about 3cm (1in). Finish off by pointing the joints with mortar.

How to Plant a Pond

The best time to plant a pond is between mid spring and early summer, when new growth is vigorous yet the plants are not too large. However, most plants can be introduced either earlier or later. Tender floaters such as *Eichhornia crassipes* and *Salvinia braziliensis* should not be introduced while there is a reasonable risk of frost.

HOW TO PLANT WATERLILIES

1 Waterlilies and other deep-water plants can be planted in the same mesh baskets used for marginal plants, but for the more vigorous waterlilies an old washing-up bowl provides more root-run. Plant as for marginals (see below).

2 Cover the soil surface with gravel. There may be space to insert a few oxygenating plants around the edge. These will probably spread and root elsewhere, but it will get them off to a good start.

3 Lower the bowl into the water. If planting early, before the leaf stalks are long, rest the bowl on a couple of bricks for a week or two, then lower to its final position. Different varieties should be planted at different depths.

HOW TO PLANT MARGINALS

1 Use a pond planting basket, and line it with a piece of hessian (sometimes sold for the purpose by water garden specialists) or a piece of horticultural fleece. Fill the container with a soil for aquatics. Insert the plant and carefully firm the soil around the roots.

2 Cover the surface with gravel. This will help to protect the soil from erosion and fish are less likely to stir it up. Gently lower the basket into the water so that it sits on the marginal shelf with about 5cm (2in) of water above the soil.

Six of the best marginals

- *Caltha palustris*
Yellow flowers in spring.
- *Houttuynia cordata*
Small white flowers in summer. Green leaves with red stems, but 'Chameleon' has multicoloured foliage.
- *Iris laevigata*
Mainly blue, white or pink flowers, depending on variety, in summer.
- *Juncus effusus* 'Spiralis'
Stems spirally twisted like corkscrew.
- *Pontederia cordata*
Spikes of pale blue flowers in summer and autumn.
- *Scirpus* 'Zebrinus'
Leaves transversely banded white and green.

ABOVE: *A well-planted pond has both deep-water plants like waterlilies and marginal plants around the edge.*
BELOW: Caltha palustris *is one of the easiest marginal or bog-garden plants to grow.*

Three of the best oxygenating plants

- *Elodea canadensis*

Not much to see – tightly packed small green leaves on submerged stems. Excellent oxygenator, but will require thinning out several times each season.

- *Myriophyllum* (several species)

Dense whorls of feathery green foliage that rises above the water. Can spread rapidly once established.

- *Tillaea recurva*

Bright green, almost moss-like growth just below surface.

Six of the best waterlilies for a small pond

- 'Froebelli' – Red.
- 'James Brydon' – Red.
- *Laydekeri lilacea* – Pink.
- 'Paul Hariot'

Yellow deepening to copper-red with age.

- *Pygmaea helvola*

Yellow, very small and suitable for miniature ponds.

- 'Rose Arey' – Pink.

Other deep-water aquatics

- *Aponogeton distachyos*

Slightly scented white flowers from spring to autumn.

- *Orontium aquaticum*

Poker-like flowers with bright yellow tips in mid and late spring.

DON'T FORGET THE DRY-SIDE

With a natural pond, the soil by the water's edge is usually very moist. The soil immediately behind a pre-formed or liner pool will be as dry as in the rest of the garden. But there are many plants that are associated with water that will tolerate dry soil, even though they may prefer it moist. Make the most of these to give the illusion of a bog garden or natural edging to an informal pond. Plants to include are astilbes, hostas, *Iris sibirica*, *I. pseudacorus*, mimulus, many primulas, and hemerocallis.

Floaters to try . . . and to avoid

Two good floaters that are unlikely to become uncontrollable are *Stratiotes aloides* and *Azolla caroliniana*. The latter spreads quickly but winter knocks it back except where winters are very mild (in cold areas it is worth overwintering a few plants in a frost-free place to start the colony again the following year).

Avoid any species of *Lemna* (duckweed). They not only spread rapidly but are very difficult to eradicate.

Routine Pond Maintenance

Although informal ponds tend to look after themselves, there are various routine measures you should undertake to help promote a healthy balance of plants and to encourage other species to inhabit the pond. Checking the water level and looking for any leaks are all-important tasks. Keeping the water clear of algae and other highly invasive plants means that the pond's other inhabitants – the ones you want to be there – get the best possible chance to thrive.

Maintaining the water level

You will need to fill up the water in the pond periodically, particularly in summer. Allowing the level to drop too much may expose the liner to the potentially harmful rays of the sun. Fill the pond in the evening with a hose. If you can raise the end of the hose above the water level, the resultant agitation will help to oxygenate the water and will be beneficial to any fish in the pond.

Checking for leaks

Some gardeners like to drain and refill the pond annually, although this is not a good idea if you keep fish, while others do it every two or three years. However, it is only necessary to drain a pond if a leak develops in the liner itself. The tell-tale sign that there is a leak is a dramatic drop in the water level, but before you drain the pond, check the edges to make sure that the liner has not collapsed at any point. If part of the liner has slipped below the desired water level, build it up again from behind, then fill the pond with fresh water.

If you are sure there is a leak, press all around the liner with your hands to locate it (the soil behind the hole will feel soft and boggy), then drain the pond to below the level of the leak. You will then need to repair the liner, using a repair kit appropriate to the type of liner material.

ABOVE: *As the water evaporates, particularly during the summer, use a hosepipe to increase the water level of the pond.*

RIGHT: *The excavated soil from this informal pool in a suburban garden has been used to make a raised bed, which is retained with local stone and log edging.*

ABOVE: *This duckweed should be removed before it spreads. It is very hardy and spreads so quickly that you need to check for it regularly.*

ABOVE: *If you leave a lettuce leaf on the surface of the water overnight, it will trap water snails that can be disposed of in the morning.*

Keeping the water clear

Most informal ponds are self-maintaining once the balance of plant and insect life is established, and you should have no major problems with water clarity.

Algal growth sometimes develops in spring and summer, however, where waterlilies and other plants with floating leaves are not mature enough to cover the required area (between 50 and 70 per cent of the water surface).

The problem may also be due to an insufficiency of oxygenating plants, but if the pond is a new one, or if you have just replaced all the water, it usually clears of its own accord. Otherwise, check the pool for dead or decaying leaves and flowers, and remove them. To clear the water quickly, use an ultraviolet clarifier.

In a formal pool where the water itself is the prime feature, eliminating algae may require more regular intervention. You can keep the water clear in a variety of ways. If the pool supports no plant or wildlife whatsoever, you can add any proprietary cleaning agent such as the chlorine that is usually used in swimming pools.

If you keep fish in a pond with plants, you may need to add an ultraviolet clarifier to keep the water clear.

Pond weeds

You are almost bound to have problems with blanketweed (*Spirogyra*), a plant that grows beneath the water surface in dense strands and is most prevalent during warm weather. You may not realize you have it until it comes to the surface, where it forms unsightly masses. It is easy to remove with a long cane, and makes good composting material.

Also in summer you may notice duckweed (*Lemna*), a tiny two-leaved plant with roots that trail in the water. It will rapidly colonize a small pond: once noticed it should be removed immediately with a net.

From time to time you may need to thin oxygenating plants by pulling out clumps with your hands, but make sure you leave enough behind to ensure water clarity. It is best to thin little and often.

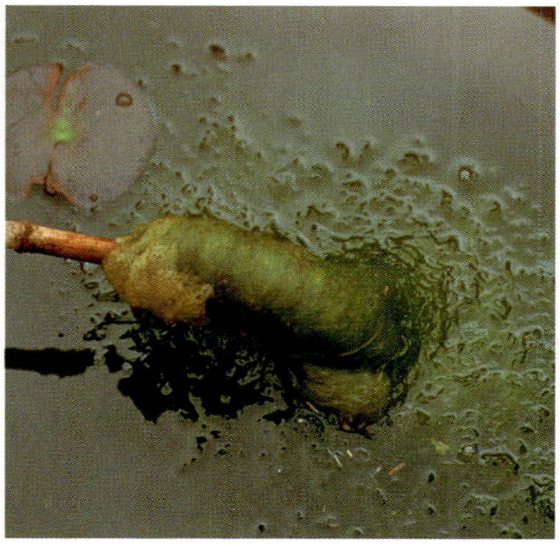

ABOVE: *To clear water of blanket weed, insert a cane into the water and twist it to wind the weed around it like candyfloss.*

TOP: *Lift out and tear apart any clumps of oxygenating plants that are congested, returning about a half to two-thirds to the water.*

Water snails

Water snails can be a problem, since they feed on plants and often nibble away at the undersides of waterlily leaves. You may notice them clinging to the sides of the pool. A few will not do any significant harm and may even help to control blanketweed, but you can reduce their numbers by floating a lettuce leaf on the surface of the water and leaving it overnight. Next morning, lift the leaf and dispose of any water snails that have accumulated there. The ramshorn snail (*Planorbis corneus*), however, is a beneficial mollusc, since it feeds on decaying matter at the bottom of the pond.

THE POND IN WINTER

A few end-of-season tasks are essential if you want to help your pond, and its plants and fish, remain in good condition. These include keeping the water clear of leaves and other debris, and lifting and dividing any overgrown plants. The pump, too, may need attention now: if you leave a pump in your pond in shallow water over winter, ice may damage it. Once the pump is out of the water, you may wish to have it serviced if necessary so that it will be ready for use in the spring.

PREPARING THE POND FOR WINTER

1 Protect the pond from the worst of the leaf fall with a fine-mesh net. Anchor it just above the water's surface. This may not be practical for a large pond, but is useful for a small one. Remove the leaves regularly, and eventually take the netting off.

2 If you are not able to cover your pond with a net, or don't like the appearance of one, use a fish net or rake to remove leaves regularly – not only from the surface but also from deeper water. Too many leaves in the water can pollute the pond.

3 Submerged oxygenating plants, such as *Elodea* and rampant growers like milfoil (*Myriophyllum*), will eventually clog the pond unless you net or rake them out periodically. This is a good time to thin them simply by raking out the excess.

4 Trim back dead or dying plants, especially where the vegetation is likely to fall into the water. To divide overgrown water plants, first remove them from the containers. It may be necessary to cut some roots to do so.

5 Some plants can simply be pulled apart by hand, but others will have developed such a tight mass of roots that you may find them too tangled and have to chop them into smaller pieces with a spade.

6 Discard any pieces of plant that you don't want for replanting, then pot up the others in planting baskets. Cover the surface of the basket with gravel to prevent the soil being washed away.

PROTECTING POND PUMPS

1 Remove submersible pumps from the water before penetrating frosts cause the water to freeze deeply, unless it is below the ice line and needed to sustain a biological filter, which some gardeners prefer to keep working.

2 Clean the pump thoroughly before you put it away. It will probably be covered with algae, which can be scrubbed off with a stiff brush.

3 Remove the filter and either replace it with a new one or clean it. Follow the manufacturer's instructions.

4 Make sure all the water is drained from the pump. If your pump is an external one, make sure the system is drained.

5 Read the manufacturer's instructions, and carry out any other servicing that is necessary before storing the pump in a dry place. If you need to send the pump away for a service, do it now instead of waiting until spring.

WAYS TO GROW ROCK PLANTS

If you have a sunny corner, a rock garden could be an attractive way to fill it. Alternatively, introduce rocks with a pond. A steeply sloped rock garden provides an opportunity to include a series of cascades that run through the rock garden to the pool beneath. It also solves the problem of what to do with the soil excavated during pond construction!

If your interests lie more with the exquisite beauty of the plants than with the landscaping aspects of a rock garden, there are plenty of ways to include alpines in areas other than a rock garden.

Combined with water

Rock gardens and ponds both require a sunny position to do well, and they associate well together. It is often possible to introduce a series of cascades linking a small pool at the top with the main pool below. Bury the connecting hose when constructing the rock garden, and use plenty of rocks to make the cascades look as natural as possible.

Very pleasing combined rock and water gardens can also be constructed without running water.

Island rock beds

Provided the lawn is reasonably large, and informal in shape, small rock outcrops can be created. You don't need many rocks for this kind of rock garden, just a few bold ones, carefully positioned so that they look as though they are protruding through the ground. For rocks to look convincing it is important to slope them into the ground, and for the strata to lie in one direction.

Rock plants in gravel gardens

Rock plants look good in gravel, so include them in a gravel garden or create a small flat gravel bed just for rock plants. Provide the same soil conditions as for a raised rockery, but on the flat. In addition, you can include a few rocks to create the impression of a scree.

ABOVE: *If you like alpines but don't want a rock garden, why not have a whole collection of sink gardens?*

LEFT: *A low rock bank is another easy way to grow rock plants, and is very simple to construct.*

Sink gardens

Alpines are perfect for sink gardens. Genuine stone sinks are ideal, but these are scarce and expensive. Perfectly attractive gardens can be created in imitation stone sinks.

Although you can simply plant 'on the flat' within the trough or sink, much more effective are 'landscaped' displays in which a section of rock face is created.

Raised beds

The great advantage of a raised bed for alpines is that you are better able to appreciate their beauty in miniature. You can build the beds with bricks or walling blocks, but natural stone is much better, especially if you can leave plenty of planting holes in the sides.

Peat beds

The vast majority of alpines grow happily in ordinary or alkaline soil, but a few require acid conditions. If these plants appeal, build a peat bed from peat blocks, bonding the blocks like bricks. Fill with a peaty mixture or an ericaceous potting soil and plant the alpines in your chosen arrangement.

HOW TO MAKE A ROCK GARDEN

1 The base is a good place to dispose of rubble, which you can then cover with garden soil – the ideal place for soil excavated from the pond.

2 It is best to use a special soil mixture for the top 15–23cm (6–9in), especially if soil excavated from the pond is used. Mix together equal parts soil, coarse grit and peat (or peat substitute), and spread this evenly over the mound.

3 Lay the first rocks at the base, trying to keep the strata running in the same direction.

4 Lever the next row of rocks into position. Use rollers and levers to move them.

5 As each layer is built up, add more of the soil mixture, and consolidate it around the rocks.

6 Ensure that the sides all slope inwards, and make the top reasonably flat rather than building it into a pinnacle. Position the plants, then cover the exposed soil with a thin layer of horticultural grit.

Choosing and Planting

A visit to any garden centre will reveal a huge selection of plants for your rock garden. One of the delights of collecting alpines is the constant surprises as new treasures are encountered, and the ability to indulge in a wide range of plants that won't take up much space.

The plants suggested here can only be an arbitrary selection of some of the best, with the emphasis on plants that are fairly widely available.

Useful for a wall

- *Acaena microphylla* (top or face)
- *Achillea tomentosa* (top)
- *Alyssum montanum* (top)
- *Alyssum saxatile* (top or face)
- *Arabis caucasica* (top or face)
- *Arenaria balearica* (top or face)
- *Aubrietia* (face)
- *Campanula garganica* (face)
- *Cerastium tomentosum* (face)
- *Corydalis lutea* (face)
- *Dianthus deltoides* (top or face)
- *Erinus alpinus* (top or face)
- *Gypsophila repens* (top or face)
- *Sedum*, many (face)
- *Sempervivum*, many (face)

Try these in a trough

- *Arabis ferdinandi-coburgi* 'Variegata'
- *Aster alpinus*
- *Gentiana acaulis*
- *Hypericum olympicum*
- *Phlox douglasii*
- *Potentilla tabernaemontani*
- *Raoulia australis*
- *Rhodohypoxis baurii*
- *Sedum lydium*
- *Sempervivum* (various)

LEFT: Alyssum saxatile.

BELOW LEFT: Dianthus deltoides *'Electra'*.
BELOW: Helianthemum *'Fire Dragon'*.

Good starter plants for a rock garden

Some of these plants are quite rampant or large – *Alyssum saxatile* and helianthemums, for example. If you are not familiar with particular plants, look them up in an encyclopedia.

- *Acaena microphylla*
- *Alyssum saxatile*
- *Antennaria dioica* 'Rosea'
- *Arabis ferdinandi-coburgi* 'Variegata'
- *Armeria maritima*
- *Campanula carpatica*
- *Campanula cochleariifolia*
- *Dianthus deltoides*
- *Dryas octopetala*
- *Erinus alpinus*
- *Gentiana acaulis*
- *Gentiana septemfida*
- *Gentiana sino-ornata*
- *Geranium subcaulescens* 'Splendens'
- *Gypsophila repens*
- *Helianthemum*

- *Hypericum olypicum*
- *Iberis sempervirens* 'Snowflake'
- *Oxalis adenophylla*
- *Phlox douglasii*
- *Phlox subulata*
- *Pulsatilla vulgaris*
- *Raoulia australis*
- *Saxifraga* (mossy type)
- *Sedum spathulifolium* 'Cape Blanco'
- *Sedum spurium*
- *Sempervivum* (various)
- *Silene schafta*
- *Thymus serpyllum* (various)
- *Veronica prostrata*

LEFT: Sempervivum ballsii.

HOW TO PLANT ALPINES

1 Position the plants while still in their pots so that you can see how they look and can move them around easily if necessary.

2 Use a trowel to take out a hole a little larger than the root-ball. You can buy narrow trowels that are particularly useful for planting in the crevices between rocks.

3 Make sure the plant is at the correct depth, then trickle gritty soil around the roots and firm it well.

4 Finish off by covering the exposed surface with more grit.

CHOOSING PLANTS

Hard landscaping (paving, walls, fences, pergolas, and so on) is what gives a garden a strong sense of design, and provides the skeleton that gives the garden its shape. But it is the soft landscaping – the plants – that provides the flesh, shape and texture of the garden. The same basic design can look very different in the hands of gardeners with different ideas on the use of plants.

ABOVE: *Mixing different types of plant can be very effective. This border contains shrubs, herbaceous plants, bulbs, and grasses.*

OPPOSITE: *No matter how attractive the design of a garden, it is the plants that make it pretty.*

Beds and Borders

Beds and borders need to be planned. The shape will affect the overall appearance, of course, but there are also practical considerations such as the amount of maintenance required, the theme to be created, as well as the crucial question of the actual plants to be used.

Formal beds and borders are normally dictated by the basic design concept, which will often determine the type of plants you can use. A formal rose garden will clearly feature roses, and only the 'filler' plants might have to be debated. A classic style with neat symmetrical beds cut into the lawn, or edged by clipped box, demands the type of formal bedding associated with this type of garden.

Herbaceous and shrub borders are much more open to interpretation, and the actual plants used will have as much affect on the overall impression created as the shape or size of the border.

In traditional large gardens there is a clear distinction between herbaceous borders and shrub borders, but few small gardens can afford this luxury and the inclusion of a 'mixed border' is the usual compromise. Here shrubs jostle for

LEFT: *By curving the corners of borders in a small garden you can generate extra planting space that helps to make the garden more interesting.*

OPPOSITE ABOVE: *A garden like this, with plenty of shrubs such as roses, require little maintenance and because the hard landscaping is minimal is relatively inexpensive to create.*

OPPOSITE BELOW: *Single-sided herbaceous borders can look right in a rural setting if you have enough space. A border like this can be colourful for many months.*

position with herbaceous plants and annuals, while summer bedding plants and spring bulbs make bids for any areas of inhabitable space left. There is nothing wrong with this type of gardening: the border looks clothed long after the herbaceous plants have died down, and there will be flowers and pockets of changing interest for a much longer period than could be achieved with shrubs alone.

Colour themes are also difficult to achieve in a small garden, and although single-colour borders can be planted in a small garden, it is best to be a little more flexible. Settle for a 'golden corner' rather than a golden border, or a blue-and-silver theme for just part of a border rather than a more extensive area.

Small beds cut into the lawn do not have to be filled with summer bedding and then replaced by spring bulbs and spring bedding. Instead plant them with blocks of perennial ground cover, or use a perennial edging and plant seasonal flowers within it.

Island Beds

Traditionally, low-growing seasonal plants have been grown in beds cut into the lawn – island beds – and taller herbaceous plants and shrubs placed in long borders designed to be viewed from one side. Island beds planted with herbaceous plants and shrubs bridge this divide, and provide planting opportunities that can be put to good use in a small garden.

Planting principles

Island beds are intended to be viewed from all sides, so the tallest plants usually go in the centre and the smaller ones around the edge. Don't be too rigid, however. Concentrate on creating a bed that you have to walk around to see the other side, rather than simply planting tall summer flowers like delphiniums in the centre. Shrubby plants, even medium-sized evergreens, might be better for the centre of the bed, with other lower-growing shrubs creating bays that can be filled with plants that die down for the winter. Your bed will then retain its function of breaking up a lawn and creating a diversion that has to be explored.

Don't be afraid to plant a small tree, such as *Malus floribunda*, in an island bed, to create much-needed height.

If seasonal bedding appeals more than shrubs and border perennials, then island beds can still be used creatively for these.

The question of shape

Most people think of island beds as informal in outline, but you can introduce rectangular beds if this suits the style of your garden.

Curved beds generally look much more pleasing, however, especially if you introduce broad and narrow areas so that there are gentle bays.

Design considerations

Use an island bed to break the line of sight. By taking it across the garden, an island bed may distract attention from an uninspiring view – whether beyond the garden or simply the fence itself. Attention is directed to the sides, and as you walk around the bed, the eye is taken into the bed rather than to the perimeters.

A series of island beds can be used to divide up a long, narrow garden. Instead of the eye being taken in a straight line to the end, the beds become a series of diversions.

BELOW: *Island beds help to break up a large lawn, and create a sense of height.*

ONE-SIDED BORDERS

Single-sided borders are useful if you want to create flowery boundaries around the perimeter and emphasize an open space within the garden, turning the garden in on itself. These borders are also useful for taking the eye to a distant focal point, and, by varying the width of the border, you can create a false sense of perspective that can appear to alter the size of the garden.

Straight and narrow beds

Most gardens have at least some straight and narrow borders around the edge of the lawn, a favourite spot for roses or seasonal bedding. If you want to cut down on the regular replanting work, plant with dwarf shrubs as backbone plants then include flowering ground cover herbaceous plants such as hardy geraniums and spring bulbs to provide flowers over a long period.

Make a border look wider by laying a mowing edge. Then use plants that will sprawl over the edge, softening the hard line and giving the impression of a wider border.

The advantages of curved borders

Straight edges are easier to mow and trim, but unless the border is wide and variation is created with the use of shrubs of various sizes, they can appear unimaginative and may take the eye too quickly along the garden, making it seem smaller. Gentle curves that create bays enable the plants to be brought further out into the garden and provide much more adventurous planting scope.

It may be possible to modify an existing straight border by cutting into the lawn. Bear in mind that mowing time is likely to be increased rather than decreased, however.

ABOVE: *Single-sided borders are the best choice for small town gardens that have high enclosing walls, especially if you can use climbers or tall plants to hide the wall.*
LEFT: *A single-sided mixed border.*

Turning corners

Don't forget that borders can turn corners. Right-angled turns seldom look satisfactory, however, so add a curve to the corner. This will give it greater depth at that point.

You can even take the border right round the garden in a continuous strip. A small square garden with a circular central lawn surrounded by border can look quite spectacular if well planted with a wide range of plants that hold interest throughout the seasons.

How to Make Beds and Borders

If you are making a garden from scratch, areas allocated to lawns, beds and borders will be laid out accordingly, but you can often improve an existing garden by altering the shape of a border, or creating beds in what is currently a large and uninspiring lawn.

HOW TO MARK OUT AN OVAL BED

For small formal beds, such as ovals and circles, it is best to sow or lay the grass over the whole area first, then cut out the beds once the grass has become established.

Start by marking out a rectangle that will contain the oval. Afterwards you can check that it is square by measuring across the diagonals, which should be the same length.

Place a peg half way along each side, and stretch a string between them. The two strings will cross at the centre point. Then cut a piece of string half the *length* of the oval and using a side peg as a pivot, insert pegs where it intersects the long string along the centre.

Make a loop from a piece of string twice the distance between one of these two pegs and the top or bottom of the oval (whichever is the furthest away).

With the loop draped over the inner pegs, scribe a line in the grass while keeping the string taut. You can make the line more visible by using a narrow-necked bottle filled with dry sand instead of a stick.

Use an edging iron to cut out the shape, then lift the grass with a spade.

HOW TO MAKE A CURVED BORDER

1 If you want a quick and easy method, and can trust your eye for an even curve, lay hosepipe where you think the new edge should be. Run warm water through it first if the weather is cold, otherwise it may not be flexible enough to lie on the ground without awkward kinks.

2 The best way to judge whether the curves are satisfactory is to view the garden from an upstairs window, and have someone on the ground who can make further adjustments if necessary.

3 When the profile is satisfactory, run sand along the marker (dry sand in a wine bottle is a convenient method). Use an edging iron to cut the new edge, then lift the surplus grass and dig the soil thoroughly before attempting to replant.

4 An alternative and a more accurate way to achieve smooth curves is to use a stick or bottle fixed to a string attached to a peg. Use this as a pivot. By adjusting the length of the string and the position of the pivot, a series of curves can be achieved. Cut the edge as before.

How to Get a Neat Edge

Emphasize the profile of your beds and borders, as well as your paths, by giving them a crisp or interesting edge. A mowing edge is a practical solution for a straight-edged border. Curved beds and borders usually have to be edged in other ways.

Some methods, like the corrugated edging strip and the wooden edge shown below are not particularly elegant, but they help to prevent the gradual erosion of the lawn through constant trimming and cutting back, and they maintain a crisp profile.

Using ornate or unusual edgings
For a period garden, choose a suitable edging. Victorian-style rope edging tiles are appropriate. If you live in a coastal area, consider using large seashells. If you enjoy your wine as well as your garden, why not put the empty bottles to use by forming an edging with them? Bury them neck-down in a single or double row, with just a portion showing.

TOP: *It is possible to buy a modern version of Victorian rope-edging.*
ABOVE: *Edgings such as this are useful if you want to create a formal or old-fashioned effect.*

How to Fit Edging Strips

Edging strips like this are available in a thin metal, soft enough to cut with old scissors, or in plastic. These strips help stop erosion of the grass through frequent edge clipping and cutting back. Although these may not be the most decorative edging strips, they are quick and easy to fit.

1 Make a slit trench along the lawn edge with a spade, then lay the strip alongside the trench and cut to length. Place the edging strip loosely into it.

2 Backfill with soil for a firm fit. Press the strip in gently as you proceed. Finish off by tapping it level with a hammer over a straight-edged piece of wood.

How to Fit Wooden Edging Roll

Wired rolls of sawn logs can make a strong and attractive edging where you want the bed to be raised slightly above the lawn, but bear in mind that it may be difficult to mow right up to the edge.

1 Cut the roll to length using wire-cutters or strong pliers to cut through the wires, and insert the edging in a shallow trench. Join pieces by wiring them together. Backfill with soil for a firm fit. Make sure that the edging is level, first by eye. Use a hammer over a straight-edged piece of wood to tap it down. Then check the height with a spirit-level. Adjust as necessary.

PLANNING BORDERS

THE SECRET OF A SUCCESSFUL BORDER IS PLANNING for a long period of interest. However large a border, it probably will not remain attractive for more than about a month if you plan it only with plants that flower together. Planning should include not only plants that make pleasing associations when flowering, but that look good even out of bloom. Also incorporate plants that flower at different seasons.

The risk of planting a series of plants that bloom at different times is an uncoordinated appearance, with plants in flower dotted about amid a swathe of foliage in varying stages of

ABOVE: *Hydrangeas look good in shrub borders or mixed borders, but the flower colour may vary according to the acidity or alkalinity of the soil.*

LEFT: *Don't be afraid to use a focal point like a birdbath in a border. It will be eyecatching even when the plants are not at their best.*

growth. Sadly, in a small garden there isn't space to devote to a spring border, summer border, and autumn border.

Some of these shortcomings can be overcome by planting a mixed border that clearly incorporates many different kinds of plants, and by always planting in bold groups rather than using isolated specimens.

If starting from scratch, plan your borders on paper first. In an existing border you will obviously want to retain as many plants as possible, but be prepared to uproot and move or discard those that are out of place.

Choosing plants is always difficult, but in the following pages you will find suggestions of some of the most useful for a small garden. Space precludes mention of more than a small selection of suitable plants, so add special favourites and others that suit *your* garden and *your* taste.

TOP: *A border showing a good mix of shrubs and perennials.*
ABOVE: *Hollies are useful for the back of a shrub border.*

How to Plant a Border

You don't have to be an artist to draw a functional planting plan. You can buy simple computer programs that will help you draw one up, but you still have to provide the plant knowledge that makes a border come alive and fulfil your own expectations. You can achieve results that are just as acceptable, and probably just as quickly, with pencil and paper.

A SCALE OUTLINE

1 Draw the outline shape of the bed and border, marking on the scale. Use graph paper so that you can easily estimate the size of a particular plant as you work.

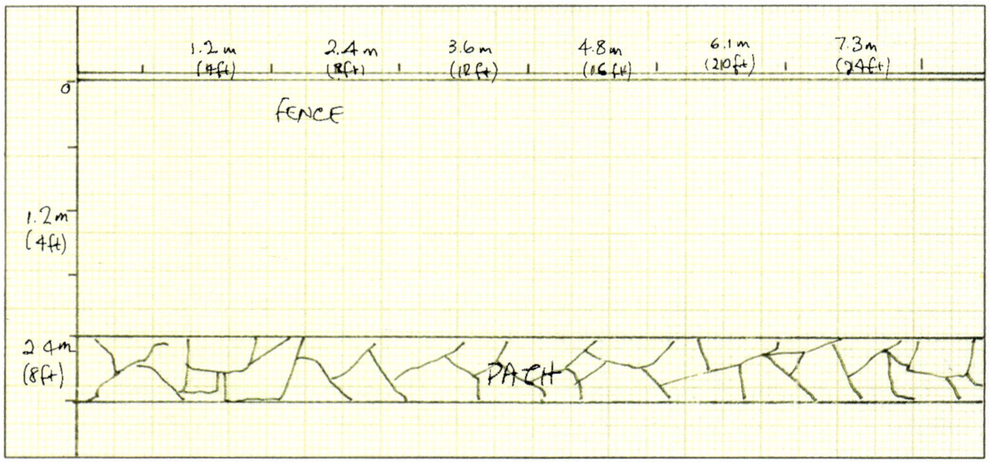

2 Make a list of plants that you want to include. Be sure to add essential details such as height, spread, and flowering season. If you find it easier to move around pieces of paper rather than use pencil and eraser initially, cut out several pieces of paper of appropriate size, with the height and flowering period marked on. You could colour them – evergreen greens, variegated green and gold stripes, and flowering plants in the colour of the blooms.

3 Either start with a basic plan with a series of spaces to be allocated (just indicate whether tall, medium or small), or shuffle around your cut-outs until they appear to form a pleasing pattern. Don't worry about whether the plants will fill the exact shape – with time they will all grow into each other, and in the meantime you can fill the gaps with annuals.

4 When satisfied with your key plants, draw these in on a more detailed planting plan. Then fill in the gaps with other plants, not necessarily on your priority list.

If you feel sufficiently artistically inclined, you can try a profile view that will give a better idea of how the border will look – though you can only make a snapshot of how it would look in one season.

HOW TO PLANT HERBACEOUS PLANTS

GUIDELINES TO GETTING IT RIGHT

- Unless the plants are large, plant in groups of about three – a bold spash usually looks better than single plants. Using single plants just because space is limited is a common mistake – the impact is often better if you use fewer kinds but more of each.
- Take into account the likely ultimate height, but remember that plants may grow taller in one garden than another.
- As a rule place the taller plants at the back (in the centre of an island bed), with the smallest at the front. But don't follow this too slavishly unless planting formal summer bedding. A few focal point plants that stand out from the rest can be very effective.
- Consider planting the border so that different parts are at their best at different times, perhaps starting with spring flowers at one end and working through to autumn at the other.
- Use foliage plants to maintain interest throughout the border.

1 Always prepare the soil first. Dig it deeply, remove weeds, and incorporate a fertilizer and garden compost if impoverished. Most herbaceous plants are sold in pots, so space them out according to your plan. Change positions if associations don't look right.

2 Water thoroughly about half an hour before knocking the plant from its pot, then remove a planting hole with a trowel. If the roots are wound tightly around the root-ball, carefully tease out a few of them first. Work methodically from the back of the border, or from one end.

3 Firm the soil around the roots to remove any large pockets of air.

4 Always water thoroughly after planting, and keep well watered in dry weather for the first few months.

Planting for Texture

Quite dramatic plantings can be achieved simply by planting blocks of the same plant – whether summer bedding, herbaceous perennials or shrubs. If the garden is seen as an area of voids and masses, blocks of colours and textures, the overall impression can be as important as individual plants. Ground cover plants are ideal for this purpose.

ABOVE: *Thyme is a useful ground cover for a sunny position, and will even tolerate being walked upon occasionally.*

CONVENTIONAL PLANTING

Many ground cover plants spread by sideways growth, sending up new plants a short distance from the parent. These are best planted like normal herbaceous or shrubby plants. Suppress weeds initially with a 5cm (2in) layer of a mulch such as chipped bark. This is also the best way to plant any kind of ground cover that forms part of a mixed border.

HOW TO PLANT GROUND COVER

If planting ground cover plants as a 'texture block', or perhaps to cover an area of ground that is difficult to cultivate, such as a steep slope, it is best to plant through a mulching sheet. You can use black polythene, but a proper mulching sheet is better as it allows water to penetrate. However, do not use the sheet method for plants that colonize by spreading shoots that send up new plants, as the sheet will prevent growth by suppressing the shoots as effectively as the weeds.

1 Prepare the ground well, eliminating weeds. Add rotted manure or garden compost, and rake in fertilizer if the soil is impoverished.

Secure the sheet around each edge. Tuck the edges firmly into the ground and cover with soil. Make two slits in the form of a cross where you want to plant.

2 Plant through the sheet as you would normally, firming the soil around the roots.

If you use small plants, planting with a trowel will not be a problem. Water thoroughly.

3 Although the mulching sheet will suppress weeds very effectively while the ground cover is still young and not able to do the job itself, it does not look attractive, so cover it with an ornamental mulch, such as chipped bark.

HOW TO PLANT SHRUBS

1 Most shrubs are sold in pots, and can be planted at any time of the year when the ground is not frozen or waterlogged. Space them out in their pots first, then adjust if the spacing does not look even.

2 Prepare the ground thoroughly, making sure it is free of weeds. Dig in plenty of organic material such as well-rotted manure or garden compost. Otherwise use a proprietary planting mix.

3 Excavate the hole and try the plant for size. Use a garden cane or piece of wood across the hole to make sure the plant is at its original depth. Add or remove soil as necessary.

4 Remove the plant from the pot. If the roots are tightly wound around the root-ball, carefully tease some of them free, to encourage rapid rooting.

5 Firm the plant in well to eliminate large air pockets. Gentle pressure with the heel is an efficient way to do this, or alternatively you can do this by hand.

6 Rake or hoe in a balanced fertilizer to get the plant off to a good start. In autumn use one that is slow acting or has controlled release, to avoid stimulating growth during the cold months. If planting in winter, wait until spring before adding the fertilizer. Water well, then mulch with a 5cm (2in) layer of organic material such as garden compost, cocoa shells, or chipped bark.

Rose Borders

Roses (*Rosa*) used to be grown on their own in devoted borders, where their beauty and delicious scent could be admired without the distraction of other plants. However, it makes sense – particularly in a small garden, where every plant must earn its keep – to combine roses with other shrubs, herbaceous perennials, annuals and spring bulbs. These additional plants are ideal for providing interest before or after the roses have finished flowering, or as happy summer colour combinations. Below is a small selection of beautiful shrub roses, as well as possible planting companions.

ABOVE: *Soft pink roses and scented lavender (*Lavandula*) make a lovely planting combination.*

Alchemilla mollis
Clump-forming perennial. Rounded, crinkly-edged leaves and sprays of small greenish yellow flowers in mid summer *45 × 45cm (18 × 18in).*

Artemisia ludoviciana
Bushy perennial. Aromatic silvery-grey lance-shaped leaves. Small silvery-white flowers in summer *90 × 60cm (36 × 24in).*

Aubrieta
Mound-forming evergreen perennial. Masses of large, violet-purple or blue flowers in spring and fresh green leaves *10 × 30cm (4 × 12in).*

Colchicum
Autumn-flowering corms. Use for late colour when many roses have ceased to be colourful. Very large crocus-shaped flowers, usually in shades of pink or mauve, sometimes white, before the leaves, in early or mid autumn. The leaves (at least twice as tall as the flowers) appear in spring and die down in summer. In flower: *10–15 × 10–20cm (4–6 × 4–8in).*

Crocus
Spring-flowering corms. Use for early colour before the roses are growing. Both large-flowered Dutch hybrids, flowering in early spring, or the smaller *C. chrysanthus* varieties, flowering in late winter or early spring, are suitable. Colours include yellow, blue, purple, and white, some being multi-coloured *8–10 × 10cm (3–4 × 4in).*

Festuca glauca
Tuft-forming semi-evergreen grass. Blue-green grassy leaves, forming

ABOVE: *Lavenders, such as this* Lavandula angustifolia, *associate happily with roses.*

neat rounded clumps. Flowers in summer are insignificant. Useful in front of roses *15 × 23cm (6 × 4in).*

Galanthus nivalis
Spring-flowering bulb. This popular bulb often blooms in late winter, otherwise early spring, so use it to provide interest before the roses begin to grow again. The many varieties all have small nodding white bell flowers *10–15 × 5–8cm (4–6 × 2–3in).*

Gypsophila paniculata
Bushy perennial. Small, linear leaves on branching stems, crowned by masses of small white flowers over a long period in summer. *60–90 × 60–90cm (24–36 × 24–36in).*

Hordeum jubatum
Short-lived perennial grass, usually treated as an annual. Arching plume-like flowers spike in summer and early autumn *30–60 × 30cm (12–24 × 12in).*

Lavandula angustifolia 'Hidcote' (syn. *L. spica* 'Hidcote Purple')
Bushy evergreen shrub. Aromatic grey-green leaves and spikes of lilac flowers from mid- to late summer *60 × 75cm (24 × 30in).*

Nepata × faassenii
Bushy, clump-forming perennial. Small grey-green leaves, topped by

ABOVE: *The fully double, peony-like flowers of* Rosa *'Constance Spry' are heavily scented.*

loose spikes of lavender-blue flowers, at their best in early summer. Other bushy species and hybrids are also very suitable for growing with roses *45 × 45cm (18 × 18in).*

Rosa 'Bourbon Queen'
Bourbon rose. Clusters of fragrant, cup-shaped, double, magenta to rose-pink flowers, mainly in summer *2.4 × 1.5m (8 × 5ft).*

Rosa 'Cardinal de Richelieu'
Gallica rose. Compact habit with fully double, deep burgundy-purple flowers in summer *1 × 1.2m (3 × 4ft).*

Rosa 'Constance Spry'
Shrub rose. Arching habit that will climb if supported. Fully double, fragrant, pink flowers in summer *2 × 1.5m (6½ × 5ft)*

Rosa rugosa
Species rose. Wrinkled leaves and cup-shaped flowers in carmine-red from summer to autumn, followed by red to orange-red hips *2 × 2m (6½ × 6½ft).*

Viola × wittrockiana
Biennials, often treated as annuals. Pansies need no introduction, and come in a variety of colours. Some varieties flower mainly in late winter and spring, others in summer *23 × 23cm (9 × 9in).*

BELOW: *This living wall of roses provides a stunning boundary to any garden. Climbing roses quickly give dense cover, providing privacy yet adding a stunning and fragrant attraction to a garden.*

Foliage and Grass Borders

With the extensive range of flowering plants available, it is easy to overlook the beauty and impact of foliage. Yet many plants are more impressive in leaf than they are in flower, their colours, forms and textures providing interest at various times of year. Foliage plants – whether they be luxuriant ferns, bold hostas, spiky grasses, or fiery maples – are an essential part of any well-planned planting scheme, providing intriguing contrasts and strong architectural impact.

Acer palmatum atropurpureum
Rounded deciduous tree. Stunning red-purple, palm-like leaves that turn red in autumn *8 × 10m (26 × 30ft).*

Ajuga reptans
Semi-evergreen carpeting plant. Many variegated varieties with multi-coloured leaves. Small blue flowers in summer *10 × 30m (4 × 12in).*

Alchemilla mollis
Clump-forming perennial. Rounded, crinkly edged pale green leaves, which often hold droplets of dew or rain. Sprays of small greenish-yellow flowers in mid-summer *45 × 45m (18 × 18in).*

Cortaderia selloana 'Aureolineata'
Evergreen perennial grass. Stiff, arching, yellow-green leaves and silvery yellow plumes on erect stems in late summer *2.2 × 1.5m (7 × 5ft).*

Bergenia purpurascens
Non-woody evergreen. Large, leathery dark green leaves, turning red in late autumn. Pink flowers in spring *45 × 30cm (18 × 12in).*

Epimedium perralderianum
Evergreen carpeting plant. Heart-shaped bright green leaves with bronze markings, turning coppery-bronze in winter. Small yellow flowers in early summer *30 × 45cm (12 × 18in).*

Euonymus fortunei 'Emerald 'n' Gold'
Evergreen shrub. One of several dwarf varieties with attractive variegated foliage, in this case green and gold *60 × 120cm (24 × 48in).*

LEFT: *A tapestry of greens in high summer, the hosta in the foreground makes its mark long after the spring-flowering daphne and the peony behind have enjoyed their main period of interest.*

BELOW: *This glossy* Hosta fortunei *var.* hyacinthina *marks a bend in the path. It looks very striking planted with a yellow-leaved berberis.*

Fatsia japonica (syn. *Aralia sieboldii*)
Rounded evergreen shrub. Bold palmate leaves and architectural habit, and small white flowers in autumn, followed by black fruit *2.4 × 2.4m (8 × 8ft).*

Festuca glauca
Semi-evergreen tufted grass. Bristle-like blue-grey leaves. Small grass flowers in early and mid-summer *15 × 23cm (6 × 9in).*

Hakonechloa macra 'Alboaurea'
Deciduous grass. Forms clumps of arching narrow golden-yellow leaves from spring till autumn *30 × 30cm (12 × 12in).*

Heuchera 'Pewter Moon'
Clump-forming perennial. Grey-

ABOVE LEFT: Fatsia japonica*, commonly known as the false castor oil plant, has dramatic, rich green leaves that reflect the light.*

ABOVE: *This border contains no flowers, but the impact of the planting comes from dwarf conifers and other foliage plants.*

LEFT: *The leaves of* Hakonechloa macra *'Alboaurea' become tinged with bronze-red along the margins in the autumn.*

marbled, lobed leaves and large, pale pink flowers in early summer *40 × 30cm (16 × 12in).*

Hosta hybrids
Mainly clump-forming perennials. Renowned for their bold foliage that comes in a variety of different shapes and colours such as green, golden yellow, grey-blue or variegated, and for their bell- or funnel-shaped flowers, usually in summer. *H. fortunei* var. *aureomarginata* has yellow-edged, olive-green leaves; *H.* 'Blue Moon' has blue-green foliage; *H.* 'Lemon Lime' is yellow-green; and *H. undulata* var. *undulata* has twisted leaves and white to yellow-white markings *15–100cm × 30–100cm (6–39in × 12–39in),* according to variety.

Matteuccia struthiopteris
Deciduous fern. Erect, pale green fronds resembling shuttlecocks *1.2 × 1m (4 × 3ft).*

Miscanthus sinensis 'Silberfeder' (syn. 'Silver Feather')
Deciduous perennial grass. Downward-arching, pale green leaves with silver midribs and erect silvery plumes in autumn on strong, erect stems *1.8 × 1.5m (6 × 5ft).*

Pennisetum villosum
(syn. *P. longistylum*)
Deciduous perennial grass. Flat or folded leaves and feathery green or white plumes (purple with age) on arching stems in late summer and early autumn *60 × 60cm (24 × 24in).*

Pleioblastus auricomus
(syn. *P. viridistriatus*)
Evergreen bamboo. Yellow, green-striped linear leaves on hollow, purple-green canes *1.5 × 1.5m (5 × 5ft).*

Rubus cockburnianus 'Golden Vale'.
Deciduous shrub. Bright golden foliage. The bare thorny stems are attractive in winter, having a white 'bloom' *100 × 100cm (40 × 40in).*

Salvia officinalis 'Purpurascens'
Evergreen or semi-evergreen dwarf shrub. Purple-flushed grey-green leaves. 'Icterina' is grey-green and yellow *60 × 75 m (2 × 2½ft).*

Stachys lanata (syn. *S. byzantina*)
Mat-forming, semi-evergreen perennial. Grey-green, furry leaves, with purple-pink flower spikes from early summer to early autumn *45 × 60cm (18 × 24in).*

Colour Themes

Colour themes can be very effective, and although it may not be practical to plant whole borders like this in a small garden, you can often use a colour theme in part of a border, devote an island bed to shades of one or two colours, or perhaps cheer up a dull corner with yellow and gold.

LEFT: *Many ceanothus grow tall, so use them where you need bold plants for the back of a blue border. There are both evergreen and deciduous kinds of ceanothus.*

BELOW LEFT: *Grey-leaved plants are useful for filling in between blue flowers. This one is* Artemisia ludoviciana.

Mixed borders

The plants suggested here will form the foundation of a colour theme for a mixed border, but you can add to them and broaden the scope by using bulbs and annuals in appropriate colours too.

Two of the most popular colour ranges are looked at here: blue and silver, and yellow and gold, both of which are ideal for small gardens.

Blue and silver

Agapanthus hybrids
Deciduous to evergreen perennial. Light to deep blue ball-shaped flower heads mid and late summer *45 × 75cm (18 × 30in).*

Artemisia absinthium
Deciduous sub-shrub. Deeply divided silvery-grey leaves. Yellow flowers in mid and late summer *1m × 60cm (3 × 2ft).*

Artemisia ludoviciana
Herbaceous perennial. Silver-grey foliage *1m × 45cm (3ft × 18in).*

Ceanothus x *burkwoodii*
Evergreen shrub. Clusters of bright blue flowers mid summer to mid autumn *2.4 × 2.1m (8 × 7ft).*

Delphinium hybrids
Herbaceous perennial. Tall flower spikes in various shades of blue *1.8m × 60cm (6 × 2ft).*

Festuca glauca
Grass. Dense tufts of blue-grey leaves *23 × 23cm (9 × 9in).*

Hibiscus syriacus 'Blue Bird'
Deciduous shrub. Lilac-blue flowers late summer to mid autumn *2.4 × 2.4m (8 × 8ft).*

Nepeta x *faassenii*
Herbaceous perennial. Spike-like heads of lavender-blue flowers all summer. Grey-green leaves *45 × 45cm (18 × 18in).*

Perovskia atriplicifolia
Shrubby perennial. Feathery sprays of violet-blue flowers in late summer and early autumn. Grey-green leaves *1.2m × 45cm (4ft × 18in).*

ABOVE: *Delphiniums are some of the best blue herbaceous border plants.*

Santolina chamaecyparissus
Evergreen shrub. Silvery, woolly leaves on mound-forming plant. Small yellow flowers in mid summer *45 × 45cm (18 × 18in).*

Senecio 'Sunshine' (syn. *Brachyglottis* 'Sunshine')
Evergreen shrub. Silver-grey foliage. Yellow daisy-type flowers in mid and late summer *1 × 1.2m (3 × 4ft).*

Stachys lanata (syn. *S. byzantina* or *S. olympica*)
Almost evergreen herbaceous perennial. Bold silvery leaves. Spikes of purple flowers in mid summer *30 × 30cm (12 × 12in).*

Yellow and gold

Achillea filipendulina
Herbaceous perennial. Flat heads of lemon-yellow flowers in mid and late summer *1 × 1m (3 × 3ft).*

Alyssum saxatile
Evergreen shrubby perennial. Golden-yellow flowers in mid and late spring. Grey-green leaves *30 × 45cm (12 × 18in).*

Anthemis tinctoria
Herbaceous perennial. Yellow daisy-like flowers early to late summer. 'E. C. Buxton' is lemon-yellow, 'Grallagh Gold' is deep golden-yellow *75 × 45cm (2½ft × 18in).*

ABOVE: Achillea filipendulina *'Gold Plate', one of the essential plants for a yellow border.*

LEFT: Hypericum calycinum *can be a rampant partner for other plants, but use it wherever you need to create a bold splash of yellow in an unpromising position.*

BELOW: *Hemerocallis come in a range of colours, but there are many good yellow varieties, such as 'Dutch Beauty'.*

Berberis thunbergii 'Aurea'
Deciduous shrub. Yellow foliage, pale yellow flowers in mid spring. Red berries in autumn *1.2 × 1.2m (4 × 4ft).*

Choisya ternata 'Sundance'
Evergreen shrub that is generally planted in a somewhat sheltered position. Yellow foliage. White flowers in mid and late spring *1.5 × 1.5m (5 × 5ft).*

Forsythia x *intermedia*
Deciduous shrub. Covered with yellow flowers in early and mid spring *2.4 × 2.1m (8 × 7ft).*

Hemerocallis hybrids
Herbaceous perennial. There are many yellow varieties, flowering throughout summer *1m × 75cm (3 × 2½ft).*

Hypericum 'Hidcote'
Evergreen or semi-evergreen shrub. Large yellow flowers from mid summer to early autumn *1.5 × 1.5m (5 × 5ft).*

Ligustrum ovalifolium 'Aureum'
Evergreen or semi-evergreen shrub. Green and gold foliage *2.4 × 2.4m (8 × 8ft)*, but can be clipped to keep it more compact.

Lonicera nitida 'Baggesen's Gold'
Evergreen shrub. Golden foliage *1.2 × 1.8m (4 × 6ft).*

Philadelphus coronarius 'Aureus'
Deciduous shrub. Yellow leaves (can become scorched in strong sun; turn green by late summer). White flowers in late spring and early summer *2.4 × 1.8m (8 × 6ft).*

Potentilla fruticosa
Deciduous shrub. Many varieties with yellow flowers all summer *1.2 × 1.2m (4 × 4ft).*

Solidago hybrids
Herbaceous perennial. Sprays of bright yellow flowers in late summer and early autumn *30cm–1.5m × 30–60cm (12in–5ft × 12in–2ft)*, according to variety.

Red Hot Borders

Creating beds and borders using such a strong, vibrant colour as red is not for the faint-hearted, but red brings warmth, drama and a touch of Mediterranean sunshine to the summer garden. Remember, too, that red-coloured foliage in the autumn and berries in the winter will bring a welcome splash of colour when the garden is, in general, rather dull. If an all-red border seems too strident for a small garden, it can, of course, be tempered with paler shades of red such as pink.

ABOVE: *Pinks and carnations (*Dianthus*) are available in a variety of striking colours including deep pink, scarlet and crimson.*

ABOVE: *Escallonias have an attractive range of flower colours from white through pink to scarlet, as this* E. *'Slieve Donard' shows.*

Aster novi-belgii 'Royal Ruby'
Clump-forming perennial. Semi-double flowers in rich red from late summer to mid autumn, just one of several good red varieties *50cm × 60cm (20 × 24in).*

Camellia hybrids
Evergreen shrubs. Glossy leaves and large single or double flowers in spring, many in shades of red 'Adolphe Audusson' (blood red) is one of the most popular and widely available varieties *1.5–3m (5–10ft),* according to variety.

Chrysanthemum hybrids
Herbaceous perennials (annual kinds are not especially suitable for hot borders). There are many hundreds of varieties, some of which appear and disappear from year to year, and may be available only in one country. Consult a specialist chrysanthemum catalogue for a selection of red varieties. Garden chrysanthemums flower in autumn *60–100cm × 45–75cm (2–3ft × 1½–2½ft).*

Crocosmia 'Lucifer'
Clump-forming perennial. Funnel-shaped, upward-facing tomato-red flowers on branched spikes in summer, and pleated, lance-shaped leaves *100 × 23cm (39 × 9in).*

Dahlia hybrids
Tuberous-rooted perennials. Many red-flowered hybrids of variable shapes, including: peony-flowered dahlias, with semi-double blooms and pompon dahlias, with rounded heads. Consult a specialist catalogue for currently available red varieties. Flowers from mid summer to autumn *60cm–2m × 60–100cm (2–6½ft × 24–39in),* according to variety.

Fuchsia hybrids
Tender deciduous shrubs (evergreen given sufficient winter warmth). Some varieties are frost-hardy. Consult a specialist fuchsia catalogue for a selection of red varieties for the garden *30–90cm × 30–90cm (1–3ft × 1–3ft),* according to variety.

Gladiolus hybrids
Upright perennials. Tall spikes of funnel-shaped flowers, many of which are red. Look at your local

ABOVE: Crocosmia *'Lucifer' brings a splendid splash of vibrant colour to the garden with its fiery red flowers.*

garden shop (store) for red varieties, or look in the catalogues of bulb specialists *45cm–1.8m × 6–23cm (18in–6ft × 6–9in)*, according to variety.

Helenium 'Bruno'
Erect perennial. Daisy-like flowers in crimson or reddish brown, with yellow-brown centres, in late summer and early autumn *1.2m × 60cm (4 × 2ft)*.

Helianthemum 'Fire Dragon'
Spreading evergreen shrub. Grey-green leaves and saucer-shaped, orange- red flowers from late spring to midsummer *30 × 30cm (12 × 12in)*.

Hemerocallis
Evergreen perennial. Narrow, arching leaves and star-shaped tubular flowers; several varieties have red flowers *70cm × 100cm (28in × 39in)*.

Lilium hybrids
Bulbous perennials. Showy, sometimes fragrant flowers in the summer, often available in red, with species such as *L. chalcedonicum*, and hybrids like 'Fire King'. There are many more from which to choose *30cm– 2m (1–6½ft)*, according to variety.

Lobelia cardinalis
Clump-forming perennial. Slender spikes of brilliant scarlet flowers in mid- and late summer, with reddish-bronze foliage *90 × 23cm (36 × 9in)*.

Lychnis chalcedonica
Erect perennial. Heads of small scarlet flowers in early and mid summer *100 × 30cm (39 × 12in)*.

Monarda 'Cambridge Scarlet'
Clump-forming perennial. Scarlet flowers in bushy clumps from mid to late summer *90 × 45cm (36 × 18in)*.

Papaver orientale
Border perennial. Large single flowers on tall stems above a rosette of foliage. There are many varieties, some in shades of pink, peach and white, but red shades dominate *90 × 60cm (3 × 2ft)*.

Pelargonium hybrids
Tender evergreen perennials. Numerous kinds, many of which are red. Check for red varieties in your local garden shop (store), or send for catalogues from specialist nurseries *20–60cm × 15–30cm (8–24in × 6–12in)*, according to variety.

ABOVE: *The crimson flowers and leafy stems of* Helenium *'Bruno' are at their absolute best in late summer.*

ABOVE: Lychnis chalcedonica *bears large heads of a deep scarlet colour. It is easy to grow and loves sunlight.*

Phorium 'Dazzler'
Evergreen perennial. Sword-shaped leaves in shades of pink, red and bronze. Reddish flowers are sometimes produced in summer *1.2–1.8 × 1m (4–6 × 3ft)*.

Potentilla atrosanguinea
Clump-forming perennial. Light to deep red, yellow or orange flowers in summer to autumn *60 × 60cm (24 × 24in)*.

Rosa hybrids
Semi-evergreen or deciduous perennial shrubs and climbers. Numerous kinds, with often scented flowers in summer and autumn, many of which are red *40cm–10m × 45cm–6m (16in–30ft × 18in–20ft)*, according to variety.

Tulipa hybrids
Bulbous perennials. Many red varieties available, all flowering in spring, and in many forms. New varieties often appear, so check at your garden shop.

White Borders

A border consisting predominantly of white flowers can create a stunning display. Cool, crisp, and elegant, a white planting scheme provides an air of harmony and tranquillity, and suits any style of garden, whether it is traditional or modern. White flowers combine well in a border with other colours, such as silver-leaved, soft grey-leaved or dark green-leaved plants for contrast.

Achillea ptarmica 'The Pearl'
Upright perennial. Covered in tight, double white flowers from early to late summer *75 × 60cm (30 × 24in).*

Anemone blanda 'White Splendour'
Tuberous perennial. Forms a carpet of white daisy-type flowers in spring *10 × 15cm (4 × 6in).*

Anemone × *hybrida* 'Honorine Jobert'
Upright perennial. White flowers with yellow centres, in late summer and early autumn *120 × 90cm (4 × 3ft).*

Anthemis punctata subsp. *cupaniana*
Mat-forming perennial. Daisy-like white flowers with yellow centres in early summer *30 × 90cm (12 × 36in).*

ABOVE: Anthemis punctata *subsp.* cupaniana, *with its appealing daisy-like flowers, is ideal for a dry sunny garden.*

Chrysanthemum × *superbum* (syn. *C. maximum*)
Clump-forming perennial. Large white daisy-type flowers, double in some varieties, borne singly on stiff stems in summer *45–90 × 60cm (18–36 × 24in)*

Cistus hybrids
Evergreen shrubs. Summer flowers in white to pink. Whites include *C.* × *dansereaui* 'Decumbens' and *C.* × *cyprius*, with pink and yellow markings and yellow centres, and *C.* × *corbariensis* (syn. *C. hybridus*) with yellow centres *15cm–2m × 60cm–2m (6in–6½ft × 2–6½ft)*, according to variety.

Convolvulus cneorum
Evergreen shrub. Silvery, silky, narrow pointed leaves and white flowers with yellow centres from late spring to early autumn *75 × 60cm (30 × 24in).*

Cornus canadensis
Ground-covering perennial. Small flowers with white bracts in late spring and early summer, sometimes followed by red berries *15cm (6in)* tall. Indefinite spread.

Cytisus multiflorus (syn. *C. albus*)
Upright then spreading deciduous shrub. A mass of pea-like white flowers in clusters from late spring to early summer *3 × 2.4m (10 × 8ft).*

Eucryphia glutinosa
Upright deciduous or semi-evergreen tree or shrub. White, cup-shaped flowers in summer as well as striking foliage in autumn *3 × 2m (10 × 6½ft).*

Gypsophila paniculata
Bushy perennial. Small, linear leaves on branching stems, crowned by masses of small white flowers over a long period in summer *60–90 × 60–90cm (24–36 × 24–36in)*

× *Halimiocistus sahucii*
Mound-forming or spreading evergreen shrub. White, saucer-shaped flowers with yellow centres in summer *45 × 90cm (18 × 36in).*

Leucojum aestivum
Clump-forming bulbous perennial. Small white, nodding flowers in late spring *60 × 29cm (24 × 9in).*

Lilium hybrids
Bulbous perennials. Striking, often highly fragrant flowers in summer.

ABOVE: Chrysanthemum × superbum 'Beethoven' *is a perfect addition to a white border.*

(30in–20ft × 3–13ft), according to variety.

Phlox paniculata 'White Admiral'
Erect perennial. Fragrant white flowers from summer to autumn *90 × 80cm (36 × 32in)*.

Spiraea 'Arguta'
Rounded deciduous shrub. Small white flowers in spring on arching shoots *2.4 × 2.4m (8 × 8ft)*.

Syringa vulgaris 'Madame Lemoine'
Upright to spreading deciduous shrub. Conical trusses of highly fragrant white double flowers, creamy-yellow in bud, in late spring and early summer *7 × 7m (22 × 22ft)*.

Viburnum plicatum
Deciduous shrub. Large heads of white flowers in late spring and early summer, followed later by red fruits *3 × 3m (10 × 10ft)*.

LEFT: *In the summer the bush* Olearia × haastii *with its daisy-like flowers resembles a miniature snowy mountain. Shown in full flower, this one is delicately fronted by a variegated grass,* Phalaris arundinacea *'Picta'*.

ABOVE: *The fragrant white flowers of* Choisya ternata *are produced in profusion in late spring, with some later flowers too.*

White lilies include *L.* 'Casa Blanca', with bowl-shaped flowers; *L. longiflorum*, which are trumpet shaped; and *L. martagon* var. *album*, with reflexed petals *45cm–2m × 30–60cm (1½–6½ft × 1–2ft)*, according to species or variety.

Olearia × haastii
Bushy evergreen shrub. Daisy-like white flowers with yellow centres from mid- to late summer *2 × 3m (6½ × 10ft)*.

Osteospermum 'Whirligig'
Spreading evergreen subshrub. Highly unusual flowers with spoon-shaped white petals and grey-blue centres *60 × 60cm (24 × 24in)*.

Philadelphus hybrids
Mainly deciduous shrubs. Fragrant white flowers in summer may be single (*P.* 'Belle Etoile'), semi-double (*P.* 'Boule d'Argent') or double (*P.* 'Virginal') *75cm–6m × 1–4m*

ABOVE: Cornus canadensis, *with its starry white flowers, followed by tight clusters of vivid red fruits, is an ideal ground-cover plant.*

Everbright Evergreens

Evergreens alone can make a dull garden. They need to be relieved by plants that renew themselves, otherwise you miss the variety that comes with fresh green leaves newly emerged from their buds or the final fling of many shrubs as they go out in a blaze of colourful glory in the autumn. But a garden without evergreens is equally dull, and the clever use of them will ensure that your garden always looks good, whatever the season.

Use a few evergreens in mixed borders and beds, so that there is some height and texture in winter, or devote an area of the garden to evergreens – a heather and dwarf conifer garden can look superb. Try evergreens for focal points and specimen trees in the lawn.

When creating an evergreen bed or border, use plants in many different shades of green, and use variegated plants between plain ones.

Aucuba japonica
Large, glossy leaves. Flowers insignificant, but red berries sometimes a bonus. Choose one of the variegated varieties *1.8 × 1.8m (6 × 6ft).*

Berberis darwinii
Small, holly-shaped leaves. Masses of attractive small orange-yellow flowers in mid and late spring *2.4 × 2.4m (8 × 8ft).*

Bergenia hybrids
Evergreen non-woody perennial, useful as ground cover in front of shrubs. Large, rounded leaves, often tinged red or purple in winter. Pink, red or white flowers in spring *30 × 60cm (1 × 2ft).*

Camellia hybrids
Glossy leaves and large single or double flowers, usually in shades of pink, red or white, in spring *2.4 × 1.8m (8 × 6ft).*

Ceanothus x *'burkwoodii'*
See *Colour themes.*

Choisya ternata 'Sundance'
See *Colour themes.*

ABOVE: Erica carnea *'Myretoun Ruby' is just one of many attractive winter-flowering plants.*

OPPOSITE: *Hebes are excellent compact, rounded plants (though some are tall). This is* Hebe × franciscana *'Variegata', suitable for even the tiniest plot.*

LEFT: *Evergreens have the advantage of looking good all year, like this combination of* Elaeagnus pungens *'Maculata' with* Hebe pinguifolia *'Pagei' in front.*

Cotoneaster dammeri
Prostrate ground cover to use in front of other shrubs. Small leaves. White flowers in early summer, red berries in autumn and winter *5–8cm × 1.5m (2–3in × 5ft)*.

Elaeagnus pungens 'Maculata'
Green leaves boldly splashed with gold in the centre. Very striking in winter sun *2.4 × 2.4m (8 × 8ft)*.

Erica
There are many species and varieties – look especially for varieties of *Erica carnea* (syn. *E. herbacea*) and *E. x darleyensis*, both winter-flowering and lime-tolerant *30 × 60cm (1 × 2ft)*.

Escallonia macrantha
Small leaves, clusters of pink or red flowers in summer *1.8 × 1.8m (6 × 6ft)*.

Euonymus fortunei
Will grow along the ground or up against a wall. Choose one of the variegated varieties, such as 'Emerald 'n' Gold' (green and gold) *30cm × 1.2m (12in × 4ft)* on the ground.

Hebe
Hebes make nicely shaped, usually rounded, plants and often have attractive flowers and sometimes colourful or variegated foliage. Heights can range from *30cm–1.2m (12in–4ft)*, with similar spreads, depending on species. Many are of borderline hardiness where frosts can be severe, so check with your local garden centre to see which ones are reliable enough for your area.

Ilex
The holly needs little introduction, but for a small garden choose one trained as a bush and a variegated variety such as 'Golden King' or 'Golden Queen' (the King is female and has berries, the Queen's male and doesn't!) *3 × 2.4m (10 × 8ft)*.

Lonicera nitida 'Baggesen's Gold'
See *Colour themes*.

Mahonia 'Charity'
Fragrant clusters of yellow flowers in early and mid winter *2.4 × 1.8m (8 × 6ft)*.

Phormium hybrids
Tall, sword-shaped leaves arising from ground level. Usually variegated cream or shades of pink or purple, according to variety. Of borderline hardiness in areas where frosts can be severe, so check with your local garden centre about which ones are suitable for your garden *1.2–1.8m × 1–1.2m (4–6ft × 3–4ft)*.

Rosmarinus officinalis
Grey-green, aromatic leaves. Small blue flowers in spring *1.8 × 1.5m (6 × 5ft)*.

Santolina chamaecyparissus
See *Colour themes*.

Senecio 'Sunshine'
See *Colour themes*.

BELOW: *Rosemary is pretty in flower, and in mild areas will often start blooming in late winter.*
LEFT: *Hollies are usually so slow-growing that most people can find space for one. This one is* Ilex aquifolium *'Aurea Marginata'.*

Viburnum tinus
Deep to mid green leaves on tidy bush. White flowers (tinged pink in some varieties) from late autumn to early spring *2.4 × 1.8m (8 × 6ft)*.

Yucca filamentosa 'Variegata'
Sword-like leaves with broad cream and yellow margins. Large bell-shaped flowers on tall spikes in mid and late summer *1.2 × 1m (4 × 3ft)*.

DWARF CONIFERS

A good garden centre will have hundreds of dwarf conifers, in a huge range of shades, shapes, and sizes. The permutations are enormous, and the best way to choose them is to go along armed with a book or catalogue that will give you likely sizes after, say, 15 years, then choose combinations that will make a pleasing group.

Colour for the Cold Months

Evergreens provide winter clothes for the garden, but they don't look very dressy and they are best interspersed with plants that renew themselves. There is no substitute for flowers and fruits, which, though more transient, are all the more appreciated.

Autumn leaf colour can be as bold and bright as many flowers, but it is worth including some autumn blooms too. A few well-placed pools of late flowers will prolong summer and keep autumn at bay.

Don't overlook colourful barks and twigs in winter, which can become focal points on a sunny day.

Chimonanthus praecox
Deciduous shrub. Scented yellow flowers on bare stems in winter *2.4 × 2.4m (8 × 8ft).*

Chrysanthemum
Look for varieties that flower late. Some flower well into late autumn and even early winter. Height varies with variety. Consult a specialist book or ask your garden centre for suitable varieties.

Colchicum speciosum and hybrids
Corms with large crocus-like flowers, mainly in shades of pink and mauve, single or double, in autumn. The foliage does not appear until spring *15 × 23cm (6 × 9in)*. The leaves can double the height.

Cornus mas
Deciduous shrub or small tree. Masses of tiny yellow flowers on bare branches in late winter and early spring *3 × 2.4m (10 × 8ft).*

Crocus speciosus
Corm. Lilac-blue typical crocus flowers in mid autumn *10 × 8cm (4 × 3in).*

Crocus tommasinianus
Corm, flowering between mid winter and early spring. Typical crocus flowers, usually lilac or purple in colour *8 × 8cm (3 × 3in).*

Cyclamen coum
Corm. Miniature cyclamen-shaped flowers with reflexed petals. Mainly shades of pink, but also white. Flowers early winter to early spring. Leaves often marbled silver *8 × 15cm (3 × 6in).*

Cyclamen hederifolium (syn. *C. neapolitanum*).
Similar to above but flowers from late summer to late autumn.

Erica
See *Everbright evergreens.*

Hamamelis mollis
Fragrant spidery yellow flowers on bare branches in mid and late winter *2.4 × 2.4m (8 × 8ft).*

ABOVE: Chrysanthemum *'Ruby Mound'.*

LEFT: *Long before spring crocuses are in flower, the blooms of* C. tommasinianus *will be putting in an appearance. These were photographed in late winter.*

Helleborus niger
Evergreen perennial border plant. Large white flowers in mid winter *30 × 45cm (12 × 18in).*

Helleborus orientalis
Evergreen perennial border plant. Large white, pink, or purple flowers in late winter and early spring *45 × 60cm (18in × 2ft).*

Iris unguicularis (syn. *I. stylosa*)
Evergreen perennial border plant. Large blue iris flowers in winter and early spring *30 × 45cm (12 × 18in).*

Jasminum nudiflorum
Sprawling shrub, usually grown against a wall or trellis. Bright yellow flowers from late autumn to early spring *2.4 × 2.4m (8 × 8ft).*

Mahonia 'Charity'
See *Everbright evergreens.*

Nerine bowdenii
Heads of pretty pink, spidery flowers on leafless stems from late summer to early winter. The foliage appears in spring *60 × 30cm (2 × 1ft).*

Prunus subhirtella 'Pendula' (syn. 'Autumnalis Pendula')
Small to medium-sized drooping deciduous tree. White flowers, sometimes tinged pink, from late autumn and throughout the winter in mild spells *3 × 3m (10 × 10ft).*

Sternbergia lutea
Bulb. Crocus-like yellow flowers in mid and late autumn *10 × 10cm (4 × 4in).*

Viburnum x *bodnantense* 'Dawn'
Deciduous shrub. Small clusters of white to pink flowers on bare stems from late autumn to early spring *2.4 × 1.5m (8 × 5ft).*

Viburnum tinus
See *Everbright evergreens.*

LEFT ABOVE: *The hellebores span winter and spring. This is* H. orientalis guttatus.
LEFT: Iris unguicularis *can be in bloom in mild spells right through the winter. The plants take a few years to settle down before flowering prolifically.*
BELOW: Nerine bowdenii *flowers in autumn, but will sometimes continue into winter.*

COLOURFUL STEMS

A specimen tree with attractive bark, perhaps placed in a lawn or in an open position and surrounded by winter-flowering heathers, can be a winter focal point. One of the white-bark birches such as *Betula jacquemontii* always looks good. If you need a really small tree, however, try *B. pendula* 'Youngii', a small weeping tree.

In a small garden, shrubs are more likely to be a practical proposition, and two of the best are *Cornus alba* 'Sibirica' (red stems) and *C. stolonifera* 'Flaviramea' (green stems).

As a half-way house between tree and shrub, pollard *Salix alba* 'Chermesina', a willow with scarlet shoots. Cut the stems hard back to a stump perhaps 1.2m/4ft tall; do this every second year.

Autumn Leaves and Berries

Autumn tints will provide a few extra weeks of border colour at a time when every bit of interest in the garden is appreciated. Berries also add a dash of spice, and some of them will remain for many months, even through to spring in a mild winter when the birds leave them alone.

Amelanchier laevis
A small deciduous tree or large shrub. Masses of white flowers in spring, sometimes black berries in summer, rich autumn foliage colour. *A. lamarckii* is very similar *3 × 2.4m (10 × 8ft)*.

Berberis thunbergii
Deciduous shrub. Yellow flowers in spring, scarlet berries and brilliant red autumn foliage. *1.2 × 1.5m (4 × 5ft)*.

Berberis wilsoniae
Deciduous shrub. Small yellow flowers in mid summer, coral red berries and red and orange foliage in autumn *1 × 1.2m (3 × 4ft)*.

Ceratostigma plumbaginoides
Deciduous sub-shrub. Clusters of small blue flowers appear from mid summer to late autumn. Leaves turn red in autumn *30 × 45cm (12 × 18in)*.

Clerodendrum trichotomum
Large deciduous shrub. Starry white fragrant flowers in late summer, followed by blue berries in crimson calyces in early and mid autumn *2.4 × 2.1m (8 × 7ft)*.

Cornus alba
Deciduous suckering shrub. Attractive autumn foliage colouring, red stems in winter *2.1 × 2.1m (7 × 7ft)*.

Cotoneaster horizontalis
Deciduous, ground-hugging shrub for front of border (can also be used against a fence or wall). Small pink flowers in early summer, followed by red berries later. Bright red foliage tints in autumn *60cm × 1.8m (2 × 6ft)*.

ABOVE: *The amelanchiers are usually grown for their white flowers in spring, but they have a second burst of colour when the leaves turn. This species is* A. laevis.

LEFT: Cornus alba *is an excellent shrub. After the brief spell of glory as the leaves colour before they fall, there is the winter-long attraction of red stems.*

Fothergilla major
Deciduous shrub. Dark green leaves, orange-yellow or red before they fall. Scented white flowers in late spring *1.8 × 1.5m (6 × 5ft).*

Ilex
See *Everbright evergreens.*

Malus 'John Downie'
Small to medium-sized deciduous tree. White apple blossom in late spring. Conical yellow and crimson crab apples in autumn *6 × 2.4m (20 × 8ft).*

Malus tschonoskii
Deciduous tree, which though tall is a candidate for a small garden by virtue of its slender, pencil-like profile. White blossom tinged pink in late spring. Dull red fruits flushed yellow (not a feature). Red and yellow autumn foliage *6 × 2.1m (20 × 7ft).*

Pernettya mucronata
Evergreen shrub. Small, sharply pointed glossy leaves. Insignificant white flowers in late spring. Clusters of berries – shades of pink, red, purple and white, according to variety – in autumn and winter. Male and female plants must be grown together to ensure fruiting *1 × 1.2m (3 × 4ft).*

LEFT: *Most sorbus are grown for their red or orange berries, but some also have white or yellow berries, and there is the bonus of spectacular leaf colour just before they fall. This is* Sorbus *'Joseph Rock'.*

Pyracantha 'Orange Glow'
Evergreen shrub, usually grown against a wall but also an attractive free-standing plant. White flowers in early summer, orange-red berries in autumn and winter. There are other suitable species and varieties *2.4 × 2.4m (8 × 8ft).*

Rhus typhina (syn. *R. hirta*)
Deciduous small tree or large shrub. Large, divided leaves, colouring orange-red and yellow before they fall *3 × 3.5m (10 × 12ft).*

Skimmia japonica
Evergreen shrub. Fragrant creamy-white flowers in spring, red berries in late summer and early autumn. Male plant needed to pollinate female *1 × 1m (3 × 3ft).*

Sorbus
Many species and hybrids make small or medium-sized trees with red or yellow berries and good autumn foliage colour. Good ones are *S. aucuparia* and hybrids, *S.* 'Embley', and *S.* 'Joseph Rock'.

ABOVE: Pernettya mucronata *is available with pink and red berries as well as white ones. This variety is 'Mulberry Wine'.*
RIGHT: *Skimmias have long-lasting red berries. This one is* S. japonica *'Nymans'.*

VARIETY WITH VARIEGATION

Variegated plants make a border look lighter and more interesting when flowers are scarce, and variegated evergreens are particularly useful at times when little is flowering.

Avoid planting too many variegated plants close together. Use them between other plants with plain foliage where the leaf colouring will be shown off to advantage.

Aralia elata 'Variegata'
Deciduous shrub or small tree. Leaflets margined and marked creamy-white ('Aureovariegata' has a broad, irregular gold margin). White flowers in late summer and early autumn *3 × 2.1m (10 × 7ft)*.

Arundinaria viridistriata (syn. *Pleioblastus auricomus*, *Pleioblastus viridistriatus*)
Bamboo. Dark green leaves broadly striped yellow. Purplish-green canes *1m × 60cm (3 × 2ft)*.

ABOVE: Hosta fortunei albopicta.
BELOW: *Only a few variegated trees are suitable. This is* Aralia elata *'Variegata'*.

Aucuba japonica (variegated varieties)
See *Everbright evergreens*.

Buxus sempervirens 'Aureovariegata'
Evergreen shrub with small leaves striped, splashed and mottled pale yellow. 'Elegantissima' has irregular creamy-white margins *1.2 × 1m (4 × 3ft)*.

Carex morrowii 'Evergold'
Sedge
Clump-forming with grass-like leaves striped yellow along the centre *25 × 30cm (10 × 12in)*.

Cornus alba 'Elegantissima'
Deciduous suckering shrub with red stems and leaves margined and mottled with white. 'Spaethii' is similar but has gold variegation *2.1 × 1.8m (7 × 6ft)*.

Elaeagnus x *ebbingei* 'Limelight'
Evergreen shrub. Large green leaves with a central splash of deep yellow *2.4 × 2.1m (8 × 7ft)*.

Elaeagnus pungens 'Maculata'
See *Everbright evergreens*.

Euonymus fortunei (variegated varieties)
See *Everbright evergreens*.

Fuchsia magellanica 'Versicolor'
Deciduous shrub. Small fuchsia-type flower in summer and into autumn. Grey-green, white, yellow, and pink variegation. Hardy except in cold areas *1.2 × 1m (4 × 3ft)*.

Hebe x *franciscana* 'Variegata'
Evergreen shrub, not suitable for very cold areas. Small rounded leaves edged cream. Mauve-blue flowers in summer *60 × 60cm (2 × 2ft)*.

ABOVE: Pachysandra terminalis *is an excellent ground cover for shade, but the plain green form looks rather boring. 'Variegata' is much more interesting.*

LEFT: Houttuynia cordata *'Chameleon'.*

BELOW: Vinca minor *'Variegata'.*

Hostas (many variegated varieties)
Herbaceous perennial *30–60cm × 30–75cm (12in–2ft × 12in–2½ft).*

Houttuynia cordata 'Chameleon'
Herbaceous perennial. Outstandingly striking, heart-shaped foliage, variegated with shades of yellow, green, bronze and red. Small white flowers in summer *30 × 45cm (12 × 18in).*

Hypericum × moserianum 'Tricolor'
Evergreen shrub. Yellow flowers about 5cm (2in) across from mid summer to mid autumn. Green and white leaves edged pink *60 × 60cm (2 × 2ft).*

Ilex (variegated varieties)
See *Everbright evergreens.*

Iris pallida 'Variegata'
Sword-like leaves, striped creamy-white and green. Blue flowers in early summer *60 × 60cm (2 × 2ft).*

Iris pseudacorus 'Variegatus'
Sword-like leaves striped green and yellow while young, turning greener with age. Blue flowers in early summer. Although associated with water, it will grow in an ordinary border though it does best in damp soil *1m × 60cm (3 × 2ft).*

Ligustrum (variegated varieties)
See *Colour themes.*

Pachysandra terminalis 'Variegata'
Evergreen sub-shrub. Green and white leaves. Insignificant white flowers in late spring *30 × 45cm (12 × 18in).*

ABOVE: *Variegation is important in the herbaceous border. This is* Iris pallida *'Variegata'.*

Phormium hybrids
See *Everbright evergreens.*

Salvia officinalis 'Icterina'
Evergreen shrub. Grey-green leaves splashed with yellow *60 × 60cm (2 × 2ft).*

Vinca minor 'Variegata'
Evergreen prostrate shrub. Green and creamy-white leaves. Pale mauve flowers *20 × 60cm (8in × 2ft).*

Weigela florida 'Variegata'
Deciduous shrub. Leaves edged creamy-white. Pink flowers in early summer *1.5 × 1.2m (5 × 4ft).*

Yucca gloriosa 'Variegata'
See *Everbright evergreens.*

PLANTING FOR QUICK RESULTS

Annuals are almost instant – many are already in flower when you buy them – border perennials are respectable after a year, but shrubs can seem infuriatingly slow to mature.

Not all shrubs are slow-growers, however, so if you want your border to look well established in three years instead of five or even ten, try those suggested here.

Even those plants that grow quickly will leave gaps in the early years. In a mixed border, fill these gaps with the quicker-growing border perennials; in a shrub border add a few bushy annuals.

Bear in mind that some shrubs that grow quickly while young may continue to grow (over-enthusiastically) once they've reached what you consider a modest size. The height and spread estimates below are based on three years (though much depends on soil and climate), but the ones listed are only likely to grow a little more than this even by 10 years. Those that grow taller can be pruned back hard to restrict their size. *Buddleia davidii*, for example, will be much better if you cut it back hard each spring.

There are many more quick-growers, however, so don't assume that your scope for an almost instant border is limited solely to those listed below.

LEFT: *Tough, low-growing, quick to mature, and very bright in flower are qualities that make* Genista tinctoria *well worth considering. This variety is 'Royal Gold'.*

Aucuba japonica
See *Everbright evergreens*.

Buddleia davidii
Deciduous shrub. Fragrant, usually lilac-blue flower clusters at ends of arching branches, from mid summer to mid autumn. Other colours include shades of red, purple, and white *2.4 × 1.5m (8 × 5ft)*.

Caryopteris x *clandonensis*
Deciduous shrub. Narrow, grey-green leaves. Clusters of bright blue flowers in late summer and early autumn *1m × 60cm (3 × 2ft)*.

Choisya ternata
See *Colour themes*.

Cistus x *corbariensis*
Evergreen shrub. Dull green leaves wavy at the edge. Bold white flowers with a yellow mark at the base of each petal, in late spring and early summer *75 × 60cm (2½ × 2ft)*.

Cytisus x *kewensis*
Deciduous shrub. Pale yellow, pea-like flowers, in profusion in late spring. Spreading shape *45cm × 1m (18in × 3ft)*.

BELOW: Hypericum calycinum *grows and spreads rapidly, so don't plant it where these characteristics can become an embarrassment. The flowers are bold and beautiful.*

ABOVE: Leycesteria formosa *is quick-growing, and highly popular with birds. They love the dark purple berries.*
RIGHT: *Weigelas come in a range of colours, but mainly pinks and reds. They grow quickly and flower young and so make an excellent choice if you want fast results.*

Erica carnea
See *Everbright evergreens.*

Fuchsia magellanica
See *Variety with variegation.*

Genista tinctoria
Deciduous shrub. Deep yellow pea-type flowers all summer *75 × 60cm (2½ × 2ft)*, but height tends to be very variable.

Hebe 'Midsummer Beauty'
Evergreen shrub. Pale green leaves, slightly reddish beneath. Sprays of lavender-purple flowers from mid summer to mid autumn. Not reliably hardy in cold areas *1 × 1m (3 × 3ft).*

Hypericum calycinum
Evergreen shrub. Large yellow, cup-shaped flowers all summer. Can be invasive *45 × 60cm (18in × 2ft).*

Lavandula (various)
Evergreen shrub. The popular lavender. Grey-green leaves and flowers in shades of blue or purple *60 × 60cm (2 × 2ft).*

Leycesteria formosa
Deciduous shrub. Cane-like stems forming a bamboo-like clump. Drooping flower tassels containing white flowers with claret bracts, followed by purple-black fruits *1.5 × 1m (5 × 3ft).*

Lupinus arboreus
Short-lived deciduous shrub. Foliage and flower spikes resemble the herbaceous lupin, but the lightly fragrant flowers are much sparser. Usually yellow, but can be lilac to purple or blue. Good for a hot, dry site *1.2 × 1m (4 × 3ft).*

Mahonia 'Charity'
See *Everbright evergreens.*

Philadelphus coronarius 'Aureus'
See *Colour themes.*

Potentilla fruticosa
See *Colour themes.*

Senecio 'Sunshine'
See *Colour themes.*

Spiraea x *bumalda* (various varieties)
Twiggy deciduous shrub. Flat flower heads, usually crimson, in late summer. Some varieties have variegated foliage *75 × 45cm (2½ft × 18in).*

Weigela hybrids
Deciduous shrub. Funnel-shaped flowers in late spring and early summer. Mainly shades of red and pink *1.8 × 1.5m (6 × 5ft).*

BELOW: Spiraea × bumalda *(syn.* S. japonica). *This is 'Anthony Waterer'.*

NO FUSS, LOW-MAINTENANCE PLANTS

There are plenty of people who do not have a lot of time to tend to their gardens. If you want to save the cost and time involved in regularly replanting with seasonal plants, grow hardy perennials and shrubs. But if you really want to cut down on maintenance, grow only those that are undemanding, with no need to prune regularly, or to keep lifting, dividing, or hacking back.

Most shrubs will require very occasional pruning, perhaps to cut out a dead or diseased shoot, or to improve the shape if growth is not symmetrical, and sooner or later border perennials will benefit from being lifted and divided, but the plants suggested here can be left for many years without attention. They will almost thrive on neglect, yet will not get out of control.

Aucuba japonica
See *Everbright evergreens.*

Berberis thunbergii
There are many varieties, including variegated, purple-leaved and gold-leaved. Shape and height also vary with variety: *B.t. atropurpurea* 'Bagatelle', for example, makes a dwarf rounded ball of growth covered with coppery-red leaves, usually less than *45cm (18in)* tall and broad, 'Helmond Pillar' is dark purple but grows into a narrow column *1.2m (4ft)* or so high but only about *30cm (12in)* wide.

Bergenia hybrids
See *Everbright evergreens.*

ABOVE: Cotoneaster horizontalis *can be grown as ground cover or as a climber.*

ABOVE: Cotinus coggygria *is sometimes called the smoke bush because of its flower heads. It can make quite a large shrub in time, but requires minimal attention.*

Choisya ternata
Both green and golden forms (see *Colour themes*) are trouble-free plants if protected from cold winds in winter.

Cornus stolonifera 'Flaviramea'
Deciduous shrub. Green leaves turn yellow before falling. Yellowish-green winter stems *1.8 × 1.8m (6 × 6ft).*

Cotinus coggygria
Deciduous shrub. Rounded shape with pale green leaves (there are also purple-leaved varieties) that have brilliant autumn colours. Feathery sprays of purple or pink flowers in mid summer *2.4 × 2.4m (8 × 8ft).*

Cotoneaster
There are many cotoneasters, from ground-huggers to shrubs *3m (10ft)* or more tall. *C. horizontalis* (*see Autumn leaves and berries*) and *C. dammeri* (see *Everbright evergreens*), are popular ground-huggers, but many others are suitable for a small garden.

Elaeagnus pungens 'Maculata'
See *Everbright evergreens.*

Erica carnea
See *Everbright evergreens.*

Fatsia japonica
Evergreen shrub. Large, hand-shaped glossy green leaves (there is a variegated variety). White, ball-shaped flower heads that appear on mature plants in mid autumn *2.4 × 2.4m (8 × 8ft).*

Griselinia littoralis
Evergreen shrub. Pale green leaves (there are variegated varieties). Not suitable for cold areas. Slow-growing *3 × 3m (10 × 10ft).*

Hebes
See *Everbright evergreens.*

Hemerocallis hybrids
See *Colour themes.*

Hibiscus syriacus
See *Colour themes*, but there are other varieties in different shades of blue, pink, and white.

Ilex
See *Everbright evergreens.*

Kniphofia hybrids
Herbaceous perennial. Large, stiff, poker-like orange or yellow flower spikes. Flowering season extends from early summer to mid autumn, according to variety *60cm–1.2m × 60cm–1.2m (2–4 × 2–4ft).*

Liriope muscari
Evergreen perennial. Clumps of broad, grassy leaves, and spikes of mauve-lilac flowers from late summer to mid autumn *45 × 30cm (18 × 12in).*

Mahonia japonica
Evergreen shrub. Glossy, dark green leaves divided into leaflets. Fragrant, lemon-yellow flowers from early winter to early spring *2.4 × 2.4m (8 × 8ft).*

Pernettya
See *Autumn leaves and berries.*

Potentilla fruticosa
See *Colour themes.*

Ribes sanguineum
Deciduous shrub. Drooping clusters of small pink or red flowers in spring *1.8 × 1.8m (6 × 6ft).*

ABOVE: *The kniphofias, sometimes called red-hot-pokers, are bold herbaceous border plants. Once well established they make large clumps. Some species are quite small, however, and different varieties flower at different times. Many kniphofias are unhappy in very cold areas and may need protection in some areas.*

Ulex europaeus
Evergreen shrub. Spiny growth, covered with deep yellow single or double flowers in spring. Flowers may also appear intermittently in winter *1.5 × 1.5m (5 × 5ft).*

Viburnum davidii
Evergreen shrub. White flowers in early summer. Turquoise-blue berries later if both male and female plants are planted *1 × 1.2m (3 × 4ft).*

Viburnum tinus
See *Everbright evergreens.*

Yucca
See *Everbright evergreens*, but the non-variegated form is equally suitable for a border or as a specimen plant.

DON'T FORGET THE DWARF CONIFERS

Conifers need negligible care, and if you choose dwarf species and varieties they will remain compact enough for a small garden. Be cautious about using them in a mixed border, however, as they seldom blend in as satisfactorily as ordinary shrubs.

Small and Dwarf Conifers

Dwarf conifers can provide year-round colour to a garden. They need practically no attention after their first year of growth, but in order for them to look their most effective they are best grown as a group with a variety of contrasting shapes, sizes and colours.

A good garden centre will have an wide range of dwarf and slow-growing conifers, but it is best to consult a specialist catalogue or book before you buy. Some described as dwarf may reach 2.4m (8ft) or so in time, and those described as slow-growing may eventually grow even larger. Make sure your dwarf conifers really are dwarf if space is at a premium.

Abies balsamea 'Nana'
Dwarf conifer, forming a dome-shaped bush. Has aromatic, dark green needle-like leaves and purplish blue cones. Exceptionally hardy *1 × 1m (3 × 3ft).*

Abies cephalonica 'Meyer's Dwarf'
Dwarf conifer that forms a spreading, flat-topped mound. Needle-like leaves are glossy deep green; cones are greenish brown *50cm × 1.5m (20in × 5ft).*

Cedrus deodara 'Golden Horizon'
Usually small, broad conifer with appealing horizontal branches hanging down at their tips. Needle-like leaves are bright yellow when young. Female cones are glaucous blue, maturing to brown *5 × 2.4m (16½ × 8ft).*

Chamaecyparis lawsoniana 'Aurea Densa'
Small or dwarf conifer. Forms a rounded shrub with bright golden yellow, scale-like leaves, needle-like when young. Cones are glaucous or rust-brown *1.2m × 1.2m (4 × 4ft).*

Chamaecyparis lawsoniana 'Bleu Nantais'
Dwarf conifer, forming a rounded cone shape. Bright glaucous foliage, initially needle-like, becoming scale-like *1.5 × 1.5m (5 × 5ft).*

Chamaecyparis obtusa 'Nana Gracilis'
Small or dwarf conifer that forms a rough pyramid. Has bright glossy green scale-like leaves. Cones age from green to brown *2 × 2m (6½ × 6½ft).*

Juniperus communis 'Compressa'
Dwarf conifer. A slow-growing dwarf with grey-green foliage, ideal for a rock garden, and can be used in small containers *60 × 15cm (24 × 6in).*

Juniperus horizontalis
Spreading conifer forming a mat of greyish green leaves, needle-like when young, then scale-like. Blue 'berries' *30cm × 2m (1 × 6½ft).*

Juniperus virginiana 'Sulphur Spray' (syn. *J. chinensis* 'Sulphur Spray')
Dwarf conifer that forms a spreading, flat-topped bush. Bright yellowish green scale-like leaves and bluish purple 'berries' *1 × 2m (3 × 6½ft).*

Picea abies 'Gregoryana'
Dwarf conifer producing a dense mound of dark green needle-like leaves. Cones age from dark green to brown *60 × 60cm (2 × 2ft).*

LEFT: Abies cephalonica *'Meyer's Dwarf' has glossy, deep green, needle-like leaves and greenish brown resinous cones.*

ABOVE: *The bright golden-yellow leaves of* Chamaecyparis lawsoniana *'Aurea Densa' are needle-like when young, becoming scale-like.*

Picea glauca var. *albertiana* 'Alberta Globe'
Small or dwarf, dome-shaped conifer. Blue-green needle-like leaves. Cones may not appear *1 × 1m (3 × 3ft).*

Picea glauca var. *albertiana* 'Conica'
Small or dwarf conifer with a dense cone shape. Permanently juvenile, blue-green needle-like leaves. Cones may not appear *4 × 2m (13 × 6½ft).*

Picea glauca 'Echiniformis'
Dwarf conifer, with a rounded cone shape. Needle-like leaves are blue-grey. Light green cones age to brown *1.5 × 1m (5 × 3ft).*

Picea pungens 'Globosa'
Dwarf conifer forming a dome or mound shape. Has slightly glaucous bristle-like leaves. Green cones age to light brown *1 × 1m (3 × 3ft).*

Picea pungens 'Montgomery'
Dwarf conifer. Forms a broad-based, cone-shaped plant, with silvery blue, bristle-like leaves. Cones age from green to light brown. Slow growing *1.5 × 1m (5 × 3ft).*

Pinus mugo 'Corley's Mat'
Dwarf conifer, forming a prostrate, spreading mat. Has long, needle-like bright green leaves, on very resinous stems. Cones are dark brown *1 × 2m (3 × 6½ft).*

Taxus baccata 'Repandens'
Small or dwarf conifer forming a mat of spreading branches. Dark green leaves, and red 'berries' in autumn *To 60cm × 5m (2 × 16½ft).*

Taxus baccata 'Standishii'
Small or dwarf conifer forming a slim column. Has bright yellowish green needle-like leaves on upright stems. Red 'berries' in autumn *1.5m × 60cm (5 × 2ft).*

Thuja occidentalis 'Ericoides'
Dwarf conifer that forms a broad, sometimes rounded obelisk. Young, scale-like leaves are green in summer, turning rich brown. Cones age from yellow to brown *1.2 × 1.2m (4 × 4ft).*

Thuja orientalis 'Aurea Nana' (syn. *Platycladus orientalis* 'Aurescens')
Dwarf conifer, making an egg-shaped plant. Aromatic, yellowish green, scale-like leaves, tinged bronze in autumn, are held in vertical, fan-like plates *60 × 60cm (2 × 2ft).*

Thuja orientalis 'Rosedalis' (syn. *Platycladus orientalis* 'Rosedalis').
Small oval conifer. Fine, heather-like leaves, yellowish in spring, gradually turning bluish-green, then purple-blue in winter *120 × 90cm (4 × 3ft).*

ABOVE: *The aromatic, scale-like leaves of* Thuja orientalis *'Sieboldii', an egg-shaped dwarf conifer, are carried in stiff vertical plates.*

RIGHT: Picea abies *'Gregoryana' produces a virtually impenetrable mound of needle-like leaves; the cones age from dark green to brown.*

Combining Heathers and Conifers

Heathers and dwarf conifers are low-maintenance plants that look particularly good together, with conifers providing useful height and variation in shape, and heathers supplying seasonal colour.

Designing a bed

Although you can make a one-sided border filled with heathers and conifers, an island bed is much more pleasing – and can be viewed from all sides. The heathers are also likely to thrive better in a more open position with plenty of sun all day – such conditions are much more akin to those of heathland.

You could design a bed for year-round interest. There are hundreds of suitable heathers and dwarf conifers that you could use, so modify the bed to suit the size of your garden and the plants available at your local garden centre.

Planting a bed like this might seem expensive initially, but bear in mind that it will probably last for decades without the need for replanting. It is a small price to pay for a really interesting, long-term, minimal-maintenance feature.

MASS PLANTING

Heathers look best when they are planted in bold natural-looking drifts. A group of perhaps ten or twenty plants of one variety will have far more impact than the same number of different varieties planted in the same area or dotted around a border. Unless the bed or border is large, choose perhaps half a dozen good varieties but plant plenty of them. This applies to both foliage and flowering varieties.

LEFT: *Some low-maintenance plants, such as these heathers and dwarf conifers in a variety of shapes and colours, are attractive all year round and need only occasional attention.*

PLANTING A CONIFER AND HEATHER MIXED BED

1 Arrange the conifers on the bed first, ensuring they look pleasing from all angles. Move them around in their containers if you are not satisfied at first. Prepare the ground thoroughly, then plant the conifers, firming them in before watering.

2 Space the heathers out around the conifers. Plant in groups or drifts of one variety at a time. Avoid planting too close together, as both heathers and conifers will spread.

BELOW: *A mixed heather and conifer bed will provide interest and at no extra upkeep. Modify the bed to suit the size of your garden and the plants available from your local garden centre.*

3 Apply a mulch of chipped bark or gravel around the plants, to hide the bare soil and make the bed look more attractive.

MAINTAINING BEDS AND BORDERS

Once you have designed and planted a new bed or border, much of the work will be complete. But, no matter how large or small the planting area, there will always be something to do to make it look better, so that it continues to please and delight all who see it.

Immediately after planting, the new border is bound to look bare – and it will remain this way for a while until the roots have become well established and the plants have begun to make some top growth. Applying a mulch – of bark chippings, for example – around the plants will not only make the border look more attractive, it will keep weeds down and help to retain warmth and moisture in the soil. Depending on the material used, the mulch will need to be renewed at least once a year if it is to remain effective.

The plants will need plenty of water at regular intervals, especially throughout the first growing season. Always water thoroughly, as shallow, impatient watering will encourage surface rooting instead of deeper roots, and make the plants even more vulnerable to drought. Try to water in the early morning or late in the day, when the plants are not exposed to full sun, otherwise their leaves may get scorched.

Although many perennials will support their flower stems without any extra staking or supports, some – like the sumptuous large-flowered peonies with their heavy buds and full flowers – will flop onto other plants, especially during a spring shower. Ideally, stakes or supports should be put in place when you are planting the border, even though they may look a little odd at first, when the plants are still small. Failing this, you will need to check regularly that plants aren't being flattened by the weather, or by other plants, and insert supports wherever you can.

Good preparation of the soil should have rid you of deep-rooted and creeping perennial weeds, such as dock and couch grass. Once the border is planted, you will have to remove any fresh growth carefully with a hand fork so you do not damage the border plants. Pull up any annual weed seedlings as soon as you see them – and certainly before they have a chance to flower and shed their seed, otherwise they will simply proliferate and you will have an even bigger problem to deal with next year.

Once they are established, you may want to give your plants an annual feed of a balanced fertilizer, to keep them growing well.

Last, but by no means least, you will need to go through the border regularly, removing flowers as they fade. This will stimulate the plants to produce another crop of flowers, so keeping the border in bloom over as long a period as possible.

LEFT: *This border builds up from the front but is not regimented as the heights vary along its length. It illustrates the effectiveness of using different forms, colours and leaf shapes.*

OPPOSITE: *A good combination of textures, shapes and colours is achieved here with cardoon (*Cynara cardunculus*) providing interesting structure with pink* Salvia sclarea.

STAKING BORDER PLANTS

Some border plants, particularly tall ones, are prone to wind damage, and sometimes a potentially beautiful plant is flattened or broken by the weather. If you stake them early, the plants will usually grow through or over the support, which will then become almost invisible.

1 Proprietary supports like this are very efficient at holding up border plants that are not particularly tall but have masses of floppy or fragile stems.

2 Proprietary supports that link together as shown are useful where you are dealing with clumps of varying sizes. They can be linked together as required.

3 Twiggy sticks pushed into the ground within and around the plant can provide a very effective means of support. Once the plant grows you won't notice them.

ABOVE: *Mixing materials breaks up a large area of garden and prevents it looking dull. A few of the plants at the back of the border are staked to protect them against adverse weather.*

4 Short canes can be used to support plants such as carnations. If you use a stout cane, loop string or twine around it as well as the plant. Use thinner split canes to keep individual flower stems or groups of stems upright.

Controlling Weeds

It is never possible to eliminate weeds entirely, but you can control them. Even weeds that are difficult to eradicate can be conquered if you persist, and annual weeds will diminish in numbers if you continue to kill off the seedlings before they can flower and shed more seed. Once the weed population has been reduced, mulching and prompt action to remove any seedlings that do appear will keep the garden almost weed-free. Be prepared for the battle to be won over time.

1 Perennial weeds that have long, penetrating roots are best dug up. First loosen the roots with a garden fork, and hold the stem close to its base as you pull up the whole plant. If you do not get out all the root, new plants may grow from the pieces left behind.

2 Hoeing is one of the best forms of weed control, but it really needs to be done regularly. Slice the weeds off just beneath the soil, preferably when the ground is dry. Keep beds and borders hoed, as well as the vegetable garden.

3 Contact chemical weedkillers are useful if you want to clear an area of ground quickly and easily. Some – which normally kill only the top growth, so are better for annual weeds than for problem perennial ones – leave the ground safe to replant after a day.

4 Some weedkillers kill the whole plant, including the roots. Large areas of ground can be sprayed, but remember that you can paint some formulations onto the leaves to kill the weed without harming neighbouring plants.

5 Mulches are very effective at controlling weeds. In the vegetable and fruit garden, various forms of plastic sheeting are a cost-effective method.

6 Where appearance matters, use an organic material such as chipped bark, garden compost or cocoa shells. If the ground is cleared of weeds first, a mulch at least 5cm (2in) thick will suppress most weeds.

MULCHES

Mulches can help improve growing conditions for plants. Properly applied, a mulch will not only prevent weed growth, it will also keep the soil warm and reduce the amount of moisture lost through evaporation. There are two main kinds of mulch: sheet mulches, made from various forms of plastic or rubber sheet, and loose ones, such as garden compost and chipped bark. Both have their uses, and you may want to add one of the more decorative loose mulches to make a sheet mulch visually more acceptable. This can be more cost effective than using a loose mulch alone.

Loose mulches
Most loose mulches are visually more appealing than sheet mulches, and the organic ones gradually rot down or become integrated into the soil by insect and worm activity, thus helping to improve the soil structure and fertility, and benefiting the plant in the longer term as well.

Loose mulches have to be thick in order to suppress weeds well. Aim for a thickness of at least 5cm (2in).

There is a variety of loose mulches to choose from. Grass cuttings are readily available in most gardens. They are not the most attractive form of mulch but can be used effectively at the back of borders. Bark is another ideal material as it is both effective and attractive. Do not use bark that is fresh, however, as the resin may harm the plants.

PRACTICAL POINTS

- Always prepare the ground thoroughly before laying a sheet mulch.
- Enrich the soil with plenty of organic material such as rotted manure or garden compost – you won't have an opportunity to do this later, once the mulch has been laid.
- Add fertilizer and water it in well – only liquid feeds are practical once the sheet is in position.
- Soak the ground thoroughly with water before applying the sheet.

APPLYING A LOOSE MULCH

1 Prepare the ground thoroughly, digging it over and working in plenty of organic material such as rotted manure or compost if the soil is impoverished.

2 Loose mulches will control annual weeds and prevent new perennial ones getting a foothold. You must dig up existing deep-rooted perennial weeds, otherwise they could grow up through the mulch.

3 Water the ground thoroughly before applying the mulch. Never apply a mulch to dry soil.

4 Spread the mulch thickly, but do not take it too close to the stems of the plant otherwise they may cause problems.

Sheet mulches

Black polythene (plastic) is one of the most commonly available forms of sheet mulch, and is especially effective at suppressing weeds. It does not, however, allow water to penetrate, so is best used in narrow strips such as alongside a hedge. The polythene (plastic) is simply cut to shape and laid on the surface of the soil. You will have to cut holes in the polythene (plastic) to allow water to pass through to the soil. If you find the appearance of black polythene (plastic) distasteful, it can be covered over by a thin layer of gravel.

Woven plastic sheets are more expensive than black polythene (plastic) but they do allow water to seep through, while keeping the light out, hence killing the weeds.

Butyl rubber is a very long-lasting waterproof mulch. It is expensive, but only a thin gauge is required. Butyl rubber is more suitable for the area immediately around trees or large shrubs than as cover for a large expanse of ground.

MULCHING WITH A SHEET

1 Sheet mulches are most useful in shrub beds that can be left undisturbed for some years, and are best used when the bed or border is newly planted. Always prepare the ground as thoroughly as you would if not using a mulching sheet. Make a slit around the perimeter of the bed with a spade, then push the edges of the sheet into this. For a vegetable plot you can use special plastic pegs, but these are too conspicuous for an ornamental bed.

2 Make cross-shaped planting slits in the sheet with a knife or scissors. If planting a shrub you will probably have to make slits large enough to take a spade. This won't matter as the sheet can be folded back into place.

3 Use a trowel or a spade to dig out the planting hole beneath each slit, then insert the plants and replace the soil. Fold back the cut edges of the polythene (plastic) to cover the soil, so that the sheet sits snugly around the plant.

4 Sheet mulches can also be used around individual trees and shrubs. The best way to apply the sheet is to cut a square or circle to size, then make a single slit from one edge to the centre. Slip the sheet around the tree or shrub – and the stake if there is one – and simply fold the polythene (plastic) back over the soil. It won't matter if the join is not perfect as you can hide it with a decorative mulch.

5 Although most of the sheet mulch will be hidden as the plants grow, it will initially be very conspicuous. A layer of a decorative mulch such as chipped bark or gravel will make it much more pleasant to look at.

Feeds and Fertilizers

Plants need care and attention if they are to flourish. Giving them a regular feed will ensure strong growth as well as abundant flower and fruit production. A balanced intake of nutrients will also make them healthy enough to withstand pests and diseases.

Balanced nutrients

Plants need a balanced intake of nutrients to survive. These take the form of minerals and trace elements, which all keep the plant healthy. In the plant's natural environment these are available in the soil, to be taken up by the roots, along with water. They are then transported within the plant to supply the leaf cells, where photosynthesis uses energy provided by sunlight to manufacture sugars and starches – vital for a healthy plant. As the plant grows, flowers and eventually dies, the decaying material then releases nutrients back into the soil.

In the garden, where far more plants are grown closely together than in nature, the competition for nutrients becomes intense; this is exacerbated if the plant is in a pot, where the roots cannot grow into new areas in search of extra food.

Types of fertilizer

There are two types of fertilizer: organic and inorganic. The organic ones are derived from natural ingredients, such as plants (seaweed or nettles), blood, fish or bone. Some last longer than the inorganic types, and tend to become available to the plant only slowly after application. Inorganic fertilizers are mineral-based and may break down more quickly after application.

BELOW: *Maintaining a well-kept border filled with healthy looking plants that have reached their full potential is achieved by following a regular feeding regime.*

Controlled-release fertilizers

The rate at which the fertilizer is released into the soil depends on temperature, soil-organism activity, the fertilizer's solubility in water and its size (the finer the particles, the more quickly nutrients are likely to be released). Some inorganic fertilizers are called 'slow-release', which means that the particles are surrounded by a soluble coating that has a breakdown period of a number of months. The nutrients are released gradually; after this more fertilizer will be needed. 'Controlled-release' fertilizers only release their nutrients when the soil temperature is warm enough for plant growth.

Liquid fertilizers

Those fertilizers that are applied as a liquid are released to and absorbed by the plants the most quickly of all

FEEDING WEEDS

It is an irony of gardening that in feeding your plants you are also feeding the weeds. But if you get the weeds under control from the start, all the nutrients that you apply will be available to the plants you actually want to grow.

(usually within 5–7 days), and are useful as a fast-acting tonic if a plant is looking ill. This is especially true of foliar feeds, which are applied directly to the leaves rather than to the soil around the roots, and are absorbed straight into the plant's system. These can have an effect within about 3–4 days, compared with up to 21 days for a general granular fertilizer applied around the roots.

The N:P:K ratio

On the pack of fertilizer, there should be some information about the nutrients it contains. The three most important elements are nitrogen (N), phosphorus (P) and potassium (K). Nitrogen promotes healthy growth of leaves and shoots; phosphorus is needed for healthy root development; and potassium improves flowering and fruit production. Put simply, N:P:K equals shoots:roots:fruits.

The ratio is given on the back of the pack because certain plants need some elements in a greater quantity than others. A foliage plant, for example, will need more nitrogen and less potassium, as it produces leaves but not a great show of flowers or fruit, whereas a fruiting tomato plant needs a huge quantity of potassium to give a good yield.

It is often necessary to change the fertilizer through the season, particularly if you have planted heavy feeders such as vegetables. Apply more nitrogen and phosphorus in the spring to promote growth, and increase the levels of potassium as the season progresses, in order to produce a good show of flowers or fruit.

Applying fertilizer

In an established garden you can apply fertilizer in granular form as a dressing around the plants early in the season, or in soluble form as the plants are watered during the spring. For a new plant, mix fertilizer with the soil as it is replaced in the planting hole around the root-ball.

FEEDING BEDS AND BORDERS

Unless rain is expected, you should water the ground well. This will make the fertilizer active more quickly in dry conditions.

1 Most established plants benefit from annual feeding. Apply a slow- or controlled-release fertilizer in spring or early summer, sprinkling it around the bushes. Sprinkle it further out where most of the active root growth is.

2 Hoe the fertilizer into the surface so that it penetrates the root area more quickly.

3 Unless rain is expected, you will need to water well. This will make the fertilizer active more quickly in dry conditions.

PLANTS FOR A PURPOSE

ONE OF THE SECRETS OF SUCCESSFUL GARDENING IS the ability to choose the right plant for a particular position or use. Plants will always thrive more readily if they are suited to the conditions. Forcing an inappropriate plant into shade if it demands sun, or planting a shade-lover in scorching sunlight, is a recipe for disappointment.

You will find plenty of ideas for plants that relish problem areas like shade or sun in the pages that follow, but sometimes the question is less which plant suits particular conditions as which fulfils a particular purpose. In the following pages you will find plants that provide the right solution, whether you want a scented shrub, climber for a pergola, or an arresting

ABOVE: *Don't be afraid to grow shrubs and plants such as lilies in pots and tubs as well as the more ubiquitous seasonal summer flowers.*

LEFT: *Climbing and rambling roses are useful for summer screens, but bear in mind that it is only seasonal cover.*

LEFT: *Clematis can be planted in shade provided they can rise above it to flower in the sun.*

OPPOSITE ABOVE: *Ivies will grow almost anywhere, in sun or shade, along the ground or up a wall or tree. Green varieties can be a trifle boring, but variegated varieties are always bright.*

BELOW: *'Exotics' can be used as focal points to bring interest to an otherwise boring area during the summer, but will probably need winter protection.*

'architectural' plant as a focal point.

There are 'exotics', some of which are quite tough, other plants will only thrive during the summer months and you will either have to protect them in winter or treat them as expendable. There are also suggestions of plants to attract wildlife.

If a particular variety has been mentioned, other varieties, perhaps in different colours or with minor variations in size or shape, will almost certainly do well in the same situation. White and pale colours tend to show up better in shade, however, and where possible varieties particularly suited to the conditions have been mentioned.

Be prepared to experiment with plants, especially with those that seem to thrive in similar situations in your area, and concentrate on those that clearly do well. Do not be afraid to abandon plants that fail to live up to expectations.

THE GARDEN'S ASPECT

The aspect of the garden is something about which you don't have any choice. Whichever direction it faces, however, there will be a range of plants suitable for growing in it. Selecting the right plants will produce a wonderful show of colour throughout the year.

Know your plants
The direction the garden faces will have a strong influence on the plants likely to thrive in it. If a plant originally hails from the warm, dry and sunny countries that border the Mediterranean, it is unlikely to grow well in a damp, shady corner. Similarly, a bog plant from a northern forest will not enjoy being placed between a south-facing wall and a path.

One of the keys to successful gardening is to match the position and the plant as closely as possible. Doing this when the plant is first acquired will save both time and money, because the plant will not have to be dug up later when it has failed to thrive and most of the growing season has been lost. A good nursery is invaluable for advice, but most plants will be labelled with the conditions they prefer.

Plants for 'morning-sun' positions
Berberis darwinii
Bergenia cordifolia
Chaenomeles × *superba*
Clematis montana
Clematis tangutica
Cotoneaster horizontalis
Deutzia scabra
Dodecatheon meadia
Euphorbia griffithii
Forsythia suspensa
Galanthus nivalis
Hamamelis mollis
Helleborus foetidus
Hypericum 'Hidcote'
Lonicera periclymenum
Pyracantha
Rosa rugosa
Vinca major

BELOW: *Choosing plants with interest in different seasons is vital for a small garden as this* Parthenocissus henryana *shows.*

Plants for shady positions
Akebia quinata
Berberis × *stenophylla*
Camellia japonica
Camellia × *williamsii*
Clematis alpina
Clematis 'Nelly Moser'
Choisya ternata
Crinodendron hookerianum
Digitalis
Euonymus fortunei
Garrya elliptica
Hedera colchica
Hedera helix
Hydrangea petiolaris
Ilex
Jasminum nudiflorum
Kerria japonica 'Pleniflora'
Mahonia japonica
Parthenocissus
Piptanthus laburnifolius
Tropaeolum specicsum

Plants for sunny positions
Aethionema grandiflorum
Campsis × *tagliabuana* 'Madame Galen'
Canna indica
Cistus × *pulverulentus* 'Sunset'
Dianthus
Dryas octopetala
Eccremocarpus scaber
Echinacea purpurea
Echinops ritro
Fritillaria imperialis
Geranium cinereum 'Ballerina'
Helenium 'Waldtraut'
Imperata cylindrica 'Rubra'
Lilium
Moluccella laevis
Osteospermum
Reseda odorata
Salvia officinalis 'Tricolor'
Sempervivum
Senecio (syn. *Brachyglottis*) 'Sunshine'

OPPOSITE: *Hydrangeas like this creamy petiolaris look good in borders. They prefer shade*

ABOVE RIGHT: *Rosemary has a wonderful scent; it may also bloom late in mild weather.*

Plants for 'afternoon-sun' positions
Abelia × *grandiflora*
Campsis radicans
Ceanothus × *deleanus* 'Gloire de Versailles'
Ceanothus impressus
Cistus × *cyprius*
Crocosmia
Deutzia scabra 'Plena'
Eccremocarpus scaber
Fremontodendron 'California Glory'
Geranium 'Johnson's Blue'
Helichrysum italicum
Hosta
Humulus lupulus 'Aureus'
Kolkwitzia amabilis
Lavandula angustifolia 'Hidcote'
Lavandula stoechas
Papaver orientale
Penstemon
Rosmarinus officinalis
Vitis coignetiae

LEFT: *The large tubular flowers of* Campsis radicans, *which flowers in late summer, contrast well with the green of the foliage.*

Plants that Prefer Shade

Shade is perhaps the universal problem in small gardens. It is difficult to find a significantly large growing area that is not within the shade of a building or a boundary fence, wall or hedge, for at least part of the day . . . and sometimes there are areas in shade for most or all of the day. Such positions are also often very dry, for obstructions that cast shade also cast a rain shadow.

With the exception of some really difficult areas, there are nearly always some plants that will establish themselves and thrive. In these difficult spots you must be prepared to give the plants a little extra help for the first year. The soil should be enriched with organic material, such as garden compost or rotted manure and fertilizer, but above all the ground must be kept moist. Regular watering in dry spells will be almost essential for the first season. After that, all the plants mentioned here will be able to look after themselves under normal conditions.

Those plants with an asterisk are suitable for dry shade. The others are unsuitable for dry sites, and some prefer moist ground.

Ajuga reptans
Almost evergreen perennial. There are several good varieties with variegated and coloured leaves. Short spikes of blue flowers in early and mid summer *15 × 23cm (6 × 9in).*

ABOVE: Ajuga reptans *is one of those accommodating plants that will thrive in sun or shade, and it will even grow in crevices between paving. There are many varieties that are attractively variegated.*

ABOVE: Astrantia major *is not an eye-catching plant from afar, but does well in shade.*

Astilbe hybrids
Herbaceous perennial. Fern-like divided foliage. Feathery plumes of pink, white, or red flowers *60–90 × 45cm (2–3ft × 18in).*

Astrantia major
Herbaceous perennial. Star-like papery-looking white or greenish-pink flowers in early and mid summer *60 × 45cm (2ft × 18in).*

**Aucuba japonica*
See *Everbright evergreens.*

**Bergenia* hybrids
See *Everbright evergreens.*

**Brunnera macrophylla*
Herbaceous perennial. Rough, heart-shaped leaves. Sprays of blue flowers like forget-me-nots, in late spring and early summer *45 × 45cm (18 × 18in).*

**Buxus sempervirens*
See *Variety with variegation.*

Camellia
See *Everbright evergreens.*

Dicentra spectabilis
Herbaceous perennial. Ferny foliage. Pink, red or white heart-shaped flowers on arching stems in late spring and early summer *45 × 45cm (18 × 18in).*

**Epimedium perralderianum*
Evergreen perennial. Young leaves bright green marked bronze-red, changing to copper-bronze in winter. Small yellow flowers in early summer *30 × 30cm (12 × 12in).*

ABOVE LEFT: *Here the blue flowers of* Brunnera macrophylla *show up well against a golden conifer.*

Helleborus
See *Colour for the cold months.*

Hosta
See *Variety with variegation.*

Hypericum calycinum
See *Planting for quick results.*

**Liriope muscari*
See *No fuss low maintenance plants.*

Lonicera nitida
See *Colour themes.* The all-green species can be used, but the yellow 'Baggesen's Gold' looks brighter in a sunless position.

**Mahonia aquifolium*
Evergreen shrub. Large, leathery divided leaves. Fragrant yellow flowers in early and mid spring *1.2 × 1.2m (4 × 4ft).*

**Pachysandra terminalis*
See *Variety with variegation.*

**Ruscus aculeatus*
Evergreen sub-shrub. Strong erect stems covered with tough green 'leaves' (actually modified stalk). Inconspicuous flowers in early and mid spring, bright red berries in autumn if male and female plants are present *1 × 1m (3 × 3ft).*

Sarcococca hookeriana humilis
Evergreen shrub. Slender, lance-shaped leaves. Very fragrant small white flowers in winter *60 × 60cm (2 × 2ft).*

Saxifraga x umbrosa
Evergreen perennial. Rosettes of green leaves from which sprays of pink flowers appear in late spring and early summer *30 × 30cm (12 × 12in).*

Skimmia japonica
See *Autumn leaves and berries.*

Symphoricarpos albus
Deciduous shrub. Small, urn-shaped pink flowers from mid summer to early autumn. White berries like marbles from mid autumn to mid winter *1.8 × 1.8m (6 × 6ft).*

Tiarella cordifolia
Evergreen perennial. Maple-shaped leaves, turning bronze in winter. Feathery spikes of white fluffy flowers in late spring and early summer *23 × 30cm (9 × 12in).*

Viburnum davidii
See *No fuss, low maintenance plants.*

Vinca minor
See *Variety with variegation.*

LEFT: Symphoricarpos albus *is a vigorous, spreading shrub, which is best not planted among choice plants because of its rampant growth pattern, but it is very satisfactory for a difficult shady position.*

RIGHT: Sarcococca hookeriana, *a winter-flowering plant that has unspectacular flowers but an arresting fragrance.*

Fern Borders

Most garden ferns flourish in a shady position, where many more flamboyant plants fail to thrive. They are fascinating and beautiful plants, and their elegance and architectural impact makes up for what they lack in colour. You can use them in a mixed border, like any other perennials, but an area devoted solely to ferns looks especially effective – and very natural.

There are many different types of attractive fern to choose from, some with bold arching shuttlecocks, others forming delicate lacy clumps. Select a mixture of shapes and sizes to make the fern border more interesting, and if you are worried about bare ground in winter, choose mainly evergreen species.

ABOVE: *The hart's tongue fern (*Asplenium scolopendrium*) is so-called because it produces long, curling leaves.*

RIGHT: *The shuttlecock fern (*Matteuccia struthiopteris*) is one of the most elegant ferns, with an attractive upright habit.*

PLANTING A FERN BORDER

Ferns are easy to grow as long as they are given the right conditions. Most prefer a moist, shady or partially shady site, and it pays dividends to prepare the ground thoroughly. Spring is a good time to plant.

1 Most ferns need a moist, humus-rich soil, so fork in as much garden compost or rotted manure as possible. This is especially important if the area is shaded by trees, or a wall that also casts a rain shadow, where the soil is usually dry.

2 If the soil is impoverished, add a balanced fertilizer and rake it into the surface. If planting in late summer or winter, do not use a quick-acting fertilizer. Wait until spring to apply, or use a controlled-release fertilizer that will release the nutrients only when the weather is warm enough for growth.

3 It is very important that ferns do not dry out, especially when newly planted. Water the pots thoroughly about half an hour before planting, to make sure the root-ball is wet enough to start with.

4 Make a hole large enough to take the root-ball, but if the roots are very tightly wound round the pot, you will need to carefully tease out some of them first. This will encourage them to grow out into the surrounding soil. If the plant is in a large pot, you may have to use a spade instead of a trowel.

5 Firm in carefully to eliminate any large air pockets that could allow the roots to dry out. Then water thoroughly so that the surrounding soil is moist down to the depth of the root-ball.

6 To help conserve moisture and maintain a high level of organic matter in the soil, mulch thickly with peat moss, leaf mould or garden compost. You will need to freshen the mulch each spring.

SUN LOVERS

Sunny spots where the ground is moist, or where the sun is intense for just part of the day before it moves around, present no problem for the majority of plants. All except the shade-loving plants are likely to thrive. But if the position is sunny nearly all day, and the soil tends to be free-draining and dry, you need plants adapted to such bright and arid conditions.

Fortunately, those plants that do well in these positions are often bright, floriferous, and very colourful. As a general rule, grey-leaved plants are well suited to these conditions, but if in doubt check.

Most of the plants suggested here tolerate dry soil well. However, give perennials and shrubs extra attention for the first season. Once they get their roots down they should be able to survive happily in a normal year.

Achillea filipendulina
See *Colour themes*.

Agapanthus hybrids
See *Colour themes*.

Alyssum saxatile
See *Colour themes*.

Artemisia arborescens
Semi-evergreen shrub. Silvery-white, much divided leaves. Yellow flowers in early and mid summer. Not reliably hardy in cold areas *1.2 × 1.2m (4 × 4ft)*.

Buddleia davidii
See *Planting for quick results*.

Caryopteris x *clandonensis*
See *Planting for quick results*.

Colutea arborescens
Deciduous shrub. Divided, pale green leaves, and yellow pea-like flowers in summer. These are followed by inflated seed pods, flushed coppery-red *2.4 × 2.4m (8 × 8ft)*.

Convolvulus cneorum
Evergreen shrub. Silvery foliage. Funnel-shaped white flowers, flushed pink beneath the petals, all summer *60 × 60cm (2 × 2ft)*.

Cytisus scoparius hybrids
Deciduous shrub. Green branches make it look evergreen. Pea-type flowers, in shades of yellow, red and pink, many multicoloured, in late spring and early summer *2.4 × 1.8m (8 × 6ft)*.

Echinops ritro
Herbaceous perennial. Divided, prickly grey-green foliage, spherical steel blue flower heads in mid and late summer *1m × 60cm (3 × 2ft)*.

ABOVE: *Osteospermums thrive in a hot, sunny situation. This one is* O. jacundum.

ABOVE LEFT: Colutea arborescens *has the bonus of interesting inflated seed pods as well as pretty yellow flowers.*

ABOVE RIGHT: Helianthemum nummularium *hybrids thrive in hot, sunny situations. They come in a variety of colours, mainly reds, pinks and yellows.*

OPPOSITE BELOW: Phlomis fruticosa *can be a rather coarse-looking plant, but it thrives in hot, dry soils.*

Eryngium variifolium
Evergreen perennial. Dark green leaves marbled white. Grey-blue flower heads with white collars, in mid and late summer *60 × 45cm (2ft × 18in).*

Genista tinctoria
See *Planting for quick results.*

Hebe
See *Everbright evergreens.*

Helianthemum nummularium hybrids
Evergreen sub-shrub. Green or grey leaves. Masses of small flowers in shades of red, orange, yellow, pink, and white, in late spring and early summer, with a second flush later in the year if the dead flowers are trimmed off *15–23 × 60cm (6–9in × 2ft).*

Kniphofia hybrids
See *No fuss, low maintenance plants.*

Lavandula
See *Planting for quick results.*

Nepeta x *faassenii*
See *Colour themes.*

Osteospermum hybrids
Evergreen sub-shrub. Still sometimes called *Dimorphothecas*. Large daisy-shaped flowers mainly in shades of purple, pink, and white, all summer. Not hardy in cold areas, but will tolerate frosts where the winters are not severe *30 × 60cm (12in × 2ft).*

LEFT: Sedum spectabile *has fleshy, succulent leaves, enabling it to grow well even in a hot, sunny position.*

Perovskia atriplicifolia
See *Colour themes.*

Phlomis fruticosa
Semi-evergreen shrub. Grey-green foliage. Clusters of quaint, bright yellow flowers at the tips of shoots, in early and mid summer *75cm × 1.2m (2½ × 4ft).*

Phormium
See *Everbright evergreens.*

Romneya coulteri
Sub-shrubby perennial. Large fragrant white flowers, *10–15cm (4–6in)* across from mid summer to mid autumn. Not recommended for cold areas *1.2 × 1.2m (4 × 4ft).*

Rosmarinus officinalis
See *Everbright evergreens.*

Santolina chamaecyparissus
See *Colour themes.*

Sedum spectabile
Herbaceous perennial. Succulent leaves. Large, flat pink flower heads in early and mid autumn
45 × 45cm (18 × 18in).

Stachys lanata
See *Colour themes.*

Ulex europaeus
See *No fuss, low-maintenance plants.*

Yucca
See *Everbright evergreens.*

ANNUALS THAT LOVE THE SUN

Most hardy annuals thrive in hot, bright conditions, and especially those with daisy-like flowers that only open when it's warm and sunny. Be generous with the annuals, especially those native to sunny climates such as South Africa.

Soil

Every plant has a preference about its ideal growing conditions, and putting a plant in the right spot will mean the difference between it thriving, and looking the best it can, or merely surviving. Some plants flourish in a damp, heavy soil; others insist on a sandy, free-draining one. Certain plants prefer to grow in soil that is higher or lower in acidity than others, while some cannot tolerate acidity at all. So, it is important to get to know the soil in your garden; you can then choose plants to suit it, which will help you achieve the best possible results.

Soil structure

Soil consists of sand, silt, clay and organic matter (humus), and the proportions in which each is present will determine the structure of the soil – its consistency and water-retaining properties. The more large sand particles it contains, the more easily water will be able to drain through it and the more quickly it will warm up in spring, allowing earlier planting. Silt particles are smaller, so water is held for longer, but they retain little in the way of nutrients. Clay particles are the smallest of all; they hold on to nutrients and water extremely well, but produce a heavy, solid soil that is cold (slow to warm up in spring, because the water has to warm up as well), and also prone to damage if it is worked when it is too wet.

The ideal soil to have is loam. This contains a perfect balance of all the elements, producing a crumbly soil, often dark in colour. It holds both moisture and nutrients well, without becoming waterlogged. This soil is rare and most gardens have a soil that favours one particle size over others.

You can improve the structure of your soil by the regular addition of organic matter, in the form of well-rotted manure or garden compost. This will add air to a heavy soil, making it easier to work, and help to keep moisture in a free-draining one.

Soil acidity

The acidity of the soil depends to a large extent on the underlying bedrock, but it can also be influenced by the amount of rainfall, the rate of drainage, and also nearby vegetation (pine trees, for example, have acid foliage).

The acidity or alkalinity of soil is usually measured on the pH scale, in units from 1 to 14. According to this, a pH of 7 indicates a neutral soil; any unit below this indicates an acid soil; any unit above it, an alkaline one. The best way to ascertain the pH level of the soil in your garden is to use a simple testing kit. It makes sense to do this before starting work on a new garden, or if some of your plants don't seem to be growing well; keen growers test their soil routinely once a year.

If your soil proves to be particularly acid, you can add a dressing of lime to make it more alkaline; if too alkaline, work in plenty of organic matter in the form of rotted manure or garden compost. However, in either case by far the best solution is to seek out plants that would naturally thrive in such soil conditions.

RIGHT: Daboecia cantabrica *'Atropurpurea', with its urn-shaped, dark pinkish-purple flowers from early summer to mid-autumn, creates a mat of colour, even in a small corner.*

TESTING THE SOIL PH

Many people garden successfully without ever testing their soil, but they are probably fortunate in gardening on ground that is not deficient in nutrients, is neither too acid nor too alkaline, and receives plenty of nutrients as part of normal cultivation. If you are not as fortunate, you can easily test for pH using one of the kits available from garden centres. Always follow the instructions on the kit if they differ from the advice given here.

1 Collect the soil sample from about 5–8cm (2–3in) below the surface. This gives a more typical reading of nutrient levels in the root area. Take a number of samples from around the garden, but test each one separately.

2 With this kit one part of soil is mixed with five parts of water. Shake together vigorously in a clean jar, then allow the water to settle. This can take between half an hour and a day, depending on the soil.

3 Draw off some settled liquid from the top few centimetres (about an inch) for your test.

4 Carefully transfer the solution to the test and reference chambers in the plastic container, using the pipette provided.

5 Select the appropriate colour-coded capsule (different ones are used for each major nutrient) and empty the powder it contains into the test chamber. Replace the cap, then shake vigorously.

6 After a few minutes, compare the colour of the liquid with the shade panel that forms part of the container. The kit contains an explanation of the significance of each reading, and what – if anything – to do.

Plants for Acid Soils

In the wild, the most acid soils are usually found on heather moorland, or in coniferous forest. The correct term for plants which prefer acid soil is calcifuges. Plants that prefer acid soil are often wrongly referred to as ericaceous plants because many acid-loving plants belong to the family. Ericaceae include heathers (*Erica*), arbutus, kalmia and, of course, rhododendron.

Plants that prefer an acid soil tend to grow poorly on alkaline ground, often becoming chlorotic.

Some excellent garden plants grow only in acid soil, so if this is the nature of the soil in your garden, you can look forward to growing some real treasures. Acid-loving plants are often associated with the tendency to be spring-flowering, as are camellias for example, but many are renowned for their foliage colour in the autumn, and if you can grow a range of heathers it is possible to have plants in flower practically all year round.

You can check on the pH of your soil to determine its acidity by using a soil-testing kit. It takes a matter of a few minutes to discover whether or not your soil is suitable for a particular plant. As a rough guide, if your soil measures more than 6.5 on the pH scale it is unsuitable for growing acid-lovers such as rhododendrons and heathers. Of course, even if this is the case, you can always grow the plants you want in containers filled with an ericaceous potting compost (soil mix).

ABOVE: Daboecia cantabrica alba *is adorned with racemes of urn-shaped, white flowers from early summer to mid-autumn.*

LEFT: *Azaleas are a form of rhododendron. Many of the deciduous forms have a wonderful scent. Like other rhododendrons, they need an acid soil and shelter from hot sun.*

Berberidis corallina
Evergreen twining climber or wall shrub. Clusters of deep red flowers in summer and early autumn, against a backdrop of deep green leathery leaves. Requires a sheltered position in cold areas *3 × 3m (10 × 10ft).*

Calluna vulgaris varieties
Low-growing evergreen shrub. Small bell-like, white to dark mauve flowers, from midsummer to late autumn. Many have colourful foliage in winter *60 × 75cm (24 × 30in).*

Camellia hybrids
See Everbright evergreens.

Cassiope varieties
Dwarf evergreen shrub. Upright or spreading stems are densely clothed in tiny dark green leaves. Small bell-ike flowers, ranging from white to white-tinged red depending on the variety, in spring *30 × 30cm (1 × 1ft).*

Cornus canadensis
Creeping shrub-like perennial. Forms a carpet of small white flowers in late spring or early summer. Red fruit in autumn *15cm (6in)* tall. Indefinite spread.

Daboecia cantabrica
Dwarf evergreen shrub. Tiny dark green leaves, and small urn-shaped rose-purple flowers in long slender bunches from summer to autumn *40 × 65cm (16 × 26in).*

Epimedium grandiflorum
(syn. *E. macranthum*)
Deciduous rhizomatous perennial. Heart-shaped leaves with autumn colours. Clusters of small flowers in spring and summer. Colours vary with varieties *30 × 30cm (1 × 1ft).*

Erica
See Everbright evergreens.

Fothergilla major
See Autumn leaves and berries.

Gentiana sino-ornata
Evergreen perennial with trailing stems. Brilliant blue trumpet-shaped flowers, striped on the outside, in autumn *15 × 30cm (6 × 12in).*

Kalmia latifolia
Evergreen shrub. An attractive shrub for early summer, flowering on an acid soil. Pink saucer-shaped flowers set off by glossy deep green foliage *90–120 × 120cm (3–4 × 4ft).*

LEFT: Epimedium grandiflorum *foliage turns shades of gold, scarlet and copper in the autumn.*

BELOW: *The blood-red flowers of* Calluna vulgaris *'Dark Beauty' will last into late autumn.*

Meconopsis betonicifolia
(syn. *M. baileyi*)
Herbaceous perennial producing sky-blue flowers on tall slender stems in summer *1.2m × 45cm (4 × 1½ft).*

Pernettya mucronata (syn. *Gaultheria mucronata*)
Evergreen shrub. Small, prickly dark green leaves, tiny white flowers in late spring and early summer, followed on female plants by large rounded berries, usually red or pink *1.2 x 1.2m (4 x 4ft).*

Rhodohypoxis baurii
Low-growing herbaceous perennial with spear-shaped leaves. In spring and summer bears small, flattish flowers, varying from white to pale pink or red *10 × 10cm (4 × 4in).*

Trillium grandiflorum
Rhizomatous perennial forming a dome-shaped plant. Has large, dark green leaves and white funnel-shaped flowers on short, arching stems from spring until summer *45 × 30cm (18 × 12in).*

Plants for Chalk (Alkaline) Soils

Although a chalk (alkaline) soil limits the range of plants you can grow, many of the loveliest garden plants thrive in chalk: clematis, honeysuckle (*Lonicera*), sweet peas (*Lathyrus*) and viburnums, as well as most bulbs. Plants that need a pH of below 7.0 are best avoided in very alkaline soils. Soil pH may vary in a single garden: it may be more alkaline near walls or patios, where lime mortar may have collected. If plants fail to thrive in these areas, replace them with chalk-loving, lime-tolerant plants.

Acanthus spinosus
Clump-forming perennial. Striking arching leaves with spiny edges, and tall spikes of white and purple tubular flowers throughout summer *1.2m × 75cm (4 × 2½ft).*

Achillea filipendulina 'Gold Plate'
Clump-forming evergreen perennial. Flat, golden yellow flowerheads on tall leafy stems in late summer and early autumn *100 × 45cm (39 × 18in).*

ABOVE: *The saucer-shaped, bright yellow flowers of* Potentilla fruticosa, *a deciduous shrub, last from late spring to late summer.*

RIGHT: *The leaves of* Phlomis fruticosa, *an evergreen summer-flowering shrub, have a felty surface which turns slighly yellow in autumn.*

Anchusa azurea (syn. *A. italica*)
Clump-forming perennial. Tall spikes of bright blue flowers in early summer *100 × 60cm (39 × 24in).*

Aquilegia alpina
Upright perennial. Clumps of ornamental, finely divided leaves and nodding blue flowers in late spring and early summer *45 × 30cm (18 × 12in).*

Aucuba japonica
Rounded evergreen shrub. Glossy, leathery oval leaves, often toothed, and small red-purple flowers in mid spring *3 × 3m (10 × 10ft).*

Campanula
Annuals, biennials and perennials. Mat-forming to tall, upright varieties. Many prefer an alkaline soil: *C. lactiflora*, with bell-shaped white to lavender-blue flowers, and the saucer-shaped white or blue *C. persicifolia 30–90 × 30cm (1–3 × 1ft)*, according to variety.

Caryopteris × clandonensis 'Heavenly Blue'
Mound-forming, deciduous sub-shrub. Silvery grey-green, lance-shaped leaves and very dark blue flowers in late summer and early autumn *1 × 1.5m (3 × 5ft).*

Cistus hybrids
Evergreen shrubs. Eye-catching white to pink flowers in summer. *C. × cyprius* has white flowers with pink and yellow markings; *C. creticus* has bright pink flowers; and *C. × skanbergii* has pale pink blooms *15cm–2m × 60cm–2m (6in–6½ft × 2–6½ft)*, according to variety.

Delphinium
Clump-forming perennial. Tall spikes of blue on white flowers in early and mid summer *1.5m × 75cm (5 × 2½ft).*

Deutzia scabra 'Plena'
(syn. *D. crenata* 'Flore Pleno')
Upright deciduous shrub. Arching shoots produce dense spikes of cup-shaped white flowers in summer *2.4 × 2m (8 × 6½ft).*

Dianthus
This large group of chalk-loving plants includes dwarfs for the rock garden, border perennials, such as garden pinks and carnations, and

ABOVE: *This beautiful biennial* Dianthus barbatus *'Scarlet Beauty' flourishes in chalk.*

ABOVE: *Rock roses (*Cistus*) are fine summer-flowering plants and can cope well with drought.*

LEFT: *The fragrant flowers of lilac (*Syringa*) range from deep pink through mauve to white. This lilac is* S. × vulgaris.

biennials, such as *Dianthus barbatus*. Size depends on species.

Erysimum cheiri (syn. *Cheiranthus cheiri*)
Bushy evergreen perennial usually treated as biennial. Fragrant single or double flowers, mainly in shades of red or yellow, flowering in late spring *23–45 × 30cm (9–18 × 12in)*.

Gypsophila
Semi-evergreen or evergreen perennials and annuals. Clouds of small, star- to trumpet-shaped, white or pink flowers in late spring to autumn *5cm–1.2m × 15cm–1m (2in–4ft × 6–39in)*, according to variety.

Helianthemum nummularium
Evergreen shrub. Pink, red or yellow single or double flowers over grey-green foliage in early and mid summer *15–23 × 60cm (6–9 × 24in)*.

Kolkwitzia amabilis
Erect then drooping deciduous shrub. Abundant clusters of bell-shaped, soft pink flowers in late spring and early summer *3 × 4m (10 × 13ft)*.

Lonicera × brownii (syn. *L. sempervirens*) 'Dropmore Scarlet'
Deciduous or semi-evergreen climber. Long, trumpet-shaped scarlet flowers in summer *4 × 3m (12 × 13ft)*.

Phlomis fructicosa
Evergreen spreading shrub. Deep yellow flowers in early and mid summer, above grey-green sage-like foliage *1.2 × 1.2m (4 × 4ft)*

Potentilla fruticosa
Deciduous shrub. Dark green leaves and saucer-shaped, bright yellow flowers from late spring to late summer *1 × 1.5m (3 × 5ft)*

Scabiosa 'Butterfly Blue'
Branched perennial. Grey-green leaves and lavender-blue flowers in mid and late summer *40 × 40cm (16 × 16in)*.

Syringa vulgaris
Deciduous shrub. Fragrant single or double flowers, in shades of blue, purple, cream, and white, in late spring or early summer *3 × 2m (10 × 8ft)*.

Verbascum hybrids
Biennials and perennials. Most have tall, slim spires of flowers in summer. *V. chaixii* has felted leaves and yellow flowers with purple centres; *V. chaixii* 'Album' is white with mauve centres; and *V. phoeniceum* is smaller, with clusters of flowers surrounded by leaves *5cm–2m × 15–60cm (2in–6½ft × 6–24in)*, according to variety.

Clay Soils

The ideal garden soil is a medium loam: it retains moisture yet is well drained, with a fine, crumbly texture. However, many soils have a high clay content. Clay soils are usually very fertile and retain moisture. While this is an advantage, a very heavy wet soil tends to be difficult to work, and can often mean that plants become waterlogged. Always choose plants carefully to suit your soil type: there are many excellent plants, described below, that will thrive happily in clay.

Abelia × grandiflora
Rounded, vigorous, semi-evergreen shrub. Arching shoots with glossy, dark green leaves and an abundance of fragrant, tubular white flowers with pink tinges, lasting from mid summer to mid-autumn *3 × 3m (10 × 10ft).*

Aruncus dioicus
Clump-forming perennial. Fern-like, toothed leaves and large feathery plumes of greenish white and creamy white flowers in early and mid summer. 'Kneiffii' is a dwarf form 1–*2 × 1.2m (3–6½ × 4ft).*

Aucuba japonica
Evergreen shrub. Glossy green leaves splashed or spotted yellow, insignificant flowers, but red fruits on female plants (plant a male variety for pollination) *2.4 × 2.4m (8 × 8ft).*

Astilbe × arendsii hybrids
Clump-forming perennials. Fern-like foliage and spikes of plume-like flowerheads in summer in various colours, including: *A.* 'Fanal', in dark crimson; *A.* 'Federsee', in deep rose-pink; and *A.* 'Feuer', in salmon-pink *50–75cm × 45cm (20–30in × 18in),* according to variety.

Berberis × stenophylla
Arching evergreen shrub. Spiny-tipped leaves and clusters of deep yellow flowers in late spring, followed by blue-black fruit *3 × 3m (10 × 10ft).*

Cardamine pratensis 'Flore Pleno'
Clump-forming perennial. Leaves arranged in neat rosettes and loose clusters of double, lilac flowers in late spring *20 × 50cm (8 × 20in).*

Chaenomeles japonica
Bushy deciduous shrub. Thorny with glossy leaves and clusters of orange

ABOVE: Rodgersia pinnata *is usually grown for the impact of its deeply veined leaves.*

RIGHT: *The panicles of* Astilbe *'Elizabeth Bloom' appear in summer above bronze leaves.*

to red flowers in spring, followed by yellow or yellow-tinged fruit *1 × 2m (3 × 6½ft).*

Crambe cordifolia
Clump-forming perennial. Large, dark green crinkled leaves and abundant tiny white, gypsophila-like flowers in late spring and mid summer *2.4 × 1.5m (8 × 5ft).*

Digitalis grandiflora (syn. *D. orientalis*)
Clump-forming biennial or perennial. Tall spikes of pale yellow flowers in early and mid summer *100 × 45cm (39 × 18in).*

Hemerocallis 'Burning Daylight'
Clump-forming perennial. Strap-shaped leaves, ending in a point at the tip, and bright orange, lily-like flowers in summer *1m × 75cm (3 × 2½ft).*

Humulus lupulus 'Aureus'
Perennial climber. Bright, golden yellow lobed leaves and insignificant green flowers in summer, followed by decorative 'fruit' in autumn *6m (20ft).*

Lathyrus grandiflorus
Perennial climber. Striking pink-purple and red, pea-like flowers from summer to early autumn *1.5m (5ft).*

Leucanthemum × superbum hybrids (syn. *Chrysanthemum maximum*)
Clump-forming perennials. Chrysanthemum-like flowers in white with golden centres from early summer to early autumn. Various cultivars, which are better than the species: the dwarf 'Snow Lady'; 'Wirral Supreme', with large double flowers; and 'Phyllis Smith', with single flowers with twisted petals *45–90cm × 60cm (18–36in × 24in),* according to variety.

Persicaria bistorta 'Superba' (syn. *Polygonum bistorta*)
Clump-forming, semi-evergreen perennial. Dense spires of soft pink flowers throughout summer *90 × 90cm (36 × 36in).*

Phlox paniculata
Erect perennial. White, red, mauve, pink flowers in summer *75 × 75cm (30 × 30in).*

Phormium hybrids
Clump-forming evergreen perennial. Robust, upright, sword-shaped leaves in various colours *1–2.4 × 1m (3–8 × 3ft),* according to variety.

Rodgersia pinnata 'Superba'
Clump-forming perennial. Deeply veined, crinkled leaves and plumes of yellowish white, pink or red star-shaped flowers which last from mid- and late summer *100 × 75cm (39 × 30in).*

Tradescantia × andersoniana
Clump-forming perennial. Clusters of three-petalled, rich purple, blue or white flowers which last from early summer to early autumn and arching, strap-shaped leaves *50 × 50cm (20 × 20in).*

ABOVE: Phormium tenax, *a clump-forming evergreen perennial, never fails to make a statement with its robust, architectural, sword-shaped leaves.*

BELOW: *In mid-summer large, feathery, creamy white plumes grace the tall, tough, sturdy stems of* Aruncus dioicus, *which is a clump-forming perennial.*

Pollution-tolerant Plants

Town and city gardens, particularly those alongside a main road, are often exposed to very high levels of pollution. Many plants suffer extensively from the effects, while others thrive, despite the exhaust deposits collecting on their leaves. If you live in a busy, built-up area, select plants that are suitable for the conditions (see below), and reduce the impact by planting a dense hedge of pollution-tolerant plants around the edge of the garden.

ABOVE LEFT: Elaeagnus × ebbingei *'Gilt Edge' makes a good screen.*

ABOVE: *Berberis have spectacular flower displays in spring, and deciduous kinds have tinted foliage in autumn.*

Amelanchier canadensis
Erect deciduous shrub. Orange-red foliage in autumn and star-shaped white flowers in spring, sometimes followed by blue-black fruit *6 × 3m (20 × 10ft).*

Aucuba japonica
Rounded evergreen shrub. Glossy, leathery oval leaves, often toothed, and small red-purple flowers in mid spring *2.4 × 2.4m (8 × 8ft).*

Berberis
Evergreen or deciduous shrubs. Attractive leaves, some holly-like and many with good autumn colour, yellow to dark orange flowers, and colourful fruit. Wide range of sizes from dwarf or mound-forming (*B. thunbergii* 'Bagatelle') to vigorous and upright (*B.* 'Goldilocks'); some are useful for hedging (*B. thunbergii*) *50cm–4m × 45cm–4m (20in–13ft × 18in–13ft)*, according to species of variety.

Buddleia davidii
Arching deciduous shrub. Dense trusses of fragrant lilac to purple flowers from summer to autumn *3 × 5m (10 × 16½ft).*

Ceratostigma willmottianum
Spreading deciduous shrub. Dark green, purple-edged leaves that turn red in autumn, and a display of blue flowers with red-purple tubes from late summer to autumn *1 × 1.5m (3 × 5ft).*

Chaenomeles hybrids
Deciduous shrubs. Spiny with cup-shaped flowers in pink, red, orange or white in early spring to summer, followed by edible fruit. Some suitable for ground cover or low hedging (*C. japonica*), others for a border (*C. speciosa* and *C. × superba* varieties) *1–3m × 2–5m (3–10ft × 6½–16½ft)*, according to species or variety.

Cotoneaster frigidus
Upright then spreading deciduous tree or large shrub. White, saucer-shaped flowers in summer, followed by orange-red fruit *5 × 5m (15 × 15ft).*

Elaeagnus × ebbingei
Rounded evergreen shrub. Attractive glossy leaves, silvery beneath, and creamy, silvery white flowers in autumn *4 × 4m (13 × 13ft).*

Elaegnus pungens
Bushy evergreen shrub. Glossy, often wavy-edged leaves and pendent, silvery white flowers in autumn, followed by brown-red fruit *4 × 5m (13 × 16½ft).*

Forsythia × *intermedia*
Deciduous shrubs. Brilliant display of early yellow flowers. 'Lynwood' and 'Spectabilis' are popular varieties; 'Karl Sax' has leaves that turn red or purple in autumn *2.4 × 2.4m (8 × 8ft)*, according to variety.

Garrya elliptica
Upright evergreen shrub or small tree. Glossy, leathery leaves and pendulous catkins from mid winter to early spring *4 × 4m (13 × 13ft)*.

Ilex aquifolium
Usually erect evergreen shrub or tree. Spiky or smooth-edged holly leaves, and red or occasionally yellow or orange berries. While the species itself is very large, many of its varieties are suitable for a small garden *4–25m × 2.4–8m (13–80ft × 8–25ft)*, according to variety.

Leycesteria formosa
Upright deciduous shrub. Spikes of white flowers from summer to early autumn, followed by red-purple berries *2 × 2m (6½ × 6½ft)*.

Ligustrum ovalifolium
Upright evergreen or semi-evergreen shrub. Glossy green leaves and white flowers in mid summer, followed by black fruit *4 × 4m (13 × 13ft)*.

Olearia × *haastii*
Bushy evergreen shrub. Daisy-like white flowers with yellow centres in mid and late summer and glossy green leaves *2 × 3m (6½ × 10ft)*.

Osmanthus × *burkwoodii* (syn. × *Osmarea burkwoodii*)
Rounded evergreen shrub. Glossy dark green leaves and tubular white flowers in mid spring, followed by blue-black fruit *3 × 5m (10 × 16½ft)*.

Philadelphus hybrids
Mainly deciduous shrubs. Fragrant white flowers in summer may be single (*P.* 'Belle Etoile'), semi-double (*P.* 'Boule d'Argent') or double (*P.* 'Virginal') *75cm–6m × 1–4m (30in–20ft × 3–13ft)*, according to variety.

Syringa vulgaris
Deciduous shrubs. Conical trusses of fragrant flowers in late spring to early summer. Lilacs may be white, pink, purplish pink, blue, creamy-yellow or white *3 × 2m (8 × ft)*, according to variety.

TOP: *Ivies (varieties of* Hedera helix*) are very tough, and can be used for ground or wall cover.*

ABOVE: *The green berries of this holly,* Ilex × altaclarensis *'Lawsoniana' are yet to turn red, but they are still an attractive feature.*

LEFT: Berberis thunbergii *'Atropurpurea' has striking, marbled, reddish-purple leaves, suffused silvery pink when young.*

Tamarix tetrandra
Arching deciduous shrub or small tree. Plumes of light pink flowers in mid and late spring and feathery foliage *3 × 3m (10 × 10ft)*.

Weigela florida
Spreading deciduous shrub. Funnel-shaped pink flowers in late spring and early summer *2.4 × 2.4m (8 × 8ft)*.

PLANTS FOR THE TROPICAL LOOK

If you are trying to create a garden based on Mediterranean influences with white-painted walls and with the emphasis on hot climate flora, you will need to use plenty of plants that give the impression that they are exotic or tender when in fact they are quite frost-tolerant.

Some of the plants suggested here are only hardy enough for warm areas where frosts are light and seldom prolonged, others are really tough.

You can of course use many of them in an ordinary border, but the ones suggested here are primarily effective as part of an area reserved for the more striking plants.

If you live in a cold area and have a greenhouse, conservatory, or even a porch, grow the more vulnerable plants in large pots and move them to this protected area for winter.

Arundinaria viridistriata
See *Variety with variegation*.

Clianthus puniceus
Evergreen climbing shrub. Divided, feathery leaves, crimson-scarlet claw-shaped flowers in early summer. Will only survive outdoors in mild districts. Can reach about *3m (10ft)*.

Cordyline australis
Palm-like plant with strap-like leaves at top of plant. *C. a. purpurea* has brownish-purple leaves. Where winters are mild and frost not severe it can be left in the ground and may grow into a tall tree. Elsewhere grow in a pot, where it will remain much smaller. Protect for the winter.

Fatsia japonica
See *No fuss, low-maintenance plants*.

Gunnera manicata
Huge leaves, like a giant rhubarb. In the ground it is large even for a big garden, but you can grow it in a tub or a patio pot to restrict its size. Keep very moist, and protect during the winter.

Kniphofia hybrids
See *No fuss, low-maintenance plants*.

ABOVE: Cordyline australis *'Alberti'*.

Lilium hybrids
You can buy bulbs and pot up your own lilies, or buy them when they are about to bloom. These may have been dwarfed chemically and will probably make better container plants. Heights vary.

Osteospermum hybrids
See *Sun lovers*.

Phormium hybrids
See *Everbright evergreens*.

Rheum palmatum
An ornamental rhubarb that reaches *2.4m (8ft)* tall in flower, but the leaves are less than half this height. White or red flowers in early summer.

ABOVE: *For the cost of a packet of seeds you can have a show like this* Ipomoea tricolor *'Heavenly Blue'*.

ABOVE: *Where winters are mild* Zantedeschia aethiopica *can be overwintered outside.*
TOP: *The big, bold leaves of* Rheum palmatum *look very exotic.*
LEFT: *Lilies are quite easy to grow in pots provided you choose suitable varieties.*

Yucca
See *Everbright evergreens*, but the green form can be just as effective as a variegated variety.

Zantedeschia aethiopica
Well-known white arum flowers, popular with florists. Can be kept outdoors where winters are mild, but is usually best grown in a pot and given winter protection. The growth dies down in winter.

Exotic annuals
Some annuals that are regarded as indoor plants can be grown in the garden for the summer.

Among the flowering plants, celosias are always eye-catching, whether you grow the plume-shaped varieties or those shaped like a cock's comb. A mixture will usually include shades of yellow, red, and pink. The coleus is one of the best foliage pot-plants to try outdoors *en-masse* – plants are very easy to raise cheaply from seed. The multi-coloured foliage matches the exotic croton in boldness and colour combinations. Make sure they are carefully acclimatized, and don't put them out too early.

Many half-hardy bedding plants are easily raised from seed – try large daisy-like flowers such as arctotis, with flowers in shades of red, orange and pink. Salpiglossis are always eye-catching, and with their velvety, funnel-shaped flowers in shades of red, purple, and yellow, usually prominently veined and marked, certainly have that 'exotic' look.

Portulacas and cleomes (with spidery-looking flower heads) are among the other half-hardy annuals to include. But be sure to make space for *Ipomoea tricolor*, with its big blue flowers often *10cm (4in)* or so across, which are bound to make a real feature climbing up a trellis.

Disposable houseplants
Use flowering pot-plants to add short-term colour to your patio. Plants like gerberas, and dwarfed chrysanthemums, are inexpensive and generally treated as disposable plants if used indoors. Sink the pot into the soil so that the plant is easily removed after flowering.

ARCHITECTURAL PLANTS

Architectural plants may seem a contradiction in terms, for one implies the rigidity of buildings and structures, the other the informality and fluidity of plant life. The term is often a puzzle to non-gardeners, yet a plant enthusiast will know instantly when he sees an 'architectural' plant.

'Sculptural' plants

'Sculptural' is perhaps a better way to describe those plants, which, though clearly possessing all the natural beauty of any first-rate plant, also have structure and stature, and above all a shape – and perhaps texture – that an architect might be pleased to use to enhance his buildings and structures in the same way as a piece of sculpture might be used.

Some herbaceous plants, such as the acanthus, have assumed architectural status – in this case because the acanthus leaf occurs so often as a pattern in classical architecture, but also because the plant has the bold stance and distinctive profile that makes it stand out from the ordinary. Most architectural plants are trees and shrubs, however, with height as well as a distinctive outline. Use architectural plants sparingly and with careful consideration, not as part of a mixed planting but rather as you would large ornaments, as punctuation points within the garden.

Use architectural plants to make a bold statement in paved and gravel gardens, or to break up an otherwise boring area of lawn.

Acanthus spinosus
Statuesque plant with large, deeply divided leaves that are both erect and arching. Mauve and white, hooded flowers on stiff spikes in mid and late summer *1 × 1m (3 × 3ft).*

Angelica archangelica
Biennial or short-lived perennial. Large, deeply divided, aromatic leaves on stiff, upright plant. Ball-like head of smaller clusters of yellowish-green flowers in mid and late summer *2.4 × 1m (8 × 3ft).*

LEFT: Acanthus spinosus *is one of those plants with dramatic leaves and equally imposing flowers, and not one that will be ignored.*

BELOW: Angelica archangelica *makes a bold plant about 1.8m (6ft) tall, with large leaves and striking globular flower heads. Use it as a focal-point plant in the herb garden.*

Catalpa bignonioides 'Aurea'
Deciduous tree. The green species is far too large for a small garden, but 'Aurea' is more compact, and can be bought trained as a shrub-like multi-stemmed tree. The golden leaves are very large and handsome *4.5 × 4.5m (15 × 15ft).*

Cordyline australis
See *Plants for the tropical look.*

Cornus controversa 'Variegata'
A small tree with wide-spreading branches spaced out to give it a layered effect. Leaves have striking silver margins *4.5 × 4.5m (15 × 15ft).*

LEFT: *Daturas (now more correctly called brugmansias) are ideal for the summer patio but they have to be taken indoors for winter frost protection.*

RIGHT: *'Charity' is one of the most imposing hybrid mahonias, with bold sprays of yellow flowers blooming through the coldest months of the year.*

Crambe cordifolia
Herbaceous perennial. Normally a plant for a large garden, but sparsely planted it will make a bold statement. Enormous leaves and huge clouds of gypsophila-like small white flowers in early and mid-summer *1.8 × 1.8m (6 × 6ft).*

Datura (syn. *Brugmansia)*
Tender shrub. Must be overwintered in frost-proof place, but often grown on patio in a large tub for summer. Large drooping leaves, big bell-shaped very fragrant flowers – usually white or cream, but there are also red and pink kinds *1.8 × 1.2m (6 × 4ft)* in tub.

Fatsia japonica
See *No fuss, low maintenance plants.*

Gunnera manicata
See *Plants for the tropical look.*

Juniperus scopulorum 'Skyrocket'
Conifer. You may also find it sold under the name of *J. virginiana* 'Sky-rocket'. Very narrow, pencil-like growth. Typical conifer foliage *4.5m × 75cm (15 × 2½ft).*

Kniphofia
See *No fuss, low maintenance plants.*

Mahonia 'Charity'
See *Everbright evergreens.*

RIGHT: Salix matsudana *'Tortuosa' is a small tree that can be as fascinating in winter as it is in summer.*

Paulownia tomentosa
A large tree totally unsuitable for a small garden. It can be grown as a large shrub, however, by annual hard pruning close to ground level, when the leaves become huge. Treated like this height will be about *2.4–3m (8–10ft)* and spread about *1.8m (6ft).*

Phormium hybrids
See *Everbright evergreens.*

Salix matsudana 'Tortuosa'
A small to medium-sized tree with spiralling and twisted stems as well as contorted leaves. Seen at its best in winter when the stems are bare *4.5 × 4.5m (15 × 15ft).*

Yucca
See *Everbright evergreens*, but a green form is just as useful as a variegated variety as an architectural plant.

Living Screens

The screening plants described here are not rows of tall conifers or large windbreaks along the boundary, which are inappropriate in a small garden, but plants that you can use to screen objects within the garden and plants that you would be happy to grow as ornamentals too.

Generally, something that requires screening will need it the year round, so evergreens naturally predominate in any list of screening plants. But sometimes a summer-only screen is acceptable. For a summer screen within the vegetable plot consider Jerusalem artichokes, which provide excellent summer cover and a crop to harvest at the end of the season!

When looking for a good screening shrub, check that it is well clothed at the base. If you are prepared to erect a trellis or internal fence, many of the plants described under *Climbers and wall shrubs* will also make excellent internal screens. A trellis covered with sweet-smelling honeysuckle will make a summer screen that is pleasing to the eye and the nose. The most popular – and best – honeysuckles are deciduous, so don't expect winter cover, but some fragrant climbing honeysuckles, such as *Lonicera japonica*, are evergreen or semi-evergreen so you will have winter cover as well as summer scent – though at the price of less spectacular flowers.

Trellises and screen block walls

Sometimes it is possible to screen an unsightly object, such as a storage tank with just two or three well-chosen shrubs. Alternatively, erect a trellis or screen wall, carefully integrated as part of the garden design, then use climbers, wall shrubs or ordinary shrubs against these. This double-masking is often the most effective because you have a whole range of climbers that can be used on a trellis, including the ubiquitous but very practical and evergreen ivy, and wall shrubs such as pyracanthas.

Garage walls

Detached garages can dominate a small garden, so you probably need to soften the impact of the walls. Climbers are a natural choice, as are wall shrubs. But you could use a garage as an ideal backdrop for espalier or fan trained fruit trees.

Many evergreen shrubs will do an excellent masking job in front of a garage wall. Let hedging plants such as *Lonicera nitida* 'Baggesen's Gold' or a golden privet (such as *Ligustrum ovalifolium* 'Aureum') grow up untrimmed until the required height has been reached. Don't attempt to clip these like a formal hedge, but prune over-enthusiastic growth occasionally, and leave them with a natural shape.

ABOVE: Griselinia littoralis *'Dixon's Cream'*.
LEFT: Griselinia littoralis.

LEFT: *For a fast-growing shrubby screen the climbing* Polygonum baldschuanicum *(syn.* Fallopia baldschuanica*) is difficult to beat.*

BELOW: Ligustrum ovalifolium *'Aureo-marginatum' (syn. 'Aureum') is a fast-growing hedging plant, much more attractive than the form with plain green leaves.*

Arundo donax
Grass. Forms tall, almost bamboo-like clump, with drooping blue-green leaves. There is also a variegated form *2.4 × 1.2m (8 × 4ft).*

Buxus
Be careful not to choose a dwarf form if you want a taller screen. This is a classic shrub to clip to shape, and is much used for topiary as well as hedges. You could clip your screen to shape.

Griselinia littoralis
See *No fuss, low maintenance plants.*

Ilex
See *Everbright evergreens.*

Ligustrum ovalifolium 'Aureum'
See *Colour themes.*

Lonicera nitida 'Baggesen's Gold'
See *Colour themes.*

Miscanthus sacchariflorus
A large grass. Narrow, arching leaves, forming a dense clump *2.4 × 1m (8 × 3ft).*

Polygonum baldschuanicum
Now more correctly *Fallopia baldschuanica.* Deciduous climbing shrub. A vigorous climber, but instead of using it as a screen up a trellis, try letting it grow over the eyesore itself, if it is an old shed, for example. Within a few years it will almost cover it. Profusion of small white or pale pink flowers in conspicuous sprays from mid summer to early autumn. Height and spread is usually dictated by its support.

Permanent Plants for Containers

The choices and permutations for summer bedding plants to use in containers are almost endless. Every year there are new varieties of seed-raised plants, and growers re-introduce some of the old and neglected tender perennials to keep up the supply of novelties.

On this page you will find ideas for permanent plants to try – those that will form part of the framework of the garden, summer and winter. Use them alongside, and not instead of, seasonal flowers. You might even be able to plant spring bulbs and summer annuals around the base of some of the shrubs suggested.

Agapanthus
See *Colour themes*.

Camellia
See *Everbright evergreens*.

Ceratostigma willmottianum
See *Autumn leaves and berries*.

Choisya ternata 'Sundance'
See *Colour themes*.

Clematis, large-flowered
Deciduous climbing shrub. Large flowers in a wide range of colours. Avoid the rampant species in a container. Try growing them in a half-tub, as described opposite.

Cotoneaster 'Hybridus Pendulus'
Deciduous shrub, grafted to form a small weeping tree. Small white flowers in early summer. Red berries in autumn *1.8 × 1m (6 × 3ft)*.

Laburnum
Small deciduous tree. Produces long tassels of yellow pea-like flowers in late spring and early summer *2.4 × 1.8m (8 × 6ft)*.

Laurus nobilis
Evergreen shrub. The popular kitchen herb, sweet bay. Sometimes attractively trained and clipped into a formal shape. About *1.8m (6ft)*.

Mahonia 'Charity'
See *Everbright evergreens*.

Miscanthus sinensis 'Zebrinus'
Grass. Forms a dense clump of vertical stems that unfurl at the top into narrow, reflexed leaves, with distinctive yellow bands. Grows to an approximate height of *1.2m (4ft)* when contained in a large tub or half-barrel.

Rhododendron
Evergreen shrub (some azaleas are deciduous). There are many rhododendrons and azaleas

ABOVE: Choisya ternata *'Sundance', an excellent garden plant and attractive in a large container.*
TOP: *Agapanthus are excellent tub plants, but need winter protection in cold areas. This variety is 'Delft'.*

RIGHT: Clematis *'Nelly Moser' (top) and 'Lasurstern'.*

(botanically types of rhododendron) dwarf enough to be grown in a container. An ericaceous compost is essential for good results. Colour and size depend on variety.

Rosmarinus officinalis
See *Everbright evergreens*.

Salix caprea 'Pendula'
Deciduous weeping tree. Also known as *Salix* 'Kilmarnock'. Small, umbrella-shaped tree with stiffly pendulous branches. Attractive catkins in spring.

Taxus baccata
Conifer. The popular yew, but choose a golden form such as 'Aurea'. This makes an irregular cone in outline. If you prefer a slimmer, more pencil-shaped profile, try *T. b.* 'Fastigiata Aurea'.

Viburnum tinus
See *Everbright evergreens*.

Yucca
See *Everbright evergreens*.

LEFT: Rhododendron *'Loder's White' in a clay pot decorated with masonry paint.*

HOW TO PLANT A CLEMATIS BARREL

A clematis barrel can look really stunning when well established. You can choose several varieties to flower at the same time, or different ones that will flower at different times and so extend the period of interest, but bear in mind that this could make pruning more difficult.

1 Fill a half barrel or other large container with a loam-based compost (soil mix). You need a large, deep container and heavy potting mixture which will support the canes as well as the plants.

2 Plant about three to four clematis in a barrel of this size. Angle the root-ball so that the plants point slightly inwards.

3 Secure the canes at the top. Tie them with string or use a proprietary plastic cane holder. Don't worry if the growth reaches the tops of the canes, it will just tumble down again and make the planting look even more dense.

Climbers and Wall Shrubs

Small gardens almost inevitably have a lot of potential space for climbers and wall shrubs. Often there are external fences or walls that can be covered, interior surfaces, such as trellises, which can be used as screens, and nearly always there are all the walls of the house. Some will be in sun for most of the day, others will remain mainly in shade, but there are plants to suit every aspect.

Where space is at a premium, the vertical space provides a wonderful opportunity to grow more plants. Climbers and wall shrubs have a small 'footprint', and if pruned or trained so that they do not encroach too far out from the support, it is usually possible to grow other plants in front of them.

The climbers suggested here are all shrubs that will form a permanent part of the garden framework, but supplement them with annual climbers for a little extra variety and colour. Most annuals can be grown up a trellis – and they should be happy in a container if there is no soil in which they can be planted.

The heights given in the following list are an indication of how tall they are likely to grow in a small garden. Many climbers grow as high and wide as their support. Some clematis will grow to more than 9m (30ft) with a suitable support – such as a tree – but settle for 1.2m (4ft) if that is the height of a fence, and grow along it instead.

Actinidia kolomikta
Climber for wall or pergola. Dark green heart-shaped leaves tipped with white and pink. Sun or partial shade *3m (10ft).*

Ceanothus
Wall shrub. Blue flowers in late spring or early summer, or in late summer and into autumn, depending on species. Some are evergreen, others deciduous. Some are of borderline hardiness where winters are cold. Sun *3m (10ft).*

LEFT: Actinidia kolomikta.

Clematis
An impressive deciduous climber. Use large-flowered hybrids against a trellis on a wall. Vigorous species such as *C. montana* can be grown along a fence or through a tree. Sun or partial shade. Large-flowered hybrids *3m (10ft).*

Euonymus fortunei
See *Everbright evergreens.*

RIGHT: *Clematis remains one of the most popular climbers. This is 'The President'.*

Garrya elliptica
Evergreen wall shrub. Grown for its long catkins in late winter and early spring. Shade or sun *2.4m (8ft).*

Hedera
The ivies need no introduction. Choose large-leaved kinds, such as *H. colchica* 'Dentata Variegata', for a pergola or arch, small-leaved varieties of *H. helix* for a wall or fence. Shade or sun *3m (10ft).*

Humulus lupulus 'Aureus'
Herbaceous perennial climber. Golden leaves. Pergola or arch. Sun or partial shade *3m (10ft).*

Hydrangea petiolaris
Vigorous climber. Flat heads of white flowers in early summer. Shade or partial shade. Needs tall wall or a tree *6m (20ft).*

Jasminum nudiflorum
See *Colour for the cold months.* Shade or partial shade. Best against a wall, perhaps secured to a trellis *3m (10ft).*

Jasminum officinale
Climber. Fragrant white flowers in summer and often into autumn. Pergola or arch *3m (10ft).*

Lonicera x *japonica*
Evergreen climber. White or pale yellow fragrant flowers from early summer to mid autumn. 'Aureoreticulata' has yellow-veined leaves. Best supported against pergola or fence *6m (20ft).*

Lonicera periclymenum
Deciduous climber. Very fragrant flowers, pale yellow flushed purple-red, ideal for pergola, arch, or trellis. Some varieties flower in late spring and early summer, others from mid summer to early autumn *3m (10ft)* but can grow much taller up a tree.

Polygonum baldschuanicum
See *Living screens.* Fence or wall.

Pyracantha
Wall shrub. White flowers in early summer, red or orange berries in autumn and into winter. Sun or shade *3m (10ft).*

ABOVE LEFT: Jasminum nudiflorum.
ABOVE: *Pyracantha – a good wall shrub.*
TOP: Garrya elliptica.

Rosa
Climbing and rambling roses need no description or introduction. There are many to choose from, and some are excellent for pergolas, arches, and against the wall around the door. Many are very fragrant. Sun or partial shade *3m (10ft).*

Vitis coignetiae
Deciduous climber. Large leaves with beautiful autumn colours. Sun or shade. Will grow very tall in a tree but can be contained on a pergola.

Wisteria
Deciduous climber, with long drooping tassels of blue or white flowers in late spring and early summer. *W. sinesis* and *W. floribunda* are both widely grown, and are suitable for a pergola, or to grow against a house wall. Sun or partial shade *3m (10ft)*, but can be much taller.

PLANTING FOR SCENT

A garden without scent is like a meal without seasoning. All the elements appear to be there, but that extra spice is missing that lifts it from the ordinary and heightens the senses.

You can overdo the seasoning, however, so avoid planting too many fragrant plants of the same kind close together. One scent will compete with another, and the more subtle ones may be lost. Rather, make sure that plants with very fragrant flowers are chosen to flower in succession over a period of months. It will not matter if two fragrant shrubs are planted side by side if one flowers after the other has finished.

Mix plants that flower in the day with those that are scented at night – perhaps a rose that gives off its heady perfume during the day with a honeysuckle or night-flowering nicotiana that comes into its own once dusk falls.

Make use of plants with aromatic leaves that release their fragrance when brushed against or deliberately crushed.

Some of the plants suggested here are ornamental plants in their own right – roses and honeysuckles are highly decorative as well as fragrant – but find space for some plants which flower at night. Although they will add nothing to the daytime display they will certainly make up for lack of visual impact by their wonderful perfume after dark.

Chimonanthus praecox
See *Colour for the cold months*.

Choisya ternata
See *Everbright evergreens*. The green variety is just as good for fragrance.

Cytisus battandieri
Large deciduous shrub. Grey leaves. Pineapple-scented yellow flower in late spring and early summer. Not reliably hardy in cold areas, and best grown as a wall shrub *3 × 2.4m (10 × 8ft)*.

Daphne mezereum
Deciduous shrub. Red, pink, purple or white flowers between late winter and mid spring *1.2 × 1m (4 × 3ft)*.

Hamamelis mollis
See *Colour for the cold months*.

Jasminum officinale
See *Climbers and wall shrubs*.

Lavandula
See *Planting for quick results*.

Lonicera periclymenum
See *Climbers and wall shrubs*.

Mahonia 'Charity'
See *Everbright evergreens*.

Rosa
Roses are among the most fragrant of all shrubs, and you can grow their many forms in beds, borders, and as climbers. Use roses lavishly for a fragrant garden. Heights vary according to species.

ABOVE: *Stocks – varieties of* Matthiola incana *– are worth planting for their fragrance.*
LEFT: *One of the strongest spring fragrances comes from* Daphne mezereum *var.* rubra.

FRAGRANT ANNUALS

If you use a lot of summer bedding plants, be sure to include some fragrant ones such as stocks (*Matthiola incana*), and ornamental tobacco plants (nicotiana hybrids), though bear in mind that many of the compact, day-opening varieties of nicotiana have nothing like the powerful scent of the taller, evening-scented ones.

Night-scented stocks (*Matthiola bicornis*) are totally unattractive by day, so grow these as a gap-filler in a border where their day-time appearance doesn't matter.

Philadelphus
Deciduous shrubs. Several good species and hybrids, all with fragrant white flowers in early summer.

Sarcococca hookeriana humilis
See *Plants that prefer shade.*

ABOVE: *Lilacs (varieties of* Syringa vulgaris*) are among the most fragrant shrubs, and although some grow tall they are not too large for a small garden.*

Skimmia japonica
See *Autumn leaves and berries.*

Spartium junceum
Deciduous shrub. Yellow, pea-type flowers in summer *2.4 × 1.8m (8 × 6ft).*

Syringa vulgaris
Deciduous shrub, the popular lilac. The varieties have very fragrant flowers mainly in shades of blue, purple, mauve, and white, in late spring and early summer *2.4 × 1.5m (8 × 5ft).*

Viburnum x *bodnantense*
See *Colour for the cold months.*

Wisteria
See *Climbers and wall shrubs.*

SCENTED FOLIAGE

Use some of the scented-leaved geraniums (pelargoniums) on the patio. You can even plant some of them at the front of a border. Many herbs, such as pineapple sage, lemon balm, and lemon verbena, make acceptable patio plants in pots.

Among the shrubs with aromatic foliage are *Artemisia arborescens, Choisya ternata, Laurus nobilis, Rosmarinus officinalis,* and *Salvia officinalis.*

Eucalyptus can be grown in a small garden if you prune it back hard each spring to grow like a shrub.

RIGHT: *Wisterias are grown mainly for visual impact, but they are also fragrant.*

ATTRACTING WILDLIFE

You don't have to turn your garden into something that resembles a meadow – some might say overgrown and weedy garden – to attract wildlife.

Lots of shrubs, border and rock plants, and annuals and biennials will attract wildlife of many kinds, from birds, bees and butterflies to wasps and weevils. Not all are welcome, of course, but for the few that you don't want to attract you will certainly gain many beautiful and beneficial animals that will help to control the pests.

You will, of course, need to create particular habitats if you want to encourage particular types of wildlife, such as a pond for aquatic creatures. And there is a lot to be said for leaving an area of grass long – perhaps where bulbs are naturalized if you want a horticultural justification – and if you let a few nettles grow behind the garden shed you will provide food plants for many kinds of caterpillars that will later grace your garden as butterflies.

Attracting wildlife in general often brings the bonus of more beneficial insects such as hoverflies and ladybirds, which will help to keep down pests such as aphids.

LEFT: Aucuba japonica *'Variegata'*.

ABOVE: Berberis thunbergii *'Atropurpurea Nana'*.

Shrubs

Aucuba (birds)
Berberis (birds, bees, butterflies)
Callicarpa (birds)
Ceanothus (bees)
Cistus (bees)
Cotoneaster (bees, birds)
Cytisus (bees)
Daphne (birds, bees)
Escallonia (bees)
Hebe (butterflies)
Hedera (bees, butterflies)
Hypericum (birds)
Ilex (birds)
Lavandula (bees, butterflies)
Leycesteria formosa (birds)
Ligustrum (bees, butterflies)
Lonicera periclymenum (butterflies)
Mahonia (birds)
Pernettya (birds)
Perovskia (bees)
Potentilla (bees)
Pyracantha (birds, bees)
Rhamnus frangula (bees, butterflies)
Ribes sanguineum (bees)
Skimmia (birds, bees)
Symphoricarpos (birds, bees)
Syringa (bees, butterflies)
Ulex (bees)
Viburnum (birds, bees)
Weigela (bees)

Border and rock plants
Achillea filipendulina (bees, butterflies)
Alyssum saxatile (butterflies)
Armeria maritima (bees, butterflies)
Aster novi-beglii (bees, butterflies)
Erigeron (bees, butterflies)
Nepeta (bees, butterflies)
Scabiosa caucasica (bees, butterflies)
Sedum spectabile (bees, butterflies)
Solidago (birds, bees, butterflies)
Thymus (bees, butterflies)

Annuals and biennials
Centaurea cyanus (bees, butterflies)
Dipsacus spp. (birds)
Helianthus annus (birds)
Hesperis matronalis (bees)
Limnanthes douglasii (bees)
Lunaria annua (birds)
Scabiosa annual (bees, butterflies)

LEFT: Sedum *'Autumn Joy'*

ABOVE: Alyssum saxatile.

BELOW: Solidago.

OTHER WAYS TO ATTRACT WILDLIFE

A thick hedge attracts far more wildlife than a fence or wall. A prickly evergreen hedge like holly will provide good nest and roost sites for many birds.

An old log pile provides refuge for many beneficial insects and can make a nest site for small mammals.

the KITCHEN GARDEN

AMBITIOUS KITCHEN GARDENS ARE SELDOM achievable in a small space. Vegetables that are hungry for space such as potatoes and cabbages may lose out to flowers. But if you are content with smaller vegetables such as lettuces, carrots, beetroot, and dwarf beans, and can relegate tall climbing beans and expansive plants like globe artichokes to the mixed or herbaceous border, it is quite practical to grow a wide range of vegetables even where space is quite restricted.

Grow a whole range of vegetables, from lettuces to peas, in containers like windowboxes

ABOVE: *Raspberries are not an ideal crop for a small garden but they can be trained so that they don't take up too much space.*

TOP: *Fruit-growing is possible even on a roof or balcony garden . . . with a little imagination.*

OPPOSITE: *This picture shows an interesting way of providing supports for tall vegetables in a small kitchen garden.*

LEFT: *One of the upright-growing apple trees ideal for a small garden or limited space. This variety is 'Walz', planted in a bed of 'Surrey' ground cover roses.*

and growing bags. Even potatoes can be harvested from pots and growing bags and tomatoes of all types have been grown with great success in growing bags. This kind of small-scale vegetable gardening is demanding, and the yields always very modest for the effort involved, but if the idea of harvesting your own fresh vegetables just before you pop them into the pot appeals, you may find it worth the effort. It can certainly be fun.

If you have a reasonably sized garden – large enough to divide off a section for a kitchen garden – growing them in the ground is the most practical way to produce your vegetables, and much of the fruit.

Fruit trees and bushes are often ornamental and can be easily integrated into the flower garden. Trained fruit trees like espalier and fan apples look attractive even with bare branches in winter.

Herbs are much more easily accommodated than vegetables. Many are highly ornamental and lots of them make good container plants. Others look perfectly in place in a border. If you want to make a real feature of your herbs, make a herb garden a key part of your garden design.

Ornamental Herbs

Formal herb gardens look impressive, but can be difficult to accommodate in a small space. However, as the illustrations below show, there are alternatives.

Bear in mind that though herb gardens are packed with interest in summer, in winter you will be left with just a few evergreen shrubs and a handful of herbs that retain their foliage and are tough enough to survive unprotected. Alternatively, incorporate your herbs in an overall garden design that carries interest through all the seasons. Here are some other ways to incorporate herbs in a small garden.

A collection in a container
A herb pot can hold half a dozen or more different herbs. Do not start to harvest until plants are growing strongly, then keep harvesting little and often to produce compact yet well-clothed plants.

Shrubby plants like bay and rosemary can be grown in tubs to decorate the patio or to display by the front or back door.

Windowbox herbs
Herbs can be grown in windowboxes and troughs provided you choose compact plants such as thymes and marjorams. Ornamental, variegated mints also look good.

Growing bags
Growing bags are not elegant, but they are useful for rampant plants like mints, which would otherwise make a take-over bid for the border.

In among the flowers
Many herbs are so decorative that they don't look amiss in beds and borders, and indeed some are planted more for their ornamental than culinary uses.

Among the herbs that look good with other border plants are chives, fennel, marjoram, and lemon balm.

ABOVE: *Have fun with your small herbs. They can be arranged informally in pots, or grouped together as in the small wheelbarrow.*

RIGHT: *An attractive herb collection can be grown in a small raised bed, but bear in mind that many of these plants will grow much larger.*

HOW TO MAKE A HERB WHEEL

If you have an old cartwheel, just paint or varnish that and set it into the ground ready to plant. Few of us have access to cartwheels, however, but an acceptable second best can be made from bricks. Adjust the size of the wheel to suit your garden. Bricks are a convenient way to make the 'spokes', but you could use dwarf dividing 'hedges' of hyssop or thyme. Place an attractive terracotta pot in the centre as the hub of the wheel, and plant with herbs, or place an upright rosemary in the centre. A rosemary may become too large after a few years, but either keep it clipped to shape and size or replace it every second or third year.

1 Mark a circle about 1.5–1.8m (5–6ft) across, using a line fixed to a peg to ensure an even shape. If it helps, use a wine bottle filled with dry sand instead of a stick to mark out the perimeter. Excavate the ground to a depth of about 15cm (6in).

2 Place the bricks on end, or at an angle, around the edge. If you place them at a 45 degree angle it will create a dog-tooth effect; bricks placed on end will look more formal. Either lay them loose in compacted earth, or bed them on mortar.

3 Lay rows of brick, cross-fashion, as shown. If the diameter does not allow for them to be laid without gaps in the centre, stand an ornament or pot in the middle if you are not planting directly into the soil in that position.

4 Top up the areas between the spokes with good garden or potting soil.

5 Plant up each section, using plants that will balance each other in size of growth if possible. You could, for instance, grow a collection of different thymes.

6 For a smart finish, carefully cover the soil with fine gravel.

PLANTING A HERB POT

A herb pot makes an attractive feature for the garden or the patio, but it is best treated as a short-term home to be replanted annually. If you allow shrubby perennial herbs to become established, you will find them extremely difficult to remove when it becomes necessary. Be especially careful of planting a large shrub in the top of a herb pot with a tapering neck. Once the plant has produced a mass of roots, the inward taper makes removal a frustrating task.

1 A herb pot is best filled in stages. Start by adding a good potting compost (soil mix) to the height of the first planting pockets.

2 Knock the plants out of their containers and push the root-balls through the holes in the planting pockets. If necessary, break off some of the root-ball so that you can get it through the hole.

3 Add more potting compost (soil mix) and repeat with the next row of planting holes. Unless the pot is very large, do not try to pack too many herbs into the top. A single well-grown plant often looks much better.

4 Large earthenware pots can look just as appealing as herb pots with planting pockets if you plant them imaginatively. If you have an old half-barrel use this instead. Place a bold shrubby herb, such as sweet bay (*Laurus nobilis*), in the centre.

5 In time, the shrubby plant may take up all the planting space at the top and you will have an attractive specimen plant. Meanwhile you should be able to fit a collection of smaller herbs around the edge. Avoid mints, which may be difficult to eliminate later.

Growing Mints

Mints are notoriously difficult to control once they make themselves at home. They send spreading and penetrating shoots beneath the surface which emerge among other plants or even on the other side of a path. They are best contained in some way.

1 A growing bag is an ideal home for mints. They will be happy for a couple of seasons, and then are easily removed and replanted for a fresh start. If the mints are in large pots, it may be necessary to remove some of the root-ball, but the plants will soon recover.

2 Instead of filling the growing bag with one kind of mint, try planting a collection of perhaps four to six different mints. This will not only look attractive, it will also add to the range of flavours available for the kitchen.

OTHER HERBS TO RESTRAIN

Although mint is the herb most notorious for being invasive, others can attempt to take over the border as well. For example, tansy (*Tanacetum vulgare*) and woodruff (*Asperula odorata*, syn. *Galium odoratum*) are among the herbs that you may want to consider planting in a plunged pot or large bucket.

Woodruff is a particularly attractive herb, with its whorls of star-shaped white flowers. The added advantage of this herb is that all parts of it are aromatic – a perfect plant for a windowbox or in pots positioned by a seating area.

3 If you want to grow your mint in a border, plant it in an old bucket or large pot. Make sure there are drainage holes in the bottom, and fill with soil or a potting compost (soil mix) before planting the mint.

4 Plunge the pot into the ground so that the rim sits just below the surface, then cover with soil to hide any signs of the pot. Lift, divide and replant annually, or every second spring, to maintain vigour.

Fruit in a Small Space

The most satisfactory way to grow tree fruits such as apples and pears in a small garden or a confined space is trained as a cordon, fan or espalier against a wall or fence. Even some bush fruits such as gooseberries can be trained as cordons or double cordons against a fence.

Blackberries and hybrid berries can be trained against a fence or over an arch, but keep the growth contained and avoid allowing thorny shoots to overhang pathways.

It is even possible to grow apples in pots on the patio, but with the new flagpole-type varieties available that grow in a narrow column, you may prefer to plant these where space is limited. They will require much less watering and attention than ordinary varieties on dwarfing rootstocks in pots.

The initial training of espaliers, fans and cordons demands patience and skill. Unless you particularly like the challenge and can wait for two or three years longer, it is best to buy a ready-trained tree.

ABOVE: *Wall-trained fruit trees take up relatively little space.*

RIGHT: *If you want apples in a small garden it is best to use one of the columnar varieties or to grow an ordinary variety on a trained system like this espalier 'Lord Lambourne'.*

BUYING FRUIT TREES

Whether a fruit tree such as an apple, peach or cherry is suitable for a small garden depends not so much on the variety of the fruit but on the rootstock. This has a profound affect on the size of the tree (as well as how soon it starts to fruit). Always check the root-stock before you buy, and if in doubt ask whether it is suitably dwarfing for a small garden.

TRAINED FRUIT TREES

Trained trees look attractive and produce a heavy crop from a restricted space. But they require regular and methodical training, sometimes twice a year. If in doubt about how to prune a particular trained fruit, consult an encyclopedia or fruit book.

Espaliers are more ornamental than cordons (some shrubs, such as pyracanthas, are occasionally trained as espaliers using the same methods).

Cordons are usually trained at an angle of about 45 degrees, secured to support canes and wires fixed to stout posts or to a fence. Many plants can be planted in a small space, and soft fruits such as gooseberries and red and white currants can be trained in this way, saving the space taken up by a bush form.

Fans can be free-standing, tied to wires supported by posts, but they are usually planted against a wall or fence. In time a fan can be trained to cover a large area, such as a garage wall.

Step-overs are single-tiered espaliers, used as a fruiting edging, perhaps within the kitchen garden.

Potted fruit

Apples can be grown in pots provided you choose a very dwarfing rootstock. The same applies to peaches. You can experiment with other bush and tree fruits, but bear in mind that this is second best to growing them in the ground.

Flagpole apples

You can buy a range of apple trees that rarely produce long sideshoots, but instead grow upright and produce most fruiting spurs along the main vertical stem. These take up little space and won't cast a heavy shadow, so they are ideal for growing in a flower bed. The blossom is pretty in spring, and the ripening fruits are ornamental later in the year.

Rhubarb

Rhubarb is ornamental enough to be grown in the flower border. You can even grow it in a large pot as a foliage plant for the patio, though this is not the best way to achieve a heavy crop.

ABOVE: *This rhubarb chard is growing in a flower bed.*

Strawberries

If you don't have much space for fruit, at least try growing strawberries. A strawberry barrel or a tower container will hold a lot of strawberries and provided you keep the container well watered it will be laden with fruit . . . which won't become splashed with mud if the weather is wet or awkward to pick. Also the fruit will be more difficult for slugs to reach.

ABOVE: *There is always space for a few strawberries if you grow them in a container like this.*

Finding Room for Vegetables

If you are a dedicated vegetable grower you will probably want to turn over a large part of your garden to the task. However, this need not mean that the garden will be unattractive. Try growing vegetables in small beds, either in a patchwork pattern or a more formal ornamental potager. If you really are restricted for space, grow crops in containers, from growing bags to hanging baskets.

Whatever form your 'vegetable plot' takes, it should never be tucked away in a dull, sunless part of the garden. Most vegetables need good light and plenty of moisture to do well. Dry ground shaded by hedges and walls seldom produces succulent vegetables.

The deep bed system

If you are happy to devote a large area to vegetables, then you can grow them traditionally, in a rectangular plot divided into long straight rows, with paths for access between each one. Alternatively, you can use the deep bed system, where the plot is divided into small beds, about 1.2m (4ft) wide and, after the initial preparation, all the work is done from narrow paths at the sides.

This method has many advantages. It gives you a bigger area for growing vegetables, by cutting down the number of space-consuming paths. Because the soil is dug deeply, and enriched with masses of bulky organic material, plant roots are encouraged to spread downwards rather than sideways. This allows you to grow plants much closer together than in a conventional row, giving you a bigger yield. Having prepared the beds, you can do all the cultivation without walking on the soil and compacting it. Soil structure and fertility are greatly improved because it is easier for worms and insects to work the manures and composts into the soil. Once the crops are underway, there is virtually no need for weeding since the plants are so close together they cover the soil surface, preventing weed growth.

ABOVE: *This raised vegetable bed in a flower garden makes an interesting feature as well as a neat productive area.*

LEFT: *Ornamental kales are usually grown for their decorative effect, but they are edible if you get tired of looking at them. This variety is 'Coral Queen'.*

Ornamental potagers

The term potager comes from jardin potager, simply being French for kitchen garden. But the term has come to refer primarily to a kitchen garden – usually with both fruit and vegetables – laid out ornamentally, perhaps with beds edged with low hedges like a parterre. Treated like this, your kitchen garden can become a prominent design element.

Growing bags

Growing bags are excellent for vegetables if all you have is a balcony or patio on which to grow them. It is quite feasible to grow lettuces, spinach, radishes, cucumbers, tomatoes, turnips, even self-blanching celery and potatoes, in growing bags.

Clearly, you won't keep the family fed with potatoes from a couple of growing bags, and the economics don't make much sense. But it is worth planting an early variety (you can move the bag into a protected area if frost threatens) so that you can enjoy those new potatoes straight from the garden.

ABOVE: *These are 'Totem' tomatoes growing in a 25cm (10in) pot.*

BELOW: *You can even grow tomatoes in a hanging basket.*

Troughs, tubs and pots

Tomatoes are one of the most successful crops for a growing bag, and, provided you choose a suitable compact variety, they are equally successful in pots.

Courgettes (zucchini) and cucumbers are also a practical choice for a tub or large pot. Potatoes can be grown in a pot for a bit of fun, but you might be better planting an aubergine (eggplant) or pepper in it.

Windowboxes and hanging baskets

The only vegetable likely to do well in a hanging basket is the tomato, but you must choose a trailing or drooping variety, and control both watering and feeding.

Windowboxes offer more scope and, apart from tomatoes (use dwarf or trailing varieties), stump-rooted carrots, radishes, onions and lettuces are among the crops that do well.

Rather than grow a hearting lettuce, which leaves a gap as the whole head is harvested at once, try a non-hearting 'cut-and-come-again' variety that you can harvest in stages.

Flowers and Vegetables

If you simply don't have the space to devote part of your garden to vegetables and herbs alone, consider integrating them with the existing ornamentals. Many vegetables are pretty in their own right – with striking foliage and flowers – and when grown in beds and borders, and intermixed with other decorative plants, they can work surprisingly well.

One of the enormous advantages of growing vegetables with flowers is that the diversity of plants helps to deter pests and diseases. Mixed planting provides a naturally balanced environment, where the flowers attract insects and other wildlife that feed on pests that feed on vegetables. Sowing marigolds among tomato plants, for example, will keep the tomatoes relatively free from attack by aphids, because the marigolds attract hover-flies, and their larvae like nothing better than an aphid feast.

Among the flowers

It is quite possible to incorporate vegetables as part of a formal bedding scheme. Red or purple rhubarb chard leaves, for example, contrast well with grey-foliaged bedding plants; carrot foliage looks attractive as a foil for bright summer bedding plants; and even one of the more decorative kinds of red-leaved lettuce will make a pretty edging for a summer bedding scheme. Unfortunately, the problem comes at harvest time, when gaps soon become rather conspicuous.

Vegetables are more acceptable as gap fillers in a herbaceous or mixed border. They fill the space admirably, and after harvesting the border is left no less attractive than it was originally. If you choose crops such as spinach or 'cut-and-come again' (oak leaf) lettuce, you can harvest the leaves without destroying the whole

LEFT: *Edging a vegetable plot with colourful flowers is the best solution if you want vegetables and ornamentals.*

ABOVE: *Rosemary (*Rosmarinus officinalis*) is a herb that tastes as good as it looks.*

ABOVE: *When young, purple sage (*Salvia officinalis *'Purpurascens') has tinged foliage.*

ABOVE: *Mint (*Mentha*) is highly invasive and should be planted in pots in the ground.*

plant. Other suitable candidates here are radishes, beetroot, asparagus peas, carrots, and leaf beet; but much depends on the size of your space and your imagination.

In a traditional cottage garden, where flowers rub shoulders with fruit, vegetables and herbs, the plants often merge into one another but the result can appear rather chaotic. If the rest of the garden is formal in style, dedicate just one area to mixed planting and make it a feature, separated with a hedge or screen.

Planting in blocks

Instead of having single vegetable plants dotted here and there among the flowers, try growing them in blocks or patches. The effect can be just as decorative, and the crops will certainly be easier to harvest, after which the space can easily be replanted. Plant the areas that had vegetables in summer with winter-flowering bulbs and spring bedding. That way, you will gain more ornamental value without sacrificing much in terms of crop.

With such small patches of ground, it takes no time at all to sow a batch of seed, tend delicate young plants, or keep weeds under control. Using this method, you may grow the same quantity of vegetables as in a conventional plot but the task will seem far less daunting.

ABOVE: *Brushing past low-growing thymes (*Thymus*), such as this one with its delicate pink flowers, will release a pungent scent.*

Climbing vegetables

Most climbing vegetables are decorative in themselves, and you can treat them in much the same way as you would any ornamental annual climbers. Make a feature of ordinary or asparagus peas by growing them against a free-standing trellis or a wall of canes and netting within the flower border. Train trailing forms of courgette (zucchini) over an archway or pergola. Or grow ridge cucumbers and scarlet runner beans on wigwams (tepees) of canes at the back of a border or along a series of rustic poles lining the path.

Page numbers in *italics* refer to illustrations.

Abelia × grandiflora, 207, 220
Abies
A. balsamea, 192
A. cephalonica, 192, *192*
Acaena microphylla, 154
Acanthus spinosus, 218, 226, *226*
Acer, 132, 172
Achillea
A. filipendulina, 175, *175*, 214, 218, 237
A. ptarmica, 178
A. tomentosa, 154
acidity, 208, 216-17
Actinidia kolomikta, 232, *232*
Aethionema grandiflorum, 207
Agapanthus, 133, 230, *230*
A. hybrids, 174, 214
Agave americana, 17
Ageratum, 124
Ajuga, 77, 133
A. reptans, 73, 172, 208, *208*
Akebia quinata, 206
Alchemilla mollis, 170, 172
alkalinity, 208, 218-19
alpines, 43, 73, 74, 152-5, 237
Alyssum, 124, *128-9*
A. montanum, 154
A. saxatile, 154, *154*, 175, 214, 237, *237*
Amelanchier
A. canadensis, 222
A. laevis, 184, *184*
Anchusa azurea, 218
Anemone, 126, 178
Angelica archangelica, 226, *226*
annuals, 103, 188, 213, 225, 234, 237
Antennaria dioica, 154
Anthemis

A. nobile see Chamaemelum nobile
A. punctata, 178, *178*
A. tinctoria, 175
anthuriums, 51
Antirrhinum, *126*
Aponogeton distachyos, 147
aquatic plants, 143, 144, 147, 149, *149*, 150
Aquilegia alpina, 218
Arabis, 154
Aralia
A. elata, 186, *186*
A. sieboldii see Fatsia japonica
arbours, *18*, *25*, 92, 121
arches, 21, 23, 100-1
architectural plants, 226-7
Arenaria balearica, 154
Armeria maritima, 154, 237
Artemisia
A. absinthium, 174
A. arborescens, 214, 235
A. ludoviciana, 170, 174, *174*
Aruncus dioicus, 220, *221*
Arundinaria viridistriata see Pleioblastus auricomus
Arundo donax, 229
Asarina, 103
aspect, 50-1, 206-7, 207
Asperula odorata, 243
Asplenium scolopendrium, *143*, *210*
Aster
A. alpinus, 154
A. novi-belgii, 176, 237
Astilbe, 208, *220*
Astrantia major, 208, *208*
Aubrietia, 154, 170
Aucuba, 236
A. japonica, 180, 188, 190, 208, 218, 220, 222
azaleas, 15, 133, *216*
Azolla caroliniana, 147

Bacopa, 124
balconies, 50-1
basements, 35, 46-7
bay *see Laurus nobilis*
beans, 102, *102*
beds, 158-60, *158-60*, 162-3, *162-3*, 196, 246
Begonia semperflorens, 124
Berberidis corallina, 217
Berberis, 82, 222, *222*, 236
B. darwinii, 180, 206
B. thunbergii, 82, 175, 184, 190, 222, *223,236*
B. wilsoniae, 184
B. × *stenophylla*, 83, 206, 220
Bergenia, 77, 133
B. cordifolia, 43, 206
B. hybrids, 180, 190, 208
B. purpurascens, 172
berries, 184-5, *185*
Betula, 15, 183
birch *see betula*
Black-eyed Susan *see Thunbergia alata*
blanket weed *see Spirogyra*
bluebells *see Hyacinthoides*
borders, 158-9, *158-9*
attracting wildlife, 237
colour and shape, 161-2, *162*, 163, *163*, 174-87, *174-87*
maintenance, 162, *162*, 196, 198
mixed, 158-9, 165, *165*
one-sided, 161, *161*
plans, 15, 158, 164-95

plant types, 170-1, *170-1*, 172-3, *172-3*, 180-1, 210-11
bougainvilleas, 17
boundaries, 24-5, 43-4, 80-97
box *see Buxus*
Brachycome, 124, *126*, *136*
Brachyglottis see Senecio
brugmansias see daturas
Brunnera macrophylla, 208, *209*
Buddleia davidii, 188, 214, 222
bulbs, dividing, 15, 49, 51, 64-5
Busy Lizzie *see Impatiens*
Buxus, *18*, 82, *83*, *130*, 186, 208, 229

cacti, 17, 50-1
Calendula, 14, 124
Callicarpa, 236
Calluna vulgaris, 48, 77, 83, 194, 217, *217*
Caltha palustris, 146, *147*
Camellia, 208, 230
C. hybrids, 176, 180, 217
C. japonica, 133, 206
C. × *williamsii*, 133, 206
Campanula, 124, *143*, 154, *170*, 218
Campsis, 207, *207*
canary creeper *see Tropaeolum peregrinum*
Canna indica, 207
Cape heathers *see Erica*
Cardamine pratensis, 220
cardoon *see Cynara cardunculus*
Carex morrowii, 133, 186
Caryopteris × *clandonensis*, 188, 212, 218
Cassiope varieties, 217
Catalpa bignonioides, 226
cathedral bells *see Cobaea scandens*
Ceanothus, 232, 236
C. impressus, 207

C. × *burkwoodii*, 174, *174*
C. × *deleanus*, 207
Cedrus deodara, 192
Centaurea cyanus, 237
Cerastium tomentosum, 154
Ceratostigma, 134
C. plumbaginoides, 184
C. willmottianum, 134, 222, 230
Chaenomeles
C. hybrids, 222
C. japonica, 220-1, 222
C. speciosa, 220-1, 222
C. × *superba*, 206, 220-1, 222
chalk soils *see* alkalinity
Chamaecyparis, 192, *193*
Chamaemelum, 37, 66, 73, 74
chamomile *see Chamaemelum*
cherry *see Prunus*
Chilean glory flower *see Eccremocarpus scaber*
Chimonanthus praecox, 182, 234
Choisya ternata, 175, *179*, 190, 230, *230*, 234, 235
planting conditions, 133, 135, 188, 206
Chrysanthemum, 182, *182*
C. hybrids, 176
C. × *superbum*, 178, *178*
cineraria, *132*
Cistus, 188, 207, *219*, 236
C. hybrids, 178, 218
Clematis, 121, *122*, 130, *205*, 230, 231, 232
C. alpina, 206
C. 'Jackmanii', *230*
C. 'Lasurstern', *230*
C. montana, 97, *97*, 206
C. 'Nelly Moser', 206, *230*
C. tangutica, 206
C. 'The President', *232*
conditions for, 102, 103, 104-5
planting conditions, 102, 103, 104-5, 106

Clerodendrum trichotomum, 184
Clianthus puniceus, 224
climbers, 43, 103, 130
choice of, 232-3
screening, 19, 24, *24*, 228-30
supports for, 40, 94, 97, 100-9, 121
uses, 13, *34*, 46
on walls, 94, 94, 97
clover *see Trifolium repens*
Cobaea scandens, 103, 105
Colchicum, 64, 170, 182
colour themes, 159
autumn, 182-5, *182-5*
blue/silver, 174-5, *174*
evergreens, 180-1, *180-1*
gold/yellow, 175, *175*
red hot, 176-7
variegation, 186-7, *186-7*
white, 178-9, *178-9*
Colutea arborescens, 212, *212*
composting, 18, 26, 63
conifers, 45, 82, 134, 181, 191-4
containers, 47, 122-41, 230-1
brightening, *21*, 138-9, 140-1
focal point, 10, *23*
frost protection, 135
fruit, 245
hanging baskets, 40, 124-5
herbs, 242
Mediterranean garden, 17
metal, 140-1
placing of, *41*, 47, 49, 128-9, 144
scented plants, 136-7
uses, *21*, 35, *35*, 53, 130-1
vegetables, 247
window boxes, 47, 126-7, *126-7*, 130
Convolvulus, 129, 136
C. cneorum, 124, 178, 212
C. sabatius, 124
cordons, 244
Cordyline australis, 224, *224*, 226
Cornus
C. alba, 48, 183, 184, *184*, 186
C. canadensis, 178, *179*, 217
C. controversa, 226
C. mas, 182
C. stolonifera, 183, 190
Cortaderia selloana, 172
Corydalis lutea, 154
Corylus avellana, 109
Cosmos atrosanguineus, 137
Cotinus coggygria, 48, 190, *190*
Cotoneaster, 236
C. dammeri, 77, 181, 190
C. frigidus, 222
C. horizontalis, 184, 190, *190*, 206
C. 'Hybridus Pendulus', 132, 230
cottage gardens, 14, *14*, 44
Cotula, 67, 73
courtyard gardens, 13, *21*
Crambe cordifolia, 221, 227
crimson glory vine *see Vitis coignetiae*
Crinodendron hookerianum, 206
Crocosmia, 176, *177*, 207
Crocus, 64, 124, 126, 170
C. speciosus, 182
C. tommasinianus, 182, *182*
cup-and-saucer vine *see Cobaea scandens*
Cupressocyparis leylandii, 82
Cyclamen, 126, 182
Cynara cardunculus, 196
Cytisus, 236
C. battandieri, 234
C. multiflorus, 178
C. scoparius hybrids, 212
C. × *kewensis*, 188

Daboecia cantabrica, *208*, *216*, 217
daffodils *see Narcissus*
Dahlia hybrids, 176
Daphne, 172, 236
D. mezereum, 234, *234*
D. odora, 136
Datura, 17, 47, 135, 227, *227*
decking, 55, 76, *76*
Delphinium, 218
D. hybrids, 174, *174*
designing on paper, 31-3
Deutzia scabra, 206, 207, 218
Dianthus, 124, *136*, *142*, *176*, 207, 218
D. barbatus, 219, *219*
D. deltoides, 154, *154*
Diascia, 124
Dicentra, 133, 208
difficult sites, 34-5
Digitalis, 206, 221
Dipsacus, 237
Dodecatheon meadia, 206
Dolichos lablab see Lablab purpureus
drought-tolerant plants, 14
Dryas octopetala, 154, 207
duckweed *see Lemna*

Eccremocarpus scaber, 103, 105, 106, 207
Echinacea purpurea, 207
Echinops ritro, 207, 212
Eichhornia crassipes, 146
Elaeagnus
E. pungens, *180*, 181, 186, 190, 222
E. × *ebbingei*, 186, 222, *222*
Elodea, 147, 150
entrances, *12, 22, 81*
Epimedium
E. grandiflorum, 217, *217*
E. perralderianum, 172, 208

Eranthis hyemalis, 64
Erica, 180, 181, 217
E. carnea, 48, 189, 190
E. gracilis, 134
E. × hiemalis, 134
Erigeron, 237
Erinus alpinus, 154

Eryngium variifolium, 213
Erysimum cheiri, 219
Escallonia, 80, 176, 181, 236
espaliers, 46, 97, 244
eucalyptus, 235
Eucryphia glutinosa, 178
Euonymus fortunei, 48, 77, *104*, 181, 206, 232
var. 'Emerald 'n' Gold', 48, 172
Euphorbia, 23, 206
everlasting peas *see Lathyrus latifolius*
exotic plants, 17, 47, 51, *205*, 224-5

Fallopia baldschuanica see Polygonum baldshuanicum
fans, 97, 244
Fatsia japonica, 172, *173*, 191, 224, 227
Felicia, 124
fences
erection of, 90-3, *90-3*
types, 88-91, *88-91*
ferns, 15, 46, 47, 124, 210-11
fertilizers, 169, 202-3
Festuca glauca, 170-1, 172, 174
flagpole apples, 245
focal points, 22-3, *22-3*, 98-9, 110-11, *110-11*, 161, *164*
forget-me-nots *see Myosotis*
formal gardens, 12-13, *12*, 82
Forsythia, 83
F. suspensa, 206
F. × intermedia, 175, 223
Fothergilla major, 185, 217
Fragaria, 124
Fremontodendron, 207
Fritillaria, 64
F. imperialis, 65, 207
F. meleagris, 126
fritillaries *see Fritillaria*
front gardens, *34*, 35, 42-5, *81*
frost protection, 135
fruit, 244-5
Fuchsia, 124
F. hybrids, 176
F. magellanica, 186, 189
furniture, 18, 19, 38-9, 41, *98*, 116-19

Galanthus, 64, 171, 206
Garrya elliptica, 206, 223, 233
Genista tinctoria, 188, 189, 213
Gentiana, 154, 217
geranium *see Pelargonium*
Geranium
G. cinereum, 207
G. 'Johnson's Blue', 207
G. subcaulescens, 154
G. × oxonianum, 104
Gladiolus hybrids, 176-7
gourds *see Lagenaria*
grape hyacinth *see Muscari*
grape vines, 40
grass
see also lawns
borders, 172-3, *172-3*
substitutes for, 66-7
gravel, uses, 16, 37, 42, 45, 78-9
Griselinia littoralis, 191, *228*, 229
ground cover plants, *54*, 55, 77
Gunnera manicata, 224, 227
Gypsophila, 219
G. paniculata, 171, 178
G. repens, 154

Hakonechloa macra, 172, *173*
Halimiocistus sahucii, 178
Hamamelis mollis, 182, 206, 234
hart's tongue fern *see Asplenium scolopendrium*
hazel *see Corylus avellana*
heath, Alpine/winter *see Erica carnea*
heather *see Calluna vulgaris*
Hebe, 43, 133, 139, 213, 236
choice of, 181, *181*, 191
H. 'Midsummer Beauty', 189
H. × franciscana, 186
Hedera, 124, *205*, 233, 236
as climber, 97, 105, 121
H. colchica, 206, 233
H. helix, 206, *223*, 233
hedges
choice of, 82-3
flowering, *80, 82*, 83
knot gardens, 12, 12-13, *12*, 82
planting, 83
problems, 42, 43
screening, 24
Helenium, 177, *177*, 207
Helianthemum, 154, *154*, 177
H. nummularium, 212, 213, 219
Helianthus annus, 237
Helichrysum, 124, 207
heliotrope, 137, *137*
Helleborus, 23, 209
H. foetidus, 206
H. niger, 183
H. orientalis, 183, *183*
Hemerocallis, 177, 221
H. hybrids, 175, *175*, 191
herb gardens, 13
herbaceous plants, 158-9, *159*, 167, 167
herbs, *6*, 20, 74, 120-1, 136, 240-3
Hesperis matronalis, 237
Heuchera, 137, 172-3
Hibiscus syriacus, 174, 191
Hippophäe rhamnoides, 48
hoeing, 199
honeysuckle *see Lonicera pileata*
hoops, 108-9, *109*
hops *see Humulus*
Hordeum jubatum, 171
Hosta, 54, 207, 209
H. hybrids, *172*, 173, *186*, 187
houseplants, 51, *51*, 123, 131, 225
Houttuynia cordata, 146, 187, *187*
Humulus, 104, 106, 121
H. lupulus, 97, 207, 221, 233
Hyacinthoides hispanica, 126
Hyacinthus, 126
Hydrangea, 164
H. macrophylla, 48
H. paniculata, 48
H. petiolaris, 104, 206, 233
Hypericum, 236
H. calycinum, 77, *188*, 189, 209
H. 'Hidcote', 175, *175*, 206
H. olympicum, 154, 155
H. × moserianum, 187

Iberis sempervivens, 155
Ilex, 165, 181, *181*, 191, 206, 229, 236
I. aquifolium, 223
I. × altaclarensis, 223
Impatiens, 47, 51, 124
Imperata cylindrica, 207

informal gardens, 14-15, *14*, 82-3
Ipomoea, 103, 105, *224*
I. lobata see Mina lobata
Iris
I. danfordiae, 130
I. laevigata, 146
I. pallida, 187, *187*
I. pseudacorus, 147, 187

I. sibirica, 147
I. unguicularis, 183, *183*
ivy *see Hedera*

Japanese gardens, 16, *16*, 24
Japanese maple, *132*
jasmine *see Jasminum*
Jasminum, 20, 105
J. nudiflorum, 183, 206, 233, *233*
J. officinale, 137, 233, 234
Juncus effusus, 146
Juniperus
J. communis, 192
J. horizontalis, 192
J. scopulorum, 227
J. virginiana, 192

Kalmia latifolia, 217
Kerria japonica, 206
kitchen gardens, 238-9
Kniphofia, 227
K. hybrids, 191, *191*, 213, 224
Kolkwitzia amabilis, 207, 219

Lablab purpureus, 103
labour-saving tips, 11
Laburnum, 132, 230
Lagenaria, 102, *103*
Lanata, 124
Lathyrus
L. grandiflorus, 221
L. latifolius, 102
L. odoratus, 103, *103*, 105, *137*
Laurus nobilis, 135, 230, 235
Lavandula, 189, 213, 234, 236
L. angustifolia, 171, *171*, 207
L. stoechas, 207
Lavatera olbia, 48
lavender, 20, 74, 83, *130*
see also Lavandula
lawns
alternatives, 49, 55, 66-7, *66-7*, 79
care, 60-3
creating, 58-9, *58-9*
edging, *55*, 57, 62
oval beds, 162, *162*
shapes, 11, 56-7
Laydekeri lilacea, 147
Lemna, 147, 149, *149*
lesser periwinkle *see Vinca minor*
Leucanthemum × *superbum*, 221
Leucojum aestivum, 178
Leycesteria formosa, 189, *189*, 223, 236
lighting, 46, 99, 112-15
Ligustrum, 175, 223, 228, 229, *229*, 236
L. ovalifolium, 82
lilies *see Lilium*
Lilium, 137, 207
L. hybrids, 177, 178-9, 224
Limnanthes douglasii, 14, 237
Liriope muscari, 191, 209
Lobelia, 124, 177
Lonicera, 104, 105, 106, 121
L. japonica, 228, 233
L. nitida, 82, *82*, 175, 209, 228, 229
L. periclymenum, 206, 233, 234, 236
L. pileata, 20, 48
L. × *brownii*, 219
love-in-a-mist *see Nigella*
low maintainance gardens, 79, 190-1
Lunaria annua, 237
Lupinus arboreus, 189
Lychnis
L. chalcedonica, 177, *177*
L. coronaria, *132*
Lysimachia, *137*

Madagascar jasmine *see Stephanotis floribunda*
Mahonia, 236
M. aquifolium, 48, 209
M. 'Charity', 227, *227*, 230, 234
features of, 134, 181, 183, 189
M. japonica, 191, 206
Malus, 185
maple *see Acer*
marginal plants, 146
marigold *see Calendula*
Matthiola
M. bicornis, 47, 234
M. incana, *234*
Matteuccia struthiopteris, 173, *210*
Meconopsis betonicifolia, 217
Mediterranean gardens, 17, *17*, 224-5
milfoil *see Myriophyllum*
Mimulus, *137*
Mina lobata, 103
Miscanthus
M. sacchariflorus, 229
M. sinensis, 173, 230
mock orange *see Philadelphus*
Moluccella laevis, 207
Monarda, 177
morning glory *see Ipomoea*
'morning-sun' positions, 206
mulches, 199, 200-1
mulching sheets, 77, 79, 168, 201
Muscari, 126
Myosotis, 124
Myriophyllum, 147, 150

Narcissus, 51, 64-5, 124, 126, *127*
nasturtium *see Tropaeolum*
Nepeta, 171, 175, 213, 237
Nerine bowdenii, 183, *183*
Nicotina, 47, 51, 120, 234
Nigella, 121
night-scented stocks *see Mathiola bicornis*

oleanders, 17, 135
Olearia × *haastii*, 48, 179, *179*, 223
Oregon grape *see Mahonia aquifolium*
ornaments, 22-3, *22-3*, *25*, 98-9, *98-9*,
110-11, *110-11*
Ornithogalum umbellatum, 126
Orontium aquaticum, 147
Osmanthus × *burkwoodii*, 223
Osteospermum, 179, 207
O. hybrids, 213, 224
O. jacundum, *212*
overhead structures, 19, 37, 38, 40-1, 50
Oxalis adenophylla, 155

Pachysandra terminalis, 48, 77, 187, *187*, 209
pansies *see Viola* × *wittrockiana*
Papaver orientale, 177, 207
Parthenocissus, 206, *206*
Passiflora, 105
passion flower *see Passiflora*

paths, 11
changing, 54
gravel, 78
materials, 72-5
weed control, 60
patios, 38-41

Paulownia tomentosa, 227
paved gardens, 13
paving
design, 68, 68, 72-3, 72, 74-5, *74-5*
lawn edging, 57, *57*
laying, 69, *69*, 73, *73*, 75, *75*
materials, 38-9, *39*, 50, 68, *68*, 70-5, *70-5*
roof gardens, 49
tiles, 50, 71, 74, *75*
peas *see Lathyrus*
peat beds, 152
Pelargonium, 17, 124, *129*, 136, 137, *137*, 235
P. hybrids, 177
Pennisetum villosum, 173
Penstemon, 207
peony, *172*
pergolas, 19, 40-1, 100-1
periwinkle *see Vinca*
Pernettya, 134, 191, 236
P. mucronata, 48, 185, *185*, 217
Perovskia, 174, 213, 236
Persicaria bistorta, 221
Petunia, 124, *128, 136,* 137
pH, 215
Philadelphus, 48, 223, 235
P. coronarius, 82, 175, 189
P. hybrids, 179, 223
Phlomis fruticosa, 212, 213, *218*, 219
Phlox
P. douglasii, 154, 155
P. paniculata, 179, 221
P. subulata, 155
Phormium, 17, 37, 97, 177, 213, 221
P. hybrids, 181, 221, 224, 227
phosphorus, 202
Picea, 192, 193, *193*
pillars, 106-7, *106-7*

Pinus mugo, 193
Piptanthus laburnifolius, 206
planning, diagrams, 28-33, 166-7, *166-7*
Pleioblastus auricomus, 173, 186
pollution-tolerance, 222-3
polyanthus *see Primula*
Polygonum baldschuanicum, 104, 121, 229, *229*, 233
Ponderata cordata, 146
ponds, 15, *15, 23*, 142, *142*, 144-51
potagers, 247
potato vine *see Solanum*
Potentilla, 83, 236
P. atrosanguinea, 177
P. fruticosa, 175, 189, 191, *218*, 219
P. tabernaemontani, 154
primrose *see Primula*
Primula, 19, 124
privet *see Lingustrum ovalifolium*
Prunus, 21, 44, 132, 183
Pulsatilla vulgaris, 155
purple sage *see Salvia officinalis*
Puschkinia scilloides, 126
Pygmaea helvola, 147
Pyracantha, 46, 185, 206, 233, *234*, 236
Pyrus salicifolia, 133

raised beds, 41, 152
Raoulia australis, 154, 155
red-barked dogwood *see Cornus alba*
red-hot pokers *see Kniphofia*
Reseda odorata, 207
Rhamnus frangula, 236
Rheum palmatum, 224
Rhodochiton atrosanguineum, 103
Rhododendron, 133, 230-1
Rhodohypoxis baurii, 154, 217
Rhus typhina, 185
Ribes sanguineum, 191, 236
rock gardens, 45, *142-3*, 143, 152-5
rock plants *see* alpines
rock roses *see Cistus*
Rodgersia pinnata, 220, 221
Romneya coulteri, 213
roof gardens, *35*, 48-9, *123*
Rosa, 104, 106, 121, 130, *159*, 233, 234
beds and borders, 13, 43, 170-1, *170-1*
climbing, 43, 94, 104, 106, *106*, 107, *171*
hedges, *82*, 83
R. hybrids, 177
R. rugosa, 171, 206
rosemary
see also Rosmarinus officinalis
hedges, 83
Rosmarinus officinalis, 181, *181*, 207, 213, 231, 235, 248
Rubus cockburnianus, 173
Ruscus aculeatus, 209
Russian vine *see Polygonum baldshuanicum*

Salix
S. alba, 183
S. caprea, 132, 231
S. matsudana, 227
Salvia, 124
S. discolor, 137
S. officinalis, 173, 187, 207, 235, 248
S. sclarea, 196
Salvinia braziliensis, 146
Santolina chamaecyparissus, 175, 213
Sarcococca hookeriana humilis, 209, *209*, 235
Saxifraga, 155, 209
Scabiosa, 124, 219, 237
scabious *see Scabiosa*
Scaevola, 124

scent, 20, 47, 130, 136-7, 234-5
Scilla
see also Hyacinthoides
S. siberica, 126
Scirpus 'Zebrinus', 146
screens
see also climbers
balconies and verandas, 51
living, 228-9
patios, 38, 40-1
roof gardens, 49
'sculptural' plants, 226
trellis, 94
uses, 10, 21, 24-6
sea buckthorn *see Hippophäe rhamnoides*
Sedum, 154
S. lydium, 154
S. spathulifolium, 155
S. spectabile, 213, *213*, 237
S. spurium, 143, 155
Sempervivum, 154, 155, *155*, 207
Senecio, 82, 189, 207
shade, 206, 208-09
awnings, 50, 120, *121*
balconies and verandas, 51
basements, 47
pergolas, 40-1
shrubs
aromatic foliage, 235
attracting wildlife, 236
borders, 158-9, *159*
boundaries, 96
in containers, 130, *130*, 132, *132*, 134, 136-7
planting, 169, *169*
uses, 49
on walls, 232-3

shuttlecock fern *see Matteuccia struthiopteris*
Siberian squill *see Scilla siberica*
Silene schafta, 155
sink gardens, *143*, 152, *152*
Skimmia, 185, *185*, 209, 235, 236
smoke bush *see Cotinus coggygria*
snake's head fritillary *see Fritillaria meleagris*
snapdragons *see Antirrhinum*
snowdrops *see Galanthus*
soil, 214-15, 216-21
Solanum, 106, 134, *134*
Soleirolia soleirolii, *54*
Solidago, 175, 237
Sorbus, 185, *185*
Spanish bluebells *see Hyacinthoides hispanica*
Spartium junceum, 235
Spiraea, 179
    S. japonica, 48
    S. × *bumalda*, 189, *189*
Spirogyra, 149, *149*
Stachys lanata, 43, 173, 175, 213
staking, 198
Star of Bethlehem *see Ornithogalum umbellatum*
step-overs, 244
Stephanotis floribunda, 105
Sternbergia lutea, 183
stone and gravel gardens, 16
storage, 26-7, *26-7*
Stratiotes aloides, 147
strawberries, 245
strelitzia, 51
striped squill *see Puschkinia scilloides*
succulents, 17, 51
sunny positions, 207, 212-13
supports, for climbers, 92-5, 100-9
Sutera cordata see Bacopa

sweet peas *see Lathyrus odoratus*
Symphoricarpos, 209, *209*, 236
Syringa, 236
    S. vulgaris, 179, 219, 219, 223, 235, 235

tamarisk *see Tamarix tetrandra*
Tamarix tetrandra, 48, 223
Tanacetum vulgare, 243
tansy *see Tanacetum vulgare*
Taxus baccata, 193, 231
Thuja, 19, 193, *193*
Thunbergia alata, 103
thyme *see Thymus*
Thymus, 124, *168*, 237, *248*
    T. serpyllum, 66-7, *66-7*, 73, 74, 155
Tiarella cordifolia, 209
Tillaea recurva, 147
tobacco plant *see Nicotina*
Trachycarpus fortunei, 17
Tradescanti × *andersoniana*, 221
tree mallow *see Lavatera olbia*
trees
    in containers, 132-3, *132-3*
    fan/espalier, 97
    problems, 43
    specimen, 183
    supporting climbers, 104-5
    uses, 24, 45
    woodland gardens, 15
trelliswork, 24, *24*, 46, 92-5, 228
Trifolium repens, 67, *67*
Trillium grandiflorum, 217
tripods, 108-9, *108-9*
Tropaeolum, 106, 124, *126*
    T. majus, 103, 105
    T. peregrinum, 103, 105
    T. speciosum, 206
tropical look, 224-5
tubers, 65
Tulipa, 64, 126, *127*
    T. hybrids, 177

Ulex, 191, 213, 236
utilities, 11, 18, 26-7

variegation, 186-7, *186-7*
vegetables, 14, 27, 102, 246-8
verandas, 50-1
Verbascum, 219
Verbena, 124, *128, 137*
Veronica prostrata, 155
Viburnum, 236
    V. davidii, 191, 209
    V. plicatum, 179
    V. tinus, 82, 133, 134, 181, 191, 231
    V. × *bodnantense*, 183, 235
Vinca
    V. major, 206
    V. minor, 124, 187, *187*, 209
vine *see Vitis coignetiae*
Viola, 74, 124, *136*
    V. × *wittrockiana*, 124, *124*, *127, 129, 137*, 171
violets, 74
Vitis coignetiae, 40, 104, 207, 233

walled gardens, 17, *34*, 46, 80, *81*
walls
    alpines, 154
    building, 86-7, *86-7*
    claire-voyée, 96
    containers on, 128-9
    design of, 84-5, *84-5*
    fixing trellis, 94-5, *94-5*
    materials, 85-6
    patio boundaries, 38
    shrubs, 232-3

    water features, 144
water features, *20*, 45-6, 96, 112, 142, 144-52
    see also ponds
water lilies, 147
    see also Laydekeri lilacea; Pygmaea helvola
water snails, 149, *149*
watering, 49
weeds, control of, *54*, 60-1, 168, 199
Weigela, 187, 223, 236
    W. hybrids, 189, *189*
wildlife gardens, 14-15, 236-7
wind breaks, 49, 51
wind tolerant plants, 48
winter aconite *see Eranthis hyemalis*
winter cherry *see Solanum*
winter heath *see Erica carnea*
Wisteria, 233, 235, *235*
woodruff *see Asperula odorata*

yew *see Taxus baccata*
Yucca, 213, 225, 227, 231
    features of, 17, 37, 97, 191
    Y. filamentosa, 133, 181
    Y. gloriosa, 133

Zantedeschia aethiopica, 225

ACKNOWLEDGMENTS

ABOVE: Dianthus barbatus *'Scarlet Beauty'*.

The publishers would like to thank all those who provided locations, materials and equipment for the special photography in this book. Specially commissioned photographs were provided by the following:
Peter Anderson: 58 (all), 59 (all), 62 (all), 63 (all), 64 (all), 125 (all), 127 top row, 127bl, 127br, 128 bottom row, 129 bottom row, 148 (all), 149 (all), 150 (all), 151 (all), 170bl, 171tr, 172t, 172b, 173tr, 192, 193 (all), 194, 198 top row, 198 br, 199 (all), 208, 209 (all), 216r, 217r, 220br. **Sue Atkinson:** 173tl, 173b, 176tr, 177tl, 178l, 179br, 212, 218l, 218r, 220, 221t, 221b, 222l, 249tr, 251l, 252b, 255b. **Jonathan Buckley:** 23bl, 48l, 48r, 92c, 92r, 93 (all), 94, 95 (all), 102, 103 (all), 104, 105 (all), 106, 107 (all), 108 (all), 109 (all), 179t, 179bl, 196, 197, 202, 206b, 207 (all), 216l, 219, 222, 223bl, 223tr, 223br, 249tl, 249c, 249b, 253b. **John Freeman:** 2, 5, 10 (all), 12b, 13t, 15t, 16, 27br, 31, 34t, 35 (all), 40b, 41t, 41b, 46b, 47b, 49b, 53, 54t, 55t, 57 (all), 60t, 60b, 61tl, 61tr, 61bl, 65 (all), 67 (all), 69 (all), 70 (all), 71 (all), 73 (all), 77 (all), 78 (all), 79 top row, 79cl, 79bl, 80, 82t, 83 top row, 83c, 83bc, 83br, 85t, 86t, 87 (all), 88tl, 88tr, 90 (all), 91tl, 91 steps, 98 (all), 99b, 100 (all), 101 steps, 110 (all), 111 (all), 116 (all), 122t, 123 (all), 130t, 130bl, 131 (all), 132t, 133 (all), 135 (all), 138 (all), 139 top row, 139bl, 139c, 143br, 144 (all), 145 (all), 146 (all), 147tr, 152b, 153 (all), 155 steps, 158, 161b, 162 (all), 163 (all), 164 (all), 165b, 167 (all), 168 steps, 169 (all), 195 (all), 198bl, 200 (all), 201 (all), 203 (all), 204tr, 204br, 205b, 208, 209, 213 (all), 231 steps, 238tr, 238br, 241 (all), 247b. **Marie O'Hara:** 19l, 27t, 124, 126, 127, 128t, 129t, 136l, 136r, 137 (all), 148 (all), 220 br, 253t, 255t. **Debbie Patterson:** 1, 4, 18, 19tc, 19tr, 19b, 20l, 20r, 21tl, 21tr, 21b, 22, 23tl, 23tr, 23br, 24t, 24b, 25tl, 25tr, 25b, 26t, 26b, 27l, 74t, 74b, 75 (all), 92l, 115b, 114t, 115 (all), 118l, 118r, 119 (all), 120, 121 (all), 139br, 140 (all), 141 (all), 171b, 250t, 251t, 252t, 254b, 254t.

The publishers would also like to thank the following picture libraries for allowing their photographs to be reproduced for this book:
Peter McHoy for the pictures on pages 12b, 46t, 47t, 61br, 66t, 66b, 68, 73bl, 79br, 82b, 83bl, 84b, 85b, 88b, 89t, 96, 97t, 97b, 113, 132bl, 134t, 134b, 147b, 153b, 154t, 154bl, 154br, 155t, 171tl, 174t, 174c, 174b, 175t, 175c, 175b, 177tr, 177b, 178r, 180t, 180b, 181t, 181c, 181b, 182t, 182b, 183t, 183c, 183b, 184t, 184b, 185t, 185bl, 185br, 186t, 186b, 187tl, 187tr, 187bl, 187br, 188t, 188b, 189tl, 189tr, 189b, 190t, 190b, 191, 208tc, 208b, 209t, 209m, 209b, 212l, 212r, 213t, 213b, 219tl, 219bl, 224t, 224b, 225tr, 225br, 225l, 226t, 226b, 227tl, 227tr, 227b, 228l, 228r, 229t, 229b, 230t, 230c, 230b, 231t, 232t, 232b, 233t, 233bl, 233br, 234t, 234b, 235t, 235b, 236, 237t, 237c, 237b, 238bl, 244r, 245l, 245r, 246b, 247t, 250b, 256. **The Harpur Garden Library** for the pictures on pages 6 (designed by Maggie Geiger, NYC), 11t (a garden in Canterbury), 11b (designed by Michael Balston), 13b (designed by Arabella Lennox-Boyd), 15t (Nooroo Mt. Wilson, NSW), 17b (designed by Trevor Frankland), 17t (designed by John Patrick, VIC), 34b (designed by Anthony Noel, London), 38t (designed by Berry's Garden Co., Golders Green), 39b (designed by Christopher Masson, London), 40t (designed by Malcolm Hillier, London), 52 (designed by Christopher Masson, London), 54b (designed by Wayne Winterrowd & Joe Eck, London), 55b (designed by Anne Alexander-Sinclair), 56t (designed by Ernie Taylor, Great Barr), 56b (a garden in Tayside), 68t (designed by Berry's Garden Co., Golders Green), 72t, 72b (designed by Hilary McMahon for Costin's Nursery, RHS Chelsea), 81b (designed by Anthony Noel, London), 81t (Fudlers Hall, Mashbury), 84t (designed by Jan Martinez, Kent), 89b (designed by Bruce Kelly, NYC), 101br (designed by Arabella Lennox-Boyd), 122b (designed by Anne Alexander Sinclair), 130br (designed by Lalitte Scott, NYC), 132br (designed by Phillip Watson, Fredericksburg, VA), 142b (designed by Simon Fraser, London), 152t (Joe Elliot, Broadwell, Gloucs), 156 (designed by Beth Chatto), 157 (designed by Ernie Taylor, Great Barr), 160 (Bank House, Borwick) and 165t (Home Farm, Balscote, Oxon). **The Garden Picture Library** for the pictures on pages 12t (Marijke Heuff), 50 (Ron Sutherland), 76 (John Duane), 112 (Jane Legate), 240t (Lynne Brotchie) and 240b (J S Sira). **Jacqui Hurst** for the pictures on pages 14, 99t, 142t, 143t, 143bl, 159t, 159b, 161t, 168tl, 204l 205t and 248. **Derek Fell** for the pictures on pages 5, 15b, 49t, 51t, 51b, 91tr, 157, 239 and 246t. **Robert Harding** for the pictures on pages 38b and **Lucy Mason** for the picture on page 147tl.

Project contributors: **Stephanie Donaldson** (the Black-and-White Pots, p. 138 and the Painted Terracotta Pots, p. 139); **Cleo Mussi** (the Miniature Pebble Circle, p. 75); **Liz Wagstaff** (the Gilded Pots, p. 115, the Verdigris Bucket, p. 140, and the Lead Chimney, p. 141); and **Karin Hossack** (the Aluminium Tin Cans, p. 141 and the Mexican Painted Pots, p. 21).